CRISIS IN THE NORDIC NATIONS AND BEYOND

Crisis in the Nordic Nations and Beyond

At the Intersection of Environment, Finance and Multiculturalism

Edited by
KRISTÍN LOFTSDÓTTIR
University of Iceland, Iceland

LARS JENSEN
Roskilde University, Denmark

Routledge
Taylor & Francis Group
LONDON AND NEW YORK

First published 2014 by Ashgate Publishing

Published 2016 by Routledge
2 Park Square, Milton Park, Abingdon, Oxon OX14 4RN
711 Third Avenue, New York, NY 10017, USA

Routledge is an imprint of the Taylor & Francis Group, an informa business

British Library Cataloguing in Publication Data
A catalogue record for this book is available from the British Library

The Library of Congress has cataloged the printed edition as follows:
Kristín Loftsdóttir, 1968-
Crisis in the Nordic nations and beyond : at the intersection of environment, finance and multiculturalism / by Kristín Loftsdóttir and Lars Jensen.
pages cm
Includes bibliographical references and index.
ISBN 978-1-4724-2538-6 (hardback)
1. Scandinavia--Social conditions--21st century. 2. Social media--Scandinavia. 3. Mass media--Influence. 4. Terrorism and mass media--Scandinavia. I. Jensen, Lars. II. Title.
HM741.K75 2014
306.094809'05--dc23

2014019294

ISBN 9781472425386 (hbk)

Contents

List of Contributors

Kimberly Cannady is Lecturer in Ethnomusicology at the Te Kōkī New Zealand School of Music (Victoria University). She received her PhD in Ethnomusicology from the University of Washington (2014), where she also worked closely with the Department of Scandinavian Studies. Kimberly's doctoral research examined music making across the Nordic North Atlantic, and she conducted fieldwork in Iceland, Denmark and the Faroe Islands. Her dissertation focused on Icelandic self-perceptions of musical legitimacy and the use of music in Iceland to further the aims of the nation state during the early twentieth-century independence movement and after the economic crisis in 2008. This research was funded by grants from the Fulbright Program (US), the American Scandinavian Foundation, and from the University of Washington. Kimberly is also a trained musician and completed a Bachelor of Music in Vocal Performance with a minor in Anthropology from the University of Utah (2006). Kimberly's current research areas include diverse forms of music making within a Nordic context as informed by postcolonial studies and nationalism. She is also developing new research in Polynesia and is particularly interested in issues of cultural heritage and music making in the Cook Islands.

Tobias Hübinette has a PhD in Korean Studies, is Associate Professor in Intercultural Education and a researcher at the Multicultural Centre. He is conducting research on and is engaged in issues concerning racism and (post) colonialism, race and Swedishness, National Socialism and Fascism, Korean-Swedish and East Asian-Swedish relations, and transnational adoption and transracial adoptees. He is also organizing a Swedish research network for critical race and whiteness studies. He has published in journals such as *Nordic Journal of Feminist and Gender Research*, *Positions: East Asia Cultures Critique*, *Journal of Intercultural Studies*, *Adoption & Culture*, *Inter-Asia Cultural Studies and International Social Work*, and *Third Text*, as well as monographs and anthologies such as *Comforting an Orphaned Nation.* Representations of international adoption and adopted Koreans in Korean popular culture (2006), Adoption med förhinder: Samtal med adopterade och adoptivföräldrar om vardagsrasism och etnisk identitet [Adoption with obstacles: Conversations with adoptees and adoptive parents on everyday racism and ethnic identity] (2008) together with Carina Tigervall, Den interkulturella blicken i pedagogik. Inte bara goda föresatser [The intercultural gaze in pedagogy. Not just good intentions] (2012) together with Katrin Goldstein-Kyaga and María Borgström, and Om ras och vithet i det samtida Sverige [On race and whiteness in contemporary

Sweden] (2012) together with Helena Hörnfeldt, Fataneh Farahani and René León Rosales.

Lars Jensen is Associate Professor at Cultural Encounters, Roskilde University. He has worked and published widely in postcolonial studies, but also works in the related fields of whiteness studies, critical race studies, (critical) cultural studies and multiculturalism. He is the co-editor with Kristín Loftsdóttir of *Whiteness and Postcolonialism in the Nordic Region: Exceptionalism, Migrant Others and National Identities* (Ashgate 2012). He is the co-editor with Prem Poddar and Rajeev Patke of *The Historical Companion to Postcolonial Literatures: Continental Europe and its Empires* (Edinburgh UP/Columbia UP 2008/2009). He has co-edited with Katherine Russo and Anne Brewster a special issue of *JEASA*, *On Whiteness: Current Debates in Australian Studies* (*JEASA 2.2* 2011). In 2012, he published a Danish monograph on Postcolonial Denmark, *Danmark: Rigsfællesskab, tropekolonier og den postkoloniale arv* (Reitzel), which he is reworking into an English edition. He is currently editing a book and a journal issue on articles commissioned after the Roskilde University conference, *After the Empires*, on postcolonial/decolonial Europe. He is also involved in the HERA funded project, *Arctic Encounters*, where he is doing research on contemporary Greenland with a focus on the overlaps between the political change, climate change, and indigenous eco-tourism.

Kristín Loftsdóttir is a Professor of Anthropology at the University of Iceland. Loftsdóttir's research has focused on whiteness, gender and racial identity in Iceland, in addition to exploring Icelandic identity in relation to international development, multiculturalism and crisis. Currently, Kristín is directing the research project '(Icelandic) Identity in Crisis' funded by RANNIS – Icelandic Centre for Research. She has previously conducted fieldwork in relation to WoDaaBe pastoralists in Niger in West-Africa, focusing on migrant work and globalization. Her books include *Whiteness and Postcolonialism in the Nordic Region: Exceptionalism, Migrant Others and National Identities* (Ashgate 2012), edited with Lars Jensen; *Teaching 'Race' with a Gendered Edge* (ATGENDER 2012) edited with Brigitte Hipfl and the monograph *The Bush is Sweet: Identity, Power and Development among WoDaaBe Fulani in Niger* (NAI 2008). She has also written about research methodology and her book (in Icelandic) *The Woman who got spear on her head: The strangeness of methodology* received Fjöruverðlaunin – Women's Literature Award as scholarly book of the year in 2010. Kristín has participated in ATGENDER – The European Women's Network and ATHENA network focusing on issues relating to post-colonialism and gender. She has co-organized with Lars Jensen the networks *The Nordic Colonial Mind* and *Nordic Identities and Crisis* (funded by NOS-HS). Currently, she is member of the PEN network (Post Colonial Europe) and of the team of the HERA funded project *Artic Encounters*. Loftsdóttir is on the board of MARK (Center for Research on Diversity and Gender) at the University of Iceland.

Satu Ranta-Tyrkkö is a postdoctoral fellow affiliated with the social work programme of the School of Social Sciences and Humanities, University of Tampere, Finland. She has done interdisciplinary ethnographic research in India with volunteer and activist social workers and/or theatre makers, including her doctoral study (2010) *At the Intersection of Theatre and Social Work in Orissa, India*. Her current research interests focus on three distinct, but at times interrelated fields: intersections of social work and arts, particularly theatre; international and postcolonial issues in social work; and ecological/eco-social issues in social work, especially in relation to extractive industries.

James G. Rice is assistant professor at the University of Iceland in disability studies and anthropology. He received his doctorate in anthropology from Memorial University of Newfoundland. The title of his dissertation is *The Charity Complex: An Ethnography of a Material Aid Agency in Reykjavík, Iceland* (2007), and the research was funded by the Social Sciences and Humanities Research Council of Canada. He has since completed post-doctoral fellowships from NOVA (Norwegian Social Research) and the University of Iceland, both of which were held at the Centre for Disability Studies, University of Iceland and focused on the intersection of disability with policy and everyday life in the context of the changing social welfare state. He is the author of a number of articles published in journals such as *Ethnology, Normal* and *Vulnerable Groups and Inclusion* and, most recently, a forthcoming chapter in the edited volume *Gambling Debt: Iceland's struggle with the New World Order*, edited by E.P. Durrenberger and G. Pálsson and published by the University of Colorado Press. He continues to teach at the University of Iceland.

Johanna Sumiala is an Adjunct Professor at the Department of Social Research/ Media and Communication Studies at the University of Helsinki, Finland. Currently, she works at the Helsinki Collegium for Advanced Studies as Kone Foundation Senior Fellow. Sumiala is a media scholar specializing in media anthropology, media and virtual ethnography, visual culture and social media. She publishes widely in Finnish and English language including such journals as *Media, Culture and Society*, *Social Anthropology*, *M/C Journal*, *Communication, Culture and Critique* and *European Journal of Cultural Studies*. She is co-editor of *Implications of the Sacred in (Post)Modern Media* (Nordicom 2006), *Images and Communities. The Visual Construction of the Social* (Gaudemus/Helsinki University Press 2007) *School Shootings: Mediatized Violence in a Global Age* (Emerald 2013). Her latest monograph is *Media and Ritual. Death, Community and Everyday Life* (Routledge 2013).

Minttu Tikka, MsSoc, is a PhD candidate at the Department of Social Research/ Media and Communication Studies, University of Helsinki. She currently works as a project researcher in a Youth Street Politics project carried out in collaboration with the Finnish Youth Research Society and University College London. She is specialized in issues of crises, social media and virtual ethnography. She has published in journals such as *Social Anthropology* (article titled 'Visualizing Globalized Fears: School Shooting Videos and Circulation of Violence on YouTube' co-written with Johanna Sumiala) and *Communication, Culture and Critique* (article titled 'Broadcast Yourself – Global News! A Netnography of the 'Flotilla' News on YouTube' co-written with Johanna Sumiala). She is also one of the editors of the first Finnish book on internet and social media methods (Vastapaino 2013).

Ebbe Volquardsen, MA is a doctoral fellow at the *International Graduate Centre for the Study of Culture (GCSC)*, Justus-Liebig-Universität Giessen (Germany) and a visiting lecturer at the Institute for Scandinavian Studies, University of Cologne. He is currently working on a doctoral dissertation about literary representations of Danish colonialism in Greenland and the former Danish West Indies, examining how these texts contribute to the production of a narrative about Denmark as a particularly humane colonial power. In his scholarship, Volquardsen focuses on the literary and cultural history of Denmark and its former colonies, Nordic exceptionalism, postcolonialism, globalization theory and global history. He obtained his master's degree in Scandinavian Studies, European Ethnology and Political Science from Humboldt-Universität zu Berlin with a thesis on nation, identity and subaltern articulation in the earliest Greenlandic novels. A revised version (in German) was published in 2011 (Ebbe Volquardsen: *Die Anfänge des grönländischen Romans. Nation, Identität und subalterne Artikulation in einer arktischen Kolonie.* Marburg: Tectum). Volquardsen is a member of the international and interdisciplinary research project 'Denmark and the new North Atlantic: Identity Positions, Natural Resources and Cultural Heritage', affiliated to the University of Copenhagen. Together with colleague Lill-Ann Körber, he is editing a volume on *The Postcolonial North Atlantic – Greenland, Iceland and the Faroe Islands* (Berliner Beiträge zur Skandinavistik; Berlin: Nordeuropa-Institut), 2014. Volquardsen is also editor-in-chief of the peer-reviewed open access journal *NORDEUROPAforum – Journal for the Study of Culture.*

Margit Ystanes is a postdoctoral fellow at the Department of Social Anthropology, University of Bergen. She obtained her PhD from the University of Bergen in 2011, with the dissertation *Precarious Trust. Problems of Managing Self and Sociality in Guatemala.* This work explores how local forms of sociality and intimacy give rise to culturally specific ways of forming and experiencing trust and mistrust – both in the intimate sphere of family life and in the public sphere of political contestation. Ystanes' current project, *Trust as a Precondition for Socio-economic Development: What can We Learn from the Case of Brazil?*, continues to investigate how trust and mistrust are formed in both private and public lives. Her research interests include trust/mistrust, contestation and political processes, the production of wealth and poverty, social inequality, racism, environmentalism, conceptualizations of nature and gender.

Acknowledgements

This volume stems from a series of workshops that were made possible by a grant in 2011 by NOS-HS (grant number 212678/F10). NOS-HS also contributed toward funds for this book. We thus want to acknowledge our gratitude to NOS-HS for making this work possible. The workshops were held under the heading *Crisis and Nordic Identity* and were the platform for a really exciting exchange of ideas. We want to thank all the workshop participants for engaging in this interesting programme with us.

Introduction
Crisis in the Nordic Nations and Beyond

Lars Jensen and Kristín Loftsdóttir

The Crises Phenomenon

Crisis has become the epitome of our time, defining this historical moment. While different aspects of contemporary society are defined as 'in crisis', there is also a sense of impending disaster, amplified by security discourses that seek to identify future risks and situations (for example, Collier, Lakow and Rabinow 2004). This sense is intensified in portrayals of a world threatened by imminent decay – witness expressions like 'zombie capitalism' (Harman 2009). The phenomenon of environmental, financial and multicultural crises identified in the title of this volume, are global in reach, yet also characterized by their localizations. When the investment bank Lehman Brothers collapsed in autumn 2008, it was 'a defining moment' as David Harvey termed it, leading to the freeze of global credit markets and lending (2010: 2). Although originating, as the Great Depression did, in Wall Street, the European economic crisis occupies a central place in the current unfolding disaster. The fiscal crisis has specific characteristics, not least the way it spills into other crises, such as the stalled project of building a pan-European polity. The threat of fragmentation of nation states into regional secession in a number of places (such as Catalunya, Scotland, and the Flemish Region, 'Padania') undermine the perceived integrity of nation states, as typically relatively affluent regions seek to break away from debt-ridden countries.

Another important dimension of the European crisis is the connection between it and the re-emergence of racism as a prominent discourse. Whereas European anti-migrant rhetoric has a significant history, and is intimately connected to European colonialism, it has been resurgent in recent decades and intensified by the economic crisis, which is arguably the culmination of a long-term crisis of the underfunded European welfare state. Anti-migration rhetoric, used in the phrase 'the crisis of multiculturalism,' has enjoyed currency, appealing to a popularist common sense notion that 'multiculturalism' has failed (Fortier 2007; Lentin and Titley 2011). This idea assumes that prior to the era of multiculturalism, European countries existed as homogeneous nation spaces. Not only do such discourses fail to engage with Europe's colonial history as background to contemporary migration (Ponzanesi 2002: 206), a similar erasure of Europe's past is evident in the discussions about Europe's historical contribution to the global environmental crisis. Race and class is closely linked to the environmental crisis (see for example Tambe 2011; Shiva 1989). Regardless of the debate over responsibility for implementing solutions that curb global warming, the environmental calamity has a humanity-threatening dimension. Paul Gilroy has labelled this impending catastrophe, 'imperilled earth' (Gilroy 2011: 19), and although this designation can be related to a series of intense troubles, there is little doubt that the environmental crisis understood broadly is a 'threat of self-destruction of all life on earth' and a 'global danger' affecting in the long term both those responsible and those not (Beck 1992: 21).

In the Face of Crises

The Nordic countries are often considered a peaceful zone largely unaffected by the crises and their effects. These countries represent some of the most affluent and least socially polarized societies in the world. They are a globalized space that actively participates in the global flows of labour, of an economic and historical system that has produced social, cultural and environmental inequalities. The record of their wider engagement is extensive, from colonialism, large-scale emigration to North America in particular, to, in more recent times, an acute sense of the importance of participating in resolving conflicts produced by this global (dis)order, whether militarily (UN contingents, the Balkan Wars, Iraq and Afghanistan), or in high profile activism in the UN system, including development aid (Jacobsen 2006; Loftsdóttir and Björnsdóttir 2012). While the acts of the Nordic countries in relation to these issues are part of a wider western and European response, they are also an illustration of a specific regional European outlook, where participation is the result of a national identity, projected onto international relations. This is as a reaction to global flows in the Nordic countries, of people, of overarching ideologies, especially neoliberalism and of the pressures on welfare societies. Nonetheless, there is a strong tendency to view the Nordic countries as somehow existing apart from global flows, as being outside power and politics, and as representing a form of Nordic exceptionalism (Loftsdóttir and Jensen 2012), even in Nordic countries with a past as global empires (Jensen 2012).

This book addresses the idea of crisis as inherently related to power dynamics by using the Nordic countries as a focal point. Whereas the essays in this collection stress the importance in investigating crisis as a concept, in which different discourses of crisis eventually confront the interlinked and social, economic and environmental reality they share, they also highlight the importance of critical perspectives from the Humanities and the Social Sciences. These perspectives are necessary to understanding the significance of 'crisis' within contemporary dynamics. In western academic thought, crisis has often been considered as transformation, or as 'rupture in the order of things' (Vigh 2008), even at times heralding a positive change as, for example, in the work of Karl Marx. At the same time, 'What and when does something become identified as crisis and for whom?' remains a key question. Henrik Vigh views crisis as constituting a context that has a certain 'terrain of action and meaning' (Vigh 2008: 8). Crisis can determine what identities and interests are at stake. This collection prioritizes an examination of these aspects within a globalized Nordic context, thus emphasizing the globalized nature of these crises, even as they share a Nordic point of departure. The book's theoretical orientation emphasizes recognizing past inequalities and examining how they filter into the present, or are contested by it. As scholars are remarking these inequalities were not only important historically in European cities and their colonial peripheries, but also in places – such as the Nordic countries – which were marginal to the metropolitan cultures, but at the same time participated actively in the production of Europe as the universal centre.

The Nordic countries have a long history, unique in the west, at the top of statistical indicators of demonstrated happiness, trust in institutional structures of society, environmental awareness, relative economic and social equality, etc. This self-image is so robust that it has worked as an ideological base for unsuccessful attempts at exporting the Nordic model to other far less affluent places. In addition it has been embraced by economists, even celebrated by *The Economist* (Special Report, 'The Nordic Countries: The Next Supermodel' (February 2013)), where it has been rendered as a safeguard against the destruction of welfare societies caused by the financial crisis. Nevertheless, the Nordic countries *have been* affected by the crises of the environment, finance and multiculturalism as well as contributed to them directly and indirectly as the chapters in this collection reflect. These crises have brought home the dilemma of receiving global flows of affluence, while also being acutely exposed to neoliberalism's deregulation of labour conditions, of environmental protective measures, and of the global movement of labour. When we started looking at crisis in the Nordic context, it quickly became apparent that one of the most productive perspectives lay in investigating the relationship between the global in the Nordic and the Nordic in the global. It also became clear that it was important to look at how the Nordic unfolds in relation to other regional identifications. Not the Nordic seen as an entity, nor as something to be looked upon in isolation in relation to the crises, but Nordic as a particular space in which the crises were manifested both as unique, as particular, and as metonymic of a wider European, Western and global crisis. With an increasingly globalized world, crises cannot be limited analytically to a national context, but have to be understood as global phenomena, where the regional, comparative level works as an interesting in-between stratum that avoids an over emphasis on the global nature of crises, or the intrinsic uniqueness of the national level. The Nordic countries represent a privileged space within the wider Europe. Dipesh Chakrabarty's (2000) expression, 'Provincializing Europe', coined a decade ago, was a part of a wider call to dismantle Eurocentrism in scholarship (see also Ang 1999) but Chakrabarty in addition emphasized that in many respects, Europe had already been provincialized, for example in terms of its status as a political-economic power. Seen from a different angle, Europe's unquestioned position as a political contender on the world scene has been replaced by struggles within the former metropolitan centres as European nations seek to adjust to their new provincialized reality in an ever more global world, where the pressures of globalization are increasingly being directed at Europe, rather than from it.

Faced with a changing Europe, the essays in this collection understand crisis as a multivocal symbol of the present, emphasizing identities, global connections and power in that regard. Minttu Tikka and Johanna Sumiala's 'Media Witnessing on YouTube – Rethinking Crisis in a Mediatized Condition' and Ebbe Volquardsen's 'Scandinavia and "the Land of UnSwedish Freedom": Jonathan Franzen, Susanne Bier and the Self-conceptions of Exceptionalism in Crisis' focus on media representations of crisis, emphasizing the overarching context of crisis discourses. Tikka and Sumiala's discussion of the global media-scape provides examples of how identities are created in public performances of crises. Volquardsen's chapter 'Scandinavia and "the Land of UnSwedish Freedom": Jonathan Franzen, Susanne Bier and Self-conceptions of Exceptionalism in Crisis' shows the deterritorialization of the notion of crisis with examples from two recent films, which he views as anchored in a postcolonial reality. James Gordon Rice's chapter '"Now is necessity": Icelandic charity during the crisis years' uses the angle of charity to show how crisis for some signals a sudden break, while it is a permanent state for others. His analysis shows how during the financial crisis in Iceland, the media shifted its discourses of poverty in Iceland by more strongly emphasizing national rethoric than before the crisis.

The chapter by Tobias Hübinette 'Racial Stereotypes and Swedish Antiracism: A Swedish Crisis of Multiculturalism?' and Kimberly Cannady's, 'Dancing on the Fissures: Alternative Senses of Crisis in the Faroe Islands' also draw attention to – in spite of considerably different approach – national identities in relation to crisis and the mobilization of these identities within globalized economies. Hübinette's chapter addresses the presumed crisis of multiculturalism, while Cannady focuses on Faroese identity in the shadow of such crisis and how music and dance foster national identity. These chapters clearly reflect the multiple angles in which crisis is evoked in relation to the nation state. Hübinette's chapter indicates how discourses of crisis of multiculturalism have to be contextualized within certain imaginations of the nation, underlining the privileges of the majority group in Sweden, while Cannady's chapter draws out the sense of marginalization in a very small Nordic nation.

Satu Ranta-Tyrkkö, Margit Ystanes and Lars Jensen's chapters highlight environmental crisis, intersecting in diverse ways with other chapters of the book, as well as clearly demonstrating the importance of stressing the globality of the Nordic nations. While Ranta-Tyrkkö in, 'Out of Sight, Out of Mind? The Mining Industry in the Peripheral Regions of Finland and Odisha, Eastern India' refers to the massive environmental destruction of mining companies in India, Ystanes discusses how environmental debates can be appropriated to promote particular development agenda with disastrous ecological consequences in her chapter, 'Saving Guatemala's "Mayan Forest": The Environmental Crisis and Contested Development'. The two chapters show the interrelationship between the social and the environmental, as well as speaking to the different subjectivities of individuals in relation to power. Jensen's chapter, 'Crisis as Opportunity – Opportunity as Crisis: Greenlandic Independence and Sustainability' reveals the contradictory effects of the environmental crisis by focusing on Greenland. While linking his insights with critical analysis of exercise of territorial power of different nation states, Jensen shows that even though destructive in the long term, the global warming paradoxically may open up possibilities in particular contexts.

The nation state and global power relationships are also central to the next chapter in the collection. Kristín Loftsdóttir's chapter '"The Enemy Outside and Within": The Crisis and Imagining the Global in Iceland', stresses the 'global' as a field of engagement looks suddenly very different in the aftermath of a financial crisis as well as highlighting how economic issues are intimately connected to the shaping of national identities. Her chapter draws attention to an increased sense of precariousness and, in line with Jensen and Ystanes, how 'crisis' can be beneficial to some actors while signalling loss of livelihoods for others.

In these adaptions of perspective, shifting from individual to national to global, and destabilizing notions of centre and circumference, our writing disassociates itself from the idea of the expert. That is, from the idea of the 'expert' being inherently bound within positivistic views of science as objective assemblage of facts removed from the field of 'politics'. While the answers to sustainable solutions require scientific knowledge, the processes by which this knowledge operates occur in the social sphere, rather than within technical solutions themselves. Our approach builds from the premise that experts and positivistic science constitute part of the problem(s) rather than being external to them, the crises result from human behaviour(s). Scholars within the humanities and social sciences are, for example, increasingly advocates for the acknowledgement that what is seen as 'environmental' is inherently social, where the emerging epoch in planetary history can accurately be described as 'anthropocene' – where the impact of humans has become equal to geological forces (Pálsson et al. 2012).

Similar things can be said about blind faith in economic mechanistic models, which were thought not only to have predictive powers but also as operating independently of the interaction between society and the economy. Science is limited by its inability to look outside the parameters of the particular crisis. It remains locked within the logic of cause and effect, and is instrumentalist in its approach. In financial and environmental crises experts have been unable to reverse the destructive elements driving those crises, and in relation to the economic crisis, mainstream economic scientists have been a contributing factor. Beyond the expertise itself, within political systems that have been designed to deal with crisis, the outlook is more dismal. Climate change science, for example, although more generally accepted than it was in the 1980s (when a consensus on global warming started to form in the scientific community) is not prioritized in national and international political agendas in any degree corresponding to the dramatic nature of the changes predicted. When the worst hurricane in local history struck the American east coast during the 2012 presidential election campaign, no presidential candidate – white or black – made use of the hurricane to address the urgency of climate change, even after science had predicted global warming will exacerbate the destructive effects of hurricanes. The financial crisis has so far only accelerated the application of the neoliberal cures, which caused the crisis in the first instance, and prolong it. Bailouts for banks are matched by private profiteering rating agencies telling states to enact legislation that will generate the kind of atmosphere, which 'the market' requires. The result has been immediate, dramatic impoverishment in southern Europe, and the destruction of the support of already shaky and rudimentary welfare societies, accompanied by a dramatic increase in utility fees and taxes. As neoliberalism in the financial crisis produced by its own speculation threatens the core of the welfare state model, ethnocentrism becomes the agent through which culturally-based ostracism takes place.

As this collection emphasizes, multiculturalism is one way to look at this impending sense of crisis with voices growing stronger in Europe claiming that multiculturalism has failed or is 'in crisis'. Here the figure of the science expert is probably not as predominant as in the other crisis discussed, but more salient as the self-identified expert in the figure of a politician or social commentator. As Alana Lentin and Gavan Titley's (2011) work shows multiculturalism has been used as a 'mobilizing metaphor for a spectrum of political aversion and racism that has become pronounced in western Europe' (3). Neoliberalism involves reified notions of culture, where 'multiculturalism' becomes pivotal, some scholars arguing that the term multiculturalism 'masks the "centrality of race and racism to neo-liberalism"' (Melamed 2006: 1). Lentin and Titley (2011) stress that social political transformation initiated by neoliberalism are reconceptualized as due to multiculturalism which as such creates a forum to continue reproducing racism in an era where direct racism acts are often condemned (3–4).

A Brave New World Order

To focus on the negative aspects of crisis ignores the possibility that it can also lead to a new order. In Bauman's reading of Antonio Gramsci, crises become 'those extraordinary situations in which the extant legal frame of social order loses its grip and hold no longer, whereas a new frame, made to the measure of newly emerged conditions responsible for making the old frame useless, is still at the designing stage' (Bauman 2011: 7–8). If this new order is irreversible climate change, unchecked neoliberalism after the demise of the idea of the welfare state, accompanied by fascist, anti-migration, populist nationalism, arguably there is little to celebrate?

If we, however, focus only on the negative outcome of the crises, we risk romanticizing the time before the crisis, ignoring the financial crash of 1929, for instance, and the smaller ones later on – crisis after all is endemic to capitalism. There was fascism, extreme nationalism, and anti-immigration policies and rhetoric – not only in the 1930s, but also in for example Enoch Powell's 'rivers of blood' anti-immigration speech in Britain in 1968, and, in the 1980s, in a range of

European countries. Nor are environmental catastrophes an exclusive sign of our time. They were abundant in earlier times, for example the mass killing of whales and seals already in the 1700s and 1800s, the prodigious felling of virgin forest in European settler societies in the 1800s. Industrial environmental disasters are also numerous, including Seveso, Harrisburg, Chernobyl and Bhopal, to mention a few of those that drew media attention (see also Nixon 2011). This collection stresses that we can analyse what 'crisis' is as a way of conceptualizing unfolding processes, which can have both positive and negative outcomes.

Examining the history of crisis and detailing the similarities in discourses in the past and the present is, however, not to diminish the concerns over the current entangled crises. Most disturbing of these is the threatened continuing survival of humans because of environmental damage. Yet the financial crisis is evidence of a similar systemic error within the ways in which 'we' have chosen to organize our societies, and the crisis of multiculturalism is the result of tensions produced at the heart of the societies arguably best socially conditioned to withstand the pressures of globalization in the shape of neoliberalism. We ask critically in what ways crisis has been conceptualized and given meaning and how such meaning can be contextualized within a particular social and historical environment, especially a north–south dynamic but also in relation to a growing inequality within the north. What identities gain salience during a crisis, and how does that relate to past and existing power relations between different groups? We recognize that averting and managing risk and catastrophes can include 'reorganization of power and authority' (Beck 1992: 24), and question how is that risk managed in what remains one of the world's most affluent locales, the Nordic countries?

Works Cited

Ang, Ien (1998) 'Eurocentric Reluctance: Notes for a Cultural Studies of the New Europe', in Kuan-hsing, Chen (ed.) *Trajectories: Inter-Asia Cultural Studies*. London: Routledge, 87–108.

Bauman, Zygmunt (2011) '"The Triple Challenge", in Postcolonial Europe', special issue of *Moving Worlds* 11 (2), 7–11.

Beck, Ulrich (1992) *Risk Society: Towards a New Modernity*. London: Sage.

Chakrabarty, Dipesh (2000) *Provincializing Europe.* Princeton: Princeton University Press.

Collier, Stephen J., Andrew Lakoff, Paul Rabinow (2004) 'Biosecurity: Towards an Anthropology of the Contemporary'. *Anthropology Today* 20 (5), 3–7.

Fortier, Anne-Marie (2007) 'Too Close for Comfort: Loving thy Neighbour and the Management of Multicultural Intimacies'. *Environment and Planning D. Society and Space* 25, 104–19.

Gilroy, Paul (2011) 'Shameful History: The Social Life of Races and the Postcolonial Archive', in Postcolonial Europe, special issue of *Moving Worlds*, 11 (2), 19–34.

Harman, Chris (2009) *Zombie Capitalism.* London: Bookmarks Publications.

Harvey, David (2010) *The Enigma of Capital: And the Crises of Capitalism.* London: Profile Books.

Ho, Karen (2009) 'Disciplining Investment Bankers, Disciplining the Economy: Wall Street's Institutional Culture of Crisis and the Downsizing of "Corporate America"'. *American Anthropologist* 111 (2), 177–89.

Jakobsen, Peter Viggo (2006) 'The Nordic Peacekeeping Model: Rise, Fall, Resurgence?' *International Peacekeeping* 13 (3), 381–95.

Jensen, Lars (2012) *Danmark: Rigsfællesskab, Tropekolonier og den Postkoloniale Arv.* Copenhagen: Reitzel.

Loftsdóttir, Kristín and Helga Björnsdóttir (2012) 'Unpolitical Wars: Presentations of Conflict in Development and Foreign Policy Discourses in Iceland'. *International Peacekeeping* 19 (1), 35–47.

— and Lars Jensen (eds) (2012) *Whiteness and Postcolonialism in the Nordic Region: Exceptionalism, Migrant Others and National Identities.* London: Ashgate.

Lentin, Alana and Gavan Titley (2011) *Crisis of Multiculturalism: Racism in a Neoliberal Age.* London: Zed Books.

Melamed, Jodi (2006) 'The Spirit of Neoliberalism: From Racial Liberalism to Neoliberal Multiculturalism'. *Social Text* 24 (4), 1–24.

Nixon, Rob (2011) *Slow Violence and the Environmentalism of the Poor.* Cambridge, MA: Harvard University Press.

Pálsson, Gísli et al. (2012) 'Reconceptualizing the 'Anthropos' in the Anthropocene: Integrating the social sciences and humanities in global environmental change research'. *Environmental Science and Policy* 28 (4), 3–13.

Ponzanesi, Sandra (2002) 'Diasporic Subjects and Migration'. In Griffin, Gabriele and Rosi Bradoitti (eds) *Thinking Differently: A Reader in European Women Studies.* London: Zed Books, 205–20.

Vigh, Henrik (2008) 'Crisis and Chronicity: Anthropological Perspectives on Continuous Conflicts and Decline'. *Ethnos* 72 (1), 5–25.

Shiva, Vandana (1989) *Staying Alive: Women, Ecology, and Development.* London: Zed Books.

Tambe, Ashwini (2011) 'Race Science and the Age of Consent in the League of Nations'. *Theory Culture Society* 28 (2), 109–30.

Chapter 1
Media Witnessing on YouTube – Rethinking Crisis in a Mediatized Condition

Minttu Tikka and Johanna Sumiala

Crisis – A Mediatized Condition

Crises are *mediatized* at multiple levels. Following the media scholar Knut Lundby's (2009: 298) insight, we argue that the manner in which global crises are reported and shaped through a range of different mediatizing techniques and mediatized actors – although not at the source – may make a significant difference to the outcome, and the experience, and may also change the course of a crisis. To give one example, Norway's 2011 terrorist attacks took place in Oslo and Utøya, but were almost immediately transformed via the range of different media into a news event on an immense scale. Substantial mediatization of public mourning and grief was initiated in, and via, the Norwegian, the Nordic and the global news media, as well as in social media (see e.g. Sumiala 2013, 2014, forthcoming). The isolatable moments of the Utøya crisis, as a fixed historical and geographical condition, were merged into the simultaneity and heterogeneity of the crisis experience at different physical, virtual, cultural, social and political distances (see e.g. Cottle 2006; Hepp 2013; Sumiala and Hakala 2010).

In this chapter, we scrutinize a crisis under a mediatized condition by examining media witnessing. We aim to illustrate how the system of media witnessing – that refers to a novel configuration of mediation, representation and experience of crisis – is able to reshape the idea of distance between crises and the people experiencing them. Those crises in question occur in locations physically far away from the Nordic countries, but touch the lives in the north more and more typically in and via the global media. Looking from the other angle, the Utøya crisis discussed above, took place in Norway, but moved people all around the world. It was the witnessing in and via the media that brought this Norwegian tragedy close to people at various distances, not only in Norway and other Nordic countries, but also in Europe and other continents. Consequently the Utøya crisis was transformed from the Norwegian tragedy into a globally shared experience of the vulnerability of life.

We also argue for the relevance of the anthropological investigation of crisis witnessing in new spatial locations, such as YouTube. We start with the premise that in order to understand how we in today's world experience and witness crisis, as an ongoing condition in our contemporary life, we need to interrogate the ways in which crisis is witnessed not only in certain physical, social and cultural locations and communities, but also, and even more so, in a range of different virtual spatial contexts including Internet and social media. These virtual contexts, we claim, provide not only new possibilities, but also challenges for anthropologists studying witnessing and how people in different parts of the globe experience, communicate and make meaning over the crisis in question.

In the history of media anthropology, anthropologists have often chosen so-called 'other cultures' as settings for their research, consistent with the tradition of anthropological scholarship which typically entails fieldwork outside the researcher's own culture (see e.g. Manzella and Yacher 2010; Rao 2010; Peterson 2010; Dracklé 2010). However, in recent years many media anthropologists note that the boundary between 'own' and 'other' culture has become increasingly hard to delineate especially due to the increased mobility and circulation of people, ideas, items and ideologies in the world (cf. Appadurai 1996; Urry 2008). Such methods have emerged – as web ethnography, netnography, or virtual ethnography/anthropology – in order to provide new methodological approaches for anthropological work to better grasp the contemporary mobile condition of social life (see e.g. Boellstroff et al. 2012; Hine 2000; 2005; Horst and Miller 2012; Kozinets 2010; Postill and Pink 2012; Wittel 2000).

The mediatized condition of witnessing invites anthropologists, who study crises, to re-visit the categories and perceptions of proximity and distance, along with the existing hierarchies between the 'real' and 'virtual' experience in relation to a crisis and the related suffering (see also Vigh 2008: 5; Ong 2012). Via our anthropological gaze we intend to develop a more nuanced understanding of media witnessing on YouTube as a cultural process and condition in a mediatized crisis.

Our empirical case, the freedom flotilla news event, in which Israeli forces raided a group of ships attempting to deliver humanitarian aid to Gaza on 31 May 2010, is chosen to illustrate the workings of media witnessing in a media-saturated world of crises. With this case (flotilla) and the context (YouTube), we argue that present-day media technology and the related cultural and social mediatization shapes 1) the spatiality, 2) the temporality, 3) the agency and, 4) the emotional attachment to the events associated with how we experience, interpret and communicate about crisis. While physically distant, the crisis on the flotilla took place thousands of kilometres away from Finnish and the Nordic waters, however, the emotional, moral, cultural and political involvement in the Israel-Palestine conflict brought the flotilla close to the Nordic hemisphere. The public interest in Sweden was particularly significant. One of the most popular Swedish authors, Henning Mankell, the creator of the crime series *Wallander*, was on board one of the boats. Mankell had also made his intentions public by announcing that he had decided to take part in the aid convoy to show his solidarity towards the Palestinians on Swedish radio. 'I think that when one talks about solidarity, one must always know that actions are what proves destiny', he said. 'It is with actions that we prove we are ready to support something we believe is important', Mankell continued (Flood 2010).

According to the International Middle East Media Center, altogether, there were 11 Swedish citizens on the boat, and among them members of parliament, activists, medical doctors, artists, academics and public intellectuals (International Middle East Media Centre 2010). The flotilla example makes it explicit that in the study of crises under mediatized conditions, we need to ask how these contemporary crises are distant, to whom they are distant, and in which ways this distance is expressed in media witnessed crises.

Another question concerns temporality. Frosh and Pinchevski (2009a: 295) argue that the contemporary life of high media saturation challenges academic research to rethink the notion of a crisis as an exceptional event to be managed, and to begin to examine it as a persistent ongoing condition, as an experimental ground of contemporary existence – a crisis-readiness to use the lexicon of Frosh and Pinchevski (2009a: 295–6). Crises typically consist of high news value material, and hence have always attracted media attention. In the current media-saturated life, rather than following a distant crisis through the news stories delivered by professional journalists that are already constructed from past events, we can now witness a crisis in and through the media in almost real-time. Different temporalities also mix. On YouTube, one may watch a video of live footage taken from the helicopter, like the Breivik slaughtering in Utøya. These live images, which were taken before the police had even entered the island, bear powerful witness to the events crossing different temporalities relating to the crisis. Media historian Terhi Rantanen (2009) stated that in the current media environment, the news is always on and consequently, so are the crises. In addition to the crisis as breaking news, 'old' crises also keep appearing and so regain visibility in the media. In the Nordic countries, the murders of Olof Palme in 1986 and Anna Lindh in 2003, as well as the sinking of the MS Estonia in the Baltic Sea in 1994, stand out as examples of past crises that continue to achieve media attention in many different forms and genres. New stories – both news and fiction – that are developed around these past crises produce new narratives and new layers of meaning in these moments of disruption and disaster.

In addition, the present-day media saturation transforms these hierarchies relating to the agency and the power to experience, to communicate and interpret these crises. Fresh, often non-professional, actors are entering the field of crisis communication, in and via new media technology, such as social media. Videos, blogs, tweets and Facebook posts are created to inform, communicate and comment on a crisis. This current type of grassroot journalism as Dan Gillmor (2006) calls it also shapes our understanding and perception of crises. Examples of this novel type of vernacular agency in crisis communication can be found in many recent crises. The Finnish school shootings in Jokela 2007 and Kauhajoki in 2008 stand out as examples in which ordinary people participated in crisis communication in numerous ways, which included sharing critical information about the events online (Sumiala and Tikka 2011). For example, the participants in the discussion forum on MuroBBS' website (a Finnish discussion forum frequented by computer enthusiasts/a Finnish hardware discussion forum) were the first to make the link between the events at the schools and their perpetrators. In both cases, the killers had posted media material online in which they had placed a warning about the crimes they were about to commit; users on the MuroBBS forum were quick to understand the connection (Sumiala and Tikka 2010).

Finally, the present-day media technology and the related cultural and social mediatization shape the emotional attachment to the events and consequently condition how we experience, interpret and communicate about a crisis. Many scholars agree that particularly relevant is the power of visual images to inflame emotions in iconizing global events and framing our knowledge and memory of international conflict and crisis (see e.g. Zelizer 2007). Kari Andén-Papadopoulos and Mervi Pantti (2011) note that this type of emotionally laden amateur imagery circulated by, what we may call grassroots photojournalists 'is often credited a new kind of closeness, that is, a 'raw' immediate, intensely subjective perspective on crisis events through the eyes of ordinary people struggling to bear witness to the scene around them' (13). These images are often perceived to carry a promise to eradicate existing boundaries of physical, social and cultural distance between spectators and sufferers seen in the media. Hence, they are afforded a heightened sense of emotional identification. The sceptics remind us that no automation should be expected here. Instead of narrowing down the distance between 'us' and the suffering 'others', 'snapparazzis' (Allan 2006: 155) taking pictures and shooting film of breaking news events may also stimulate sensationalism and voyerism, perhaps even dehumanize their subject matter. Drawing on Roger Silverstone's (2006) work Andén-Papadopoulos and Pantti (2011: 13) claim that emotional register, closeness and intimacy do not as such guarantee ethical and moral commitment and responsibility. How the relationship between the media witnesses and the suffering others is structured should, according to Andén-Papadopoulos and Pantti be perceived as contingent and deeply dependent on the specific parameters of how the sufferer is depicted in a particular amateur visual image and how the scene of suffering is narrated in that particular media discourse.

Media Witnessing

Since 9/11 in 2001, media witnessing has become one of the key concepts in the study of contemporary crises, catastrophes and conflicts of intensive mediatization (e.g. Anden-Papadopoulos 2013; Ellis 2009; Frosh and Pinchevski 2009a; Katz and Liebes 2007; Liebes and Blondheim 2005; Ong 2012; Peters 2009a; Rothenbuhler 2010; Scannell 2001). This development has emerged in concert with technological changes in the media environment. To give an example, in the case of the murder of the Swedish Foreign Minster Anna Lindh in 2003, media witnesses were delivered, first and foremost, by professional media actors, such as journalists. However, in the case of Utøya, the role of amateur media users in social media became more prominent. Also, new witnesses to an old crisis can be circulated via new media technologies, hence today we may find YouTube videos paying tribute to the death of the Swedish Prime Minister Olof Palme, a crisis that occurred some 20 years prior to the birth of YouTube (cf. Sumiala 2013).

To simply state it, media witnessing is the witnessing performed in, by and through the media. It refers to how media producers, texts and images, as well as audiences are positioned as witnesses of the realities of distant others (cf. Frosh and Pinchevski 2009b). Media witnessing requires 1) an agent who witnesses, 2) a witnessing representation and 3) an audience who receives and/or accepts the witness. Moreover, it changes the condition of witnessing by reformulating the categories of 'being there'. In the case of Sweden, for example, the physical distance between the people on the freedom flotilla and those following the events on their screens back at home can be assumed to be reduced by there being Swedish activists and well-known public figures on the boat, who offered a possibility to identify with the crisis at a different, more intimate level (Cottle 2009). So, instead of something bad happening to 'them' far away, it was happening to one of the Swedes as 'us'.

Ashuri and Pinchevski (2009: 133–5) distinguish the two key approaches to theorizing media witnessing: 1) the implicated witness and 2) the vicarious witness. The notion of an implicated witness emphasizes the distinction between witnessing agents and mere spectators, between those who were there and the ones who 'only' watched the event through the media. In this approach, one qualifies as a witnessing agent, predominantly, by the virtue of being present. This is in line with Peters' approach, since for him media witnessing always 'remains tied in some fragile way to the mortal limits of the human sensorum' and at its core is 'a hint of the real' (Peters 2009b: 45, 48). Vicarious witnessing, on the other hand, acknowledges a crucial connection between the media, namely the visual media that provides visual evidence, and the audience whose role is to receive and/or accept that evidence. Media representations, in this view, have the potential to create witness positions between people engaged in the broadcast and the imagined lives of strangers represented in, for example, a film. In this view, the broadcast or the film may become the witnessed 'event', at which the audience is co-present in time and coextensive in space (Frosh 2009: 52).

Moreover, witnessing is profoundly rooted in the ethical questions of suffering, judgement, solidarity and empathy. According to Roger Silverstone (2002), the result of media witnessing is that audiences now assume a moral stance and responsibility. For many scholars (e.g. Chouliaraki 2006; Moeller 2002; Tester 2001), the research on media witnessing contains a normative moral dimension that aspires to give a voice to the voiceless, and visibility to specific victims. According to Jonathan Ong (2012), a more detailed description of the process of media witnessing is needed, starting from the interaction between media producers and those represented (the victims), to the textual study of representations, continuing to the exploration of different emotional and cognitive responses of audiences from different social categories, as well as recording how the sufferers regard their own representations by taking their different social conditions into consideration as well.

Virtual Ethnography on Crisis

As an ethnographic place, YouTube, the site of the fieldwork in this chapter has certain implications for media anthropological work on a crisis (see e.g. Pink 2009). In the traditional media sphere dominated by the print media, radio and television, audiences receive the contents and make their interpretations based on them, but they are not able to actively shape the environment and the content produced in that environment themselves. However, to draw on Christine Hine (2000: 38), Internet users are dually involved in the construction of the web, 'through the practices by which they understand it and through the content they produce'. This much holds true in the world of YouTube, where users actively participate in the shaping of both content and the infrastructure of the platforms by surfing, clicking, commenting, uploading, downloading, sharing and liking. At the same time, the actions of people leave novel types of traces on YouTube. These signs create a new context of research (see e.g. Burges and Green 2009).

In the online environment of YouTube, the idea of studying a crisis in the present is given a new meaning. As a mobile sphere, YouTube is in constant flux, and while material is produced and uploaded, it is also continuously updated, manipulated and removed. For a virtual ethnographer, this means that s/he should be able to seize on the events as they are happening. The reconstruction of the traces and events afterwards on YouTube is often proved to be impartial, due to the ever changing character of this platform. Another key issue debated among media anthropologists is whether or not one should conduct ethnographic work solely in an online environment. In other words, we need to ask: is online fieldwork enough? To give an example, Ong (2012: 1) promotes a 'holistic' approach that is able to combine what he calls text-centred and audience-centred approaches in the study of present day crises, and the related distant suffering. Whether it is evident that in many cases, the combination of online and offline ethnographic fieldwork, when complemented with interviews of people using the media, has great value (Postill and Pink 2012; Boyd forthcoming; Orgad 2008; Lange 2007), we may find certain cases in which online ethnography provides unique material for the anthropological study of a crisis.

In this chapter, we want to argue for the advantages of virtual ethnography for an anthropological approach when studying a phenomena in flux, as well as argue for the adequacy of the method in which the media in question, namely YouTube, is approached – not so much as a medium of communication, but as a virtual culture in which the ethnographer enters, as s/he starts working on a crisis in a virtual environment. In this line of thinking, the virtual world of YouTube is addressed not only as a reflection of the 'reality' offline, or something completely separate or isolated compared with the 'real' physical world (cf. Hine 2000: 43). Instead, virtual ethnography, conducted in an online environment like YouTube, is perceived as a site of meaningful social action and cultural reconstruction. To follow Tom Boellstorff's (2008) insight, we should perceive virtual worlds as legitimate contexts of culture and interpret them as the 'actual' worlds. This, we argue, is very much the situation in this media anthropological study of crisis.

The Case

Our virtual fieldwork on YouTube was undertaken by tracing the freedom flotilla news event. The sequence of events at the flotilla from the early hours on Monday 31 May 2010 was the following: the Israeli navy warships intercepted the journey of the Gaza Freedom Flotilla (delivering humanitarian aid to Gaza citizens) in international waters, which had been blocked by the Israeli government, with Egyptian government support, since 2007. At that moment, the flotilla consisted of six ships and was carrying a cargo of thousands of tons of humanitarian aid equipment. There were 748 aboard, from approximately 40 countries, aged between one and 86 years old, including activists, journalists, doctors, writers, politicians and researchers (Sudgen 2010). As a result of Israel's raid, nine Turkish activists were killed aboard the *M/V Mavi Marmara* and dozens of others were injured. The passengers on the smallest and fastest ship of the flotilla, *Challenger I*, witnessed the attack of the Israeli warships on the *Mavi Marmara*, and the ship quickly withdrew from the formation. The purpose of this manoeuvre was to give the reporters aboard more time to send out news on the events through the ship's satellite Internet connection. After a chase, the Israeli commandos stopped the ship and boarded it. The Israeli warships raided the *Mavi Marmara* in the small hours of the morning on Monday, and the whole event was over in about an hour. The news of the raid spread immediately all around the world, both in mainstream media and on social networks – including YouTube (UN 2010).

The journey of the Gaza Freedom Flotilla was planned long before its departure. In fact, it was the ninth voyage of the Gaza Freedom Movement, which first took place in August 2008. Eight previous missions were considerably smaller in the number of boats, cargo and passengers. For this, the ninth flotilla of the Free Gaza Movement collaborated with other organizations. The self-declared aim of their mission was to draw public attention to the situation of the Gaza Strip, to break the blockade and to deliver humanitarian assistance to Gaza (UN 2010: 18–19).

As with all ethnographic research, virtual ethnographic research is characterized by openness and an endeavour to avoid a strict, pre-structured design. In addition, a high level of self-reflexivity is also necessary. Our fieldwork on YouTube integrally involved a thick description of our observations in the form of field notes, as well as the documentation and the recording of data, especially in the form of YouTube videos. Instead of uploading videos ourselves, we did what a majority of YouTube users do: we followed the online activities of active 'YouTubers' and other media by watching videos and tracing the link paths made up by the videos. According to Jakob Nielsen (2006), and frequently referred to 90-9-1 rule of thumb in participation of social media, out of 100 users on social media networks, only one is an active user, nine are random users and 90 are just there to follow what others are doing (Snickars and Vondreau 2009: 12; Van Dijck 2009: 44). Besides, by recording our observations in detail and documenting different content, we also, by our presence, participated in the construction of the internal YouTube hierarchies. Different actors, and contents, on YouTube become more visible and strengthen their position according to the number of views. By opening and watching videos in Finland, we, as researchers, also produced another view with each of our clicks, and so took part in reinforcing the YouTube hierarchies and the related social construction of the events.

We conducted our fieldwork on YouTube from 1–17 June 2010. Before this, we prepared to access the field by familiarizing ourselves with YouTube culture, both theoretically and empirically. In the last days of May 2010, we were waiting for a media event to occur. When the news of the raid spread, we were immediately ready to start our virtual ethnography. Therefore, we were also able to observe the unfolding crisis on/through YouTube in real-time. The starting point in our research was to carry out our fieldwork in the context of a world under study (see Boellstorff 2008). In other words, even though we acknowledged the different backgrounds as contextual frames that shaped production and reception of the crisis by different groups of users, the goal in this media anthropological study was not to discuss flotilla crisis within the framework of political communication. Nor was it to examine what possible political motives, connected with the wider Middle East conflict, might be discoverable in the background of the different producers of the YouTube contents. Instead, we studied the events as they presented themselves to us, as virtual ethnographers and as viewers participating in the news event from a distance, in the north. In this context, we also reflected on our own backgrounds, as Nordic, middle class, white academic women living geographically, historically and culturally far away from the actual events on the sea. While we could easily frame and understand the flotilla crisis as an event in a long history of ongoing crises and conflict in the Middle East, our attachment to the events remained relatively remote and somewhat abstract. This is not to say that we were emotionally immune to the violence of the crisis, but that we were witnessing those acts from a distance in relation to our emotional life histories. As Ong (2012) underlines, even though the analysis is focused on media representations – that is, texts and images used in communicating about the crisis in question, it is important to recognize how these texts and images are interpreted. This again depends on the personal involvement of the audience at the events, and it varies accordingly.

A note on authenticity is also needed. In virtual ethnography research, the questions concerning the origin and authenticity of the media representation of the crisis become problematic. It is possible to attempt to trace the identity, age or ethnic background of the video uploaders on their channels, but the ethnographer will often have to settle for whatever material the creators have offered of themselves. On the other hand, as is the case with most online material, we, as participants of this culture, can only rely on what the makers of the videos, Facebook updaters, bloggers or twitters reveal to us about themselves.

Our work on this global news event consisted of navigating on YouTube sites for several hours on a daily basis, making notes as well as performing different searches with the YouTube search engine and recording them. After testing different combinations of the search word, we chose the word pair 'Israeli flotilla', since it produced results that were centred on this specific event. We also kept a detailed, daily watch for videos that were connected with the related news listed in the YouTube category of 'News and Politics', in order to observe the relationship between this news event and other breaking news. The default language in performing this ethnographic research on YouTube was English and the location was worldwide. These choices have their consequences, as language and location are always related to issues of power and hegemony. If we would have traced the event, for example, in Arabic, Hebrew, Turkish or Finnish, or by using the YouTube location of Israel, our observations might have been different. Furthermore, by choosing English as the default language, we as ethnographers are engaged with testimonies aimed at audiences who are situated within the Western 'zone of safety' (Ong 2012: 11). When we began the ethnography on Tuesday, 1 June 2010, there were already several news pieces covering the topic on YouTube. The 'Israeli flotilla' search produced 2840 videos at that time. A day and a half had passed since the raid, during which much had happened.

Information on the raid and the victims that had died in it aroused a strong reaction on the very day it occurred. The raid was internationally condemned and thousands of people demonstrated against it all over the world. This produced a continuous flow of fresh news on the subject. The number of search results kept growing for more than a week, until reaching its peak of 7870 hits on 9 June 2010. After that date, there was a mild decline and the material saturated the medium. The number of hits remained at slightly over 6000 videos, upon the conclusion of our ethnography research. We also examined the most watched videos in YouTube's 'News and Politics' category during the same time period. Our observation was that news on the subject was featured most prominently for about five days after the events. After that, other news gradually took its place.

Witnessing on YouTube

With the spread of the Internet and social networking sites, such as YouTube, new modalities of media witnessing have emerged. The most distinct feature of YouTube witnessing is visuality, especially concerning the moving image. In this sense, YouTube shares many similarities with conventional television (cf. Katz 2009). But unlike conventional television, YouTube invites authors and viewers to participate in the process of witnessing on a new scale, thus establishing novel connections between the witnessing agents and testimonials, along with audiences receiving and accepting these testimonies (cf. Andén-Papadopoulos 2013). YouTube encourages audiences, or rather, users to comment on the evidence and testimonial materials and to share those materials via its channels (cf. Pantti and Tikka 2013).

Besides the opportunity to publish and comment on witnessing videos, YouTube also offers a diverse and constantly growing selection of ways in which YouTube account owners – whether professional or amateur, can participate in disseminating witness materials: videos as witnessing representations can be shared through emails, Facebook or Twitter, where users can respond to them. These witnessing pieces can also be embedded into other websites, declared offensive, suggested to other viewers of similar videos or subscribed to through one's own channel, thus creating new networks of mediated witnessing. All in all, YouTube's culture is closely linked to the cycling and the recycling of testimonials and participants, remediation, or rather pre-mediation, as Richard Grusin (2009: 63–4) characterized YouTube. The idea of sharing witnesses is found in the typical 'share it!' slogan of YouTube, which thus links participants to the chain of circulation of media witnessing by 'the intensification and multiplication of technical and social media networks' (Grusin 2009: 63). To summarize, YouTube offers the viewer a myriad of witness paths to follow. Instead of one dominant public sphere for media witnessing, YouTube is filled with numerous 'little public spheres' from which anyone can choose their own path (see Marcinkowski 2008). The ephemeral and vernacular character of YouTube, which dissolves media witnessing into a number of encounters between different witnessing agents, witnessing texts and witnessing audiences, compels us to rethink the notion media witnessing on a new scale. Issues, such as 'authenticity', 'authority', 'truth', 'intimacy' and 'moral justification', that are characteristically associated with witnessing call for further elaboration when discussed in the context of this emerging culture of media witnessing under crisis conditions.

Witnessing on the Flotilla

Witnessing Agents and Representations

In order to identify the key actors and practices contributing to, and participating in, media witnessing, we tracked the flotilla news by following certain categories and key words, such as the above mentioned search term, 'Israeli flotilla'. We also cross-analysed the results from the YouTube's search engine and the 'News and Politics' category from the perspective of the users who had uploaded videos. The results indicated the three main operators that had produced the most videos on the subject and whose videos had been viewed the most were: 1) professional news agencies, 2) the Israeli Defence Forces Spokesperson's Unit (username *Idfnadesk*) and 3) 'YouTubers'. The distribution among these operators reflects the typical YouTube participant structure, as proposed by Burgess and Green (2009). The news agencies that centrally appeared in the analysis of the empirical material were Russia Today (RT) and Al Jazeera English (AJE). The second operator, who had a key role in the building up of the flotilla news, was the Spokesperson's Unit for the Israeli Defence Forces (IDF), which joined YouTube on 29 December 2008. The third key actor producing flotilla news was the heterogeneous group of so-called ordinary users. We refer to them here as YouTubers. According to Patricia Lange (2007, 5), YouTubers 'participate in the operation of the site, actively producing videos and comments to it'. Users with a strong presence in this category included, for example, *91177info*, *Axis4peace2* and *OmniChristianVids2*, who actively produced videos connected with news or commented on the events with their videos.

The agents who witness, witnessing representations and the audience who receives the witness compound an interconnected assemblage. To state it simply, based on our material, we could see that the physical events were filmed both by activists and the Israeli naval forces. This video material was soon sent by activists to the news agencies and uploaded onto YouTube by the Israel Defence Forces Spokesperson's Unit. Professional news media then used this visual material in their bulletins. Following this, YouTubers used news videos of professional news agencies and Idfnadesk's material to produce their own videos again. The analysis of the videos shows that different actors took the same material and used it to create their own testimonials of the event.

Professionals

The witnessing role of the professional news media was twofold, and fits both of the approaches of implicated witness and vicarious witness, as mentioned above and discussed by Frosh and Pinchevski (2009). As mentioned earlier, some of the passengers were journalists, one of whom, Jamal Elshayyal, was a reporter for Al Jazeera English. In a video filmed on the *Mavi Marmara*, Elshayyal reports on the situation on board. The claim to authenticity in this material is strong, as the reporter is at personal risk in being onboard, instead of observing the situation from a distance (see e.g. Andén-Papadopoulos 2013: 354). For Peters' (2009a), the immediate and physical experience of witnesses is important because 'liveness serves as an assurance of access to truth and authenticity' (Peters 2009a: 36). Any mediation reduces the happening event into a representation that is a mere copy. Thus, Elshayyal, among other journalists on the flotilla, qualifies as a witnessing agent, because he meets the criteria of 'being there' that is emphasized in the notion of implicated witness.

However, it is exactly the incessant repeatability brought about by digitalization that enables the system of media witnessing. Apart from being a witnessing agent according to the view of the implicated witness, Elshayyal was also a witness depicted in the news reports. This leads us to the notion of the vicarious witness, where visual media, here Al Jazeera English and Russia Today, provide the visual evidence of the crisis. Elshayyal's presence on the *Mavi Marmara*, his filmed reporting, the disorganized situation around him and the shaking camera create an effect of truth. The same visual evidence was also used in Russia Today's video titled *On-board Video of Gaza Freedom Flotilla Storm, Aid Workers and Israeli Troops Clash* that is compiled from clips filmed by the passengers and surveillance cameras. The video shows soldiers with guns, a navy helicopter and there is chaotic footage from on board the ship with people running around and the wounded lying on the ground. One of the voices speaking on this video is Elshayyal's. This RT video serves as an eyewitness account of the reality on board at the time of the interception. Out of all the material, this video element, with its strong reality effect, came to mark 'the truth' of the event (cf. Andén-Papadopoulos 2013: 342). Many other news channels also broadcasted the same material over and over again.

Professional news agencies broadcast news covering events for those of us who are not there (see e.g. Bird 2010). The compositions of these YouTube news videos varied from 'on board' videos to more conventional forms. Another of Russia Today's videos was titled *Gaza Flotilla Attacked: Israeli Troops Storm Aid Ships, up to 20 Feared Dead.* It was released on the day of the attack at 09:01 GMT. The news video clip is 11:38 minutes long and it shares the form with the traditional TV-news format. The video begins with a studio anchor's introduction to the subject and continues with detailed information that is presented by a correspondent from Ashdod Port, Israel. As the correspondent is giving a report on a smaller screen, the big screen behind her is showing dramatic visual material, filmed by passengers and surveillance cameras on the the *Mavi Marmara* during the attack. The news video also includes many interviews and comments, for example, from the Head of the Gaza Hamas Government, the Hamas Government's deputy foreign minister, a former Palestinian minister, Gaza activists and a British Muslim Initiative spokesperson from the ship. The commentaries were repeatedly framed by visual material from the *Mavi Marmara*, as well as video clips from the demonstrations in Turkey. The entire news video was framed by the logo and colours of Russia Today. The composition of this video follows the elements of traditional TV news: an anchor in the studio and a local correspondent covering the events, video clips from the scene and interviewees telling the story from different perspectives.

YouTubers

The other category of witnessing agents is the YouTubers. The logic behind media witnessing is that it simultaneously invites people to both bear witness and to produce testimonies themselves (Frosh and Pinchevski 2009a). Thus, YouTubers have simultaneous and multiple roles. They bear witness to the event as the audience – the ultimate addressees of the crisis, but they also play a role in creating testimonies of the event, and hence, consequently, participating in performing the crisis. This heterogeneous group of active YouTube users acted in line with this logic and started to produce their own crisis testimonies. Users such as axis4peace2, for instance, edited and remediated the visual flotilla material filmed by the Israel Defence Forces and activists that was already circulating on YouTube, and used it to comment on the events. The videos have been named, for example, as follows:

Proof Israel Attacked and Killed before they Boarded Freedom Flotilla and *Fake Videos of Israel about the Freedom Flotilla Attack Exposed (Must See!!!)*. The user strongly criticizes Israel's actions in these videos.

Besides using the material filmed on board, YouTubers also participated as witnesses to the crisis event by making videos that contextualized the event into the wider conflict concerning Israel and Palestine. One of the videos titled The Reality in Israel described the lives of Israeli children who were under the constant fear of missile strikes from Gaza, by showing bomb holes in their playgrounds. The opposite side was taken in the video of SaudiSpirit. This video shows pictures of the flotilla's cargo, toys and wheelchairs, with text commentaries and sentimental music. The video questions the IDF's claim that there were weapons in the cargo, and that the activists had hostile intentions. These videos showed how in the present age of social media, ordinary people as grass-roots journalists are socialized to join in the performance of a crisis, and hence take emotional, moral and ethical positions in witnessing the event. In the case of flotilla news, YouTubers not only participated and witnessed the crisis through their videos, but they also played a role in creating it.

Audiences

The visual material filmed onboard can be perceived as the vigorous witnessing representation that was available to audiences worldwide. Video footage filmed by the passengers, which was rather blurry and shot quickly with a handheld camera, was repeatedly shown in the AJE and RT news broadcasts. In these videos, we see speedboats flanking the ship, commandos abseiling onto the ship from helicopters, people lying on the deck wearing life jackets, and we see the general chaos. The material published by the Israeli Defence Forces show the fighting between the passengers and the commandos, and the commandos descending onto the ship from helicopters. The material from the IDF also included a video filmed from a helicopter, with events on the ship as viewed from above. The people aboard the ship appear only as tiny dots. In the video footage from the ship's security cameras, we see both commandos with their weapons and passengers in their life jackets. The same footage was circulated by different actors and were harnessed to tell different, and often opposing, narratives. But by contrast to other current crises, such as natural disasters, this material was not filmed by accident or through happenstance. Both sides carefully prepared and produced their witnessing representations. Cameras were used as visual weaponry (Sontag 2003; see also Andén-Papadopoulos 2013) in order to witness and report the crimes of the opposite side. The number of journalists and cameras on the flotilla, as well as the cameras attached to soldiers' helmets, elucidates the engagement of these actors in the system of perpetual crisis-readiness and their need to invite audiences to witness the event through the media.

These representations that were mixed, edited, shared and circulated on YouTube were seen thousands of times by the active audiences. Even though only a fraction of the audiences started to make their own videos on the event (like YouTubers), there were also those who 'only' watched the news on YouTube; they can be counted as bearing active witness to the crisis. In contrast to the mundane witnessing via television, a relatively passive medium, the social media environment requires certain level of activity, where the viewer has to navigate and click in order to view these short video clips (cf. Ellis 2009). As mentioned above, 'clicks' also create the hierarchies inside YouTube, where videos are ranked on how many times they are watched.

Having said this, the audiences witness the events vicariously on/through YouTube. These representations create various witness positions that are also of conflicting nature. Representations as witnessing invite the viewers to accept or reject the evidences and testimonies given in these news videos. The issue of emotional and geographical distance needs to be readdressed here. For the people living in the area of the Middle East, the events on the flotilla are part of the long continuum of crises. When loss, suffering and (media) war become facts of social life, a very particular way of participating in media witnessing is created (cf. Vigh 2008). This can be seen, for example, in some of the YouTubers' videos, where the flotilla event was commented on by a video response about children in the Middle East living in constant fear of missile fire. To follow Henrik Vigh (2008: 12), rather than seeing social processes implode and disintegrate, what we see in situations of prolonged crisis is that the state of emergency becomes a 'situation of emergence' (Bhabha 1994: 41), whereby social life is interpreted and unfolds within the terrain of risk and uncertainty. For others, the Middle East crisis stretches well beyond the borders and boundaries of any particular geographical area. Many were emotionally affected by this crisis through complex historical, ethnic, political, economic, and religious attachments (cf. Cottle 2009).

Media Witnessing on YouTube – Rethinking Categories?

To conclude with, we suggest that the view on YouTube as a *machinery of media witnessing* invites new perspectives in the anthropological and cultural analysis for contemporary crises and one that challenges scholarship to rethink the questions of spatiality, temporality, emotional attachment and the practice in this condition of mediatization. Whereas, the traditional concept of a crisis carries the idea of exceptionality and the necessity of management, the crisis in a mediatized condition seems to be intertwined with the heterogeneous simultaneity of experience and witness (cf. Calhoun 2004).

We argue the stake in media witnessing on YouTube, is the transformation of categories of witnessing in relation to the issues of distance and proximity, temporalities of past, present and future, and the roles and visual and emotional practices of agents who participate in media witnessing of the crisis. Our virtual ethnography indicates that media witnessing on YouTube opens up in many directions. Some of them concern the practices and hierarchies relating to the agency in witnessing – questions raised include: which actors are able and willing to bear witness to a crisis and what kind of implications are embedded in these position changes as media witnessing emerges? In the case of the flotilla, both professionals and amateurs could equally create and share media witnesses as visual evidence of the crisis in question. When looking at amateur witnesses we may claim that the participation of amateurs in media witnessing widened the professional crisis reporting, as it resisted the normative interpretations of professional news and thereby opened up an affective and political space within it (see also Andén-Papadopoulos 2013: 353). When looking at the professionals and their procedures for witnessing, we argue that the newsrooms, in this case, Russia Today and Al Jazeera English in particular, were in constant crisis-readiness to witness the events on board. Further, the audiences were incorporated into the logic of media witnessing, since YouTube offered a platform for ordinary people to bear witness as well as to produce testimonies on the events, independent of their physical location. Thus, we may say, that media witnessing on YouTube took place simultaneously in, by and through, a variety of media sites and platforms. It brought the local to the global, and vice versa. Media witnessing as a practice on the flotilla invited a multiplicity of actors, from professional journalists to ordinary people to become involved with the crisis on different levels.

Moreover, in addition to what we may call the rethinking of media witnessing in a crisis, as different actors holding a range of different positions (professional, amateur, etc) were invited to bear witness to this same platform, we also need to recognize the contextual variation in these witnessing positions. This brings us to a question of emotional and moral distance versus proximity in relation to the witnessed events. As articulated in the study, the members of the audience held different witness positions depending on their geographical, emotional and cultural involvement, their closeness or their distance to events as a physical and symbolic reality. These issues have to do with politics and the culture of media witnessing and their association with the history and politics of the crisis in the Middle East. According to the media scholar Lilie Chouliaraki (2011), instead of treating values of human vulnerability, collective responsibility and global injustice – all associated with media witnessing – as universal, it should be acknowledged that there are various contextually-limited definitions that should be debated in the communicative space of media witnessing with radical plurality.

The 'calculus of death', institutionalized in the professional world of media production emphasizes the viewpoints and the suffering of those culturally close to 'us' (Pantti, Wahl-Jorgensen and Cottle 2012). Following this reasoning, it can be said that the presence of the Swedish activists on board the multinational flotilla made the events an important news topic in the Nordic region, and particularly within the Swedish media sphere. From the mainstream media, people in Sweden were able to read the eyewitness accounts from people like the author Henning Mankell, with whom they were already familiar through the media. The notion of 'being there' or 'implicated witness' to use the lexicon of Ashuri and Pinchevski (2009) certainly refers to those present on board, but we would like to suggest that we need to expand this idea even further as we extend our view of YouTube as a spatial location in the crisis.

Cultural geographer Doreen Massey states that places are 'constructed out of a particular constellation of social relations, meeting and weaving together at a particular locus' (1994: 154). Drawing on our ethnographic work, we argue that YouTube offered this site as a place for different interests to engage in struggle. Indeed, YouTube works for the coexistence of the many voices of witnessing in the same time-space as well as an 'ethical and democratic space that upholds equality of voice, [and] hospitality for vulnerable others' (Ong 2012: 13). Videos uploaded by a broad array of amateur and professional actors bear witness to the activists inside the vessel waiting for the attack, of the Israeli navy soldier commanding the flotilla to turn around, of the journalistic newsroom accounts of the events, of the demonstrations in Turkey, as well as the discomforting stories by ordinary YouTubers on everyday lives in Israel and Palestine. By watching these videos, an audience from different backgrounds and contextual histories whether Nordic or Southern were offered a possibility to relate to the culturally or politically more or less distant other as an 'other with her or his own humanity' (Silverstone 2004: 4). Whereas mainstream media may enforce the categories of cultural closeness and a distance based on geopolitical interests, social media such as YouTube may be seen to offer a space that is open for understanding, imagination and judgement in new spatial and temporal constellation (cf. Silverstone 2004; Chouliaraki 2011). However, instead of harmony this space has many chaotic features that spring from the struggle over the 'truth' (Sumiala and Tikka 2014, forthcoming). As representations of a witness with a myriad of angles, YouTube videos on the flotilla painted a picture of the flotilla crisis as a condition by contextualizing it simultaneously in the complex history of the Middle East, as well as on a personal level on the plurality of witnessing agents with different and even opposite motives and emotional and moral attachments on board and outside the world of YouTube. By approaching a crisis as ongoing context, and as a condition, we were enabled to analyse the layers of media witnessing in crisis, as well as the spatiality and the temporality that influenced the processes and the dynamics associated with it. A final note on temporality: eventually, a certain dramatic situation is brought to an end. The Swedish delegates arrive home in the north; in this case the flotilla crisis was concluded. Yet, uncertainty and loss remained, and still remain in a range of media representations circulating in different visual and textual forms on YouTube and elsewhere in the media (cf. Vigh 2008). Members of the heterogeneous global audience look at these videos from different witness positions and the related emotional and moral attachments. They do not share the same realities or experiences associated with the crisis. They do not even understand the implications of the crisis in a similar matter. What is held in common is that they all are incorporated in the dynamics of witnessing on YouTube in one way or the other. Consequently, they all insist on the power of YouTube as the crucial context for 'the truth' and the associated moral justification and judgement in today's crisis of a mediatized condition.

Works Cited

Allan, Stuart (2006) *Online News: Journalism and the Internet.* New York: Open University Press.

Andén-Papadopoulos, Kari (2013) 'Media Witnessing and the "Crowd-sourced Video Revolution"'. *Visual Communications* 12 (3), 341–57.

— and Mervi Pantti (2011) 'Introduction', in Andén-Papadopoulos, Kari and Mervi Pantti (eds) *Amateur Images and Global News.* Bristol: Intellect, 9–20.

Appadurai, Arjun (1996) *Modernity at Large: Cultural Dimensions of Globalization.* Minnesota: University of Minnesota Press.

Ashuri, Tamar and Amit Pinchevski (2009) 'Witnessing as a Field', in Frosh, Paul and Amit Pinchevski (eds) *Media Witnessing: Testimony in the Age of Mass Communication.* Houndmills: Palgrave, 133–57.

Bhabha, Homi K. (1994) *The Location of Culture.* London: Routledge.

Bird, Elizabeth S (2010) 'The Anthropology of News and Journalism: Why Now?', in Bird, Elizabeth S. (ed.) *The Anthropology of News and Journalism. Global Perspectives.* Bloomington, Indiana: Indiana University Press, 1–18.

Boellstorff, Tom (2008) *Coming of Age in Second Life: An Anthropologist Explores the Virtually Human.* New Jersey: Princeton University Press.

—, Bonnie Nardi, Celia Pearce and T.L. Taylor (2012) *Ethnography and Virtual Worlds.* New Jersey: Princeton University Press.

Boyd, Danah (forthcoming) 'Making Sense of Teen Life: Strategies for Capturing Ethnographic Data in a Networked Era', in Hargittai, Eszter and Christian Sandvig (eds) *Digital Research Confidential: The Secrets of Studying Behavior Online.* Cambridge MA: The MIT Press, viewed 5 May 2013, http://www.danah.org/papers/2012/Methodology-DigitalResearch.pdf.

Burgess, Jean and Joshua Green (2009) *YouTube: Online Video and Participatory Culture.* Cambridge: Polity Press.

Calhoun, Graig (2004) 'A World of Emergencies: Fear, Intervention and the Limits of Cosmopolitan Order'. *Canadian Review of Sociology/Revue Canadienne de Sociologie*, 41 (4), 373–95.

Castells, Manuel (2009) *Communication Power.* Oxford: Oxford University Press.

Chouliaraki, Lilie (2011) '"Improper Distance": Towards a Critical Account of Solidarity as Irony'. *International Journal of Cultural Studies*, 14 (4), 363–81.

— (2006) *Spectatorship of Suffering*, London: Sage.

Coombs, Timothy W. (2007) *Ongoing Crisis Communication: Planning, Managing, and Responding*, 2nd ed. Los Angeles: Sage.

Cottle, Simon (2009) *Global Crisis Reporting. Journalism in the Global Age.* Maidenhead: McGraw.

— (2006) *Mediatized Conflict: Developments in Media and Conflict Studies.* Maidenhead: McGraw.

van Dijck, José (2009) 'Users Like You? Theorizing Agency in User-generated Content'. *Media Culture and Society* 31 (1), 41–58.

Drackl√©, Dorle (2010) 'Gossip and Resistance: Local News Media in Transition: A Case Study from Alentejo, Potugal', in Bird, Elizabeth S. (ed.) *The Anthropology of News and Journalism: Global Perspectives.* Bloomington: Indiana University Press, 199–214.

Ellis, John (2000) *Seeing Things: Television in the Age of Uncertainty*. London: I.B. Tauris.

— (2009) 'Mundane witness', in Frosh, Paul and Amit Pinchevski (eds) *Media Witnessing: Testimony in the Age of Mass Communication.* Houndmills: Palgrave, 73–88.

Flood, Alison (2010) 'Author Henning Mankell Aboard Gaza Flotilla Stormed by Israeli Troops'. *The Guardian,* 31 May, viewed 2 September 2013, http://www.theguardian.com/books/2010/may/31/henning-mankell-israel-flotilla-gaza.

Frosh, Paul (2009) 'Telling Presences: Witnessing, Mass Media, and the Imagined Lives of Strangers', in Frosh, Paul and Amit Pinchevski (eds) *Media Witnessing: Testimony in the Age of Mass Communication.* Houndmills: Palgrave, 49–72.

— and Amit Pinchevski. (2009a) 'Crisis-readiness and Media Witnessing'. *The Communication Review* 12 (3), 295–304.

— and — (2009b) 'Introduction. Why Media Witnessing? Why Now?', in Frosh, Paul and Amit Pinchevski (eds) *Media Witnessing: Testimony in the Age of Mass Communication.* Houndmills: Palgrave, 1–19.

Gillmor, Dan (2006) *We the Media: Grassroots Journalism by the People for the People*. Sebastopol, CA: O'Reilly Media.

Grusin, Richard (2009) 'YouTube at the End of New Media', in Snickars, P. and P. Vonderau (eds) *The YouTube Reader*. National Library of Sweden: Stockholm, 60–67.

Hepp, Andreas (2013) *Cultures of Mediatization.* Cambridge: Polity Press.

Hine, Christine (2000) *Virtual Ethnography.* London: Sage.

— (2005) *Virtual Methods: Issues in Social Research on the Internet*. Oxford: Berg.

Horst, Heather and Daniel Miller (eds) (2012) *Digital Anthropology*. London: Berg.

International Middle East Media Centre (2010) '11 Swedish Citizens Aboard the Freedom Flotilla' 26 May, International Middle East Media Center, viewed 2 September 2013, http://www.imemc.org/article/58769.

Katz, Elihu (2009) 'The End of Television'. The ANNALS of the American Academy of Political and Social Science. September, 625, 6–18.

— and Tamar Liebes (2007) 'No More Peace! How Disaster, Terror and War have Upstaged Media Events'. *International Journal of Communication* 1, 157–66.

Kozinets, Robert (2010) *Netnography: Doing Ethnographic Research Online.* Los Angeles, CA.: Sage.

Lange, Patricia (2007) 'Commenting on Comments: Investigating Responses to Antagonism on YouTube'. Paper presented to the Society for Applied Anthropology Conference, Tampa, Florida, March. Viewed 12 February 2010, http://sfaapodcasts.files.wordpress.com/2007/04/update-apr-17-lange-sfaa-paper-2007.pdf.

Liebes, Tamar and Menahem Blondheim (2005) 'Myths to the Rescue: How Live Television Intervenes in History', in Rothenbuhler, E. and M. Coman (eds) in *Media Anthropology.* Thousand Oaks: Sage 188–198.

Lundby, Knut (ed.) (2009) *Mediatization. Concept, Changes, Consequences*. New York: Peter Lang.

Manzella, Joseph C. and Leon I. Yacher (2010) 'News and Myth in Venezuela: the Press and the Chávez revolution', in Bird, Elizabeth S. (ed.) *The Anthropology of News and Journalism: Global Perspectives.* Bloomington: Indiana University Press, 71–85.

Marcinkowski, Frank (2008) 'Public Sphere and Fragmentation of the Public Sphere', in Wolfgang Donsbach (ed.) *The Blackwell International Encyclopedia of Communication.* Blackwell, 4041–8.

Massey, Doreen (1994) *Space, Place and Gender*. Minnneapolis: University of Minnesota Press.

Moeller, Susan (2002) 'A Hierarchy of Innocence: the Media's Use of Children in the Telling of International News'. *Press/Politics* 7, 36–56.

Nielsen, Jacob (2006) 'Participation Inequality: Encouraging More Users to Contribute', 9 October 2006, Nielsen Norman Group, viewed 3 February 2012, http://www.useit.com/alertbox/participation_inequality.html.

Ong, Jonathan C. (2012) '"Witnessing" or "Mediating" Distant Suffering? Ethical Questions across Moments of Text, Production, and Reception'. *Television and New Media*, viewed 2 May 2013 http://tvn.sagepub.com/content/early/2012/08/14/1527476412454687.full.pdf+html.

Orgad, Shani (2008) 'How Can Researchers Make Sense of the Issues Involved in Collecting and Interpreting Online and Offline Data?', in Markham, Annette and Nancy Baym (eds) *Internet Inquiry: Conversations about method.* Thousand Oaks CA: Sage, 33–53.

Pantti, Mervi, Kari Wahl-Jorgensen, Simon Cottle (2012) *Disasters and the Media.* New York: Peter Lang.

— and Minttu Tikka (2013) 'Cosmopolitan Empathy and User-generated Disaster Appeal Videos on YouTube', in Benski, Tova and Eran Fisher (eds) *Internet and Emotions.* New York: Routledge.

Peterson, Mark Allen (2010) 'Getting the News in New Delhi: Newspaper Literacies in an Indian Mediascape', in Bird, Elizabeth S. (ed.) *The Anthropology of News and Journalism: Global Perspectives.* Bloomington: Indiana University Press, 168–81.

Peters, John Durham (2009a) 'Witnessing', in Frosh, Paul and Amit Pinchevski (eds) *Media Witnessing: Testimony in the Age of Mass Communication.* Houndmills: Palgrave McMillan: 23–41.

— (2009b) 'An Afterword: Torchlight Red on Sweaty Faces', in Frosh, Paul and Amit Pinchevski (eds) *Media Witnessing: Testimony in the Age of Mass Communication.* Houndmills: Palgrave, 42–8.

Pink, Sarah (2009) *Doing Sensory Ethnography.* London: Sage.

Postill, John and Sarah Pink (2012) 'Social Media Ethnography: the Digital Researcher in a Messy Web'. *Media International Australia,* (145) viewed 15 May 2013, http://blogs.bournemouth.ac.uk/research/files/2013/04/Postill-Pink-socialmedia-ethnography.pdf.

Rao, Ursula (2010) 'Empowerment through Local News Making: Studying the Media/Public Interface in India', in Bird, Elizabeth S. (ed.) *The Anthropology of News and Journalism: Global Perspectives.* Bloomington: Indiana University Press, 100–115.

Rantanen, Terhi (2009) *When News was New?* Oxford: Blackwell.

Rothenbuhler, Eric (2010) 'Media Events in the Age of Terrorism and the Internet'. *The Romanian Review of Journalism and Communication* (V) 2, 34–41.

Scannell, Paul (2001) 'Editorial'. *Media, Culture and Society* 23 (6), 699–705.

Silverstone, Roger (2006) *Media and Morality: On the Rise of the Mediapolis.* Cambridge: Polity.

— (2002) 'Complicity and Collusion in the Mediation of Everyday Life'. *New Literary History* 33 (4), 761–80.

Snickars, Pelle and Patrich Vonderau (eds) (2009) *The YouTube Reader.* Stockholm: National Library of Sweden.

Sontag, Susan (2003) *Regarding the Pain of Others.* New York: Picador/Farrar.

Sudgen, Joanna (2010) 'Gaza ships: the Passenger List.' 1 June, *The Times*, viewed 21 October 2010, http://www.timesonline.co.uk/tol/news/world/middle_east/article7141720.ece.

Sumiala, Johanna (2014) 'Mediatization of Death', in Lundby, Knut (ed.) *The Handbook of Mediatization of Communication* 21. Berlin: Walter de Gruyter (forthcoming).

— (2013) *Media and Ritual: Death, Community and Everyday Life.* London: Routledge.

— and Salli Hakala (2010) 'Crisis: Mediatization of Disaster in the Nordic Media Sphere', in Broddason, þorbjörn, Ullamaija Kivikuru, Birgitte Tufte, Lennart Weibull and Helge Østbye (eds) *The Nordic Countries and the World: Perspectives from Research on Media and Communication.* Göteborg: Nordicom.

— and Minttu Tikka (2014) Flotilla News from YouTube! New Avenues of Anthropological News Research (submitted for publication).

— and — (2013) 'Broadcast Yourself – Global News!

A Netnography of the 'Flotilla' News on YouTube'. *Communication, Culture and Critique*, 6 (2), 201–352.

— (2011) 'Visualizing Globalized Fears: School Shooting Videos and Circulation of Violence on YouTube'. *Social Anthropology/Anthropologie Sociale* 19 (3), 254–67.

— (2010) '"Web First" to Death – the Media Logic of the School Shootings in the Era of Uncertainty'. *Nordicom Review* 31 (2), 17–29.

Tester, Keith (2001) *Compassion, Morality and the Media.* Buckingham: Open University Press.

United Nations. General Assembly, Human Rights Council. (2010) Report of the International Fact-finding Mission to Investigate Violations of International Law, Including International Humanitarian and Human Rights Law, Resulting from the Israeli Attacks on the Flotilla of Ships Carrying Humanitarian Assistance. United Nations, viewed 5 November 2010, http://www2.ohchr.org/english/bodies/hrcouncil/docs/15session/A.HRC.15.21_en.pdf.

Urry, John (2008) *Mobilities.* Cambridge: Polity.

Vigh, Henrik (2008) 'Crisis and Chronicity: Anthropological Perspectives on Continuous Conflict and Decline'. *Ethnos* 73 (1), 2–24.

Wittel, Andreas (2000) 'Ethnography on the Move: from Field to Net to Internet'. *Forum Qualitative Sozialforschung/Forum: Qualitative Social Research* 1 (1), viewed 10 June, 2011, http://www.qualitative-research.net/index.php/fqs/article/viewArticle/1131.

Zelizer, Barbie (2007) 'On "Having Been There": "Eyewitnessing" as a Journalistic Key Word'. *Critical Studies in Media Communication*, 24 (5), 408–28.

Chapter 2

Scandinavia and 'the Land of UnSwedish Freedom': Jonathan Franzen, Susanne Bier and Self-conceptions of Exceptionalism in Crisis

Ebbe Volquardsen

This chapter addresses self-conceptions of exceptionalism in the United States and in Northern Europe. The notion that one nation, one region or one group is exceptional, conflicts with globalization theory. Because of migrating people, goods and ideas, the world is understood to become more homogeneous (Appadurai 2008; Comaroff and Comaroff 2012). However, globalization incorporates a globalization of risks, conflict (Beck 2007) and uncertainty (Bauman 2000), too. As contemporary Western societies are increasingly characterized by crisis and insecurity, there appears to emerge a need to highlight the unique features of the 'Self'. Phrases like 'American Exceptionalism' and 'Nordic Exceptionalism' have become common in political discourse from the 2000s, and are at once subject to a critical negotiation within popular culture, literature and film. In the following discussion, I will show how the American and the Nordic self-conceptions of exceptionalism are interdependent. The analysis starts in America with an examination of a satirical television show by American stand-up comedian, Wyatt Cenac. Together with Jonathan Franzen's novel *Freedom*, it serves as an example of artistic approaches to a discursive strategy, which uses images of Scandinavia as a category of distinction in order to consolidate the libertarian idea of 'American Exceptionalism'. The second part of the chapter concerns Scandinavian visual arts' current reevaluation of the narratives, which form the basis for notions of 'Nordic Exceptionalism'. Here, I will demonstrate how Susanne Bier's feature films *Efter Brylluppet* (*After the Wedding*) and *Hævnen* (*In a Better World*) contribute to the critical negotiation of a Nordic self-conception, characterized by altruism, and ethical and moral superiority.

The Stockholm Syndrome

Since a raid on a Swedish bank branch in the summer of 1973, the term 'Stockholm syndrome' has been used to describe the psychological phenomenon, when victims of hostage-takings show solidarity with their captors, and develop sympathy for them. 'The Stockholm Syndrome' is also the title of a travelogue by comedian Wyatt Cenac, which was broadcasted in the satirical news programme *The Daily Show* on *Comedy Central* in 2009.[1] The title choice is apt for two reasons. Firstly, Cenac in fact travelled to Sweden, where he wanted to film a documentary on the 'socialist nightmare' he expected to find in Scandinavia. Secondly, without expecting to he took pleasure in what he saw. Like the hostages in the Stockholm bank branch, Cenac associated with the 'oppressor', in his case the Swedish welfare state. This is how the dramatic composition of the satirical report reads, which has to be contextualized as a response of a politically liberal television show to statements by neo-conservative hosts like Neil Cavuto and Bill O'Reilly.[2] The latter, in particular, had in commenting on Barack Obama's tax and health policy repeatedly warned about a possible American socialist future. In this context, he would ask his American audience, if 'we really want to change America into Sweden?'[3] Cenac, meanwhile, left his viewers with the impression that such a development would indeed have its good points.

To him, the oft-demonized Sweden appeared as the more moderate and rational – and therefore better – variant of western democracy. In a staged controversy with Social Democratic ex-minister, Leif Pagrotsky, Cenac juxtaposed Swedish welfare achievements such as free access to education and health care to products of American popular culture, which appeared comparatively ridiculous. He interviewed satisfied and well-paid Swedish factory workers and shot an 'at home' interview with Swedish pop star Robyn, in a style inspired by the American reality show, *MTV Cribs*. Compared with the mansions of rappers like 50 Cent or Snoop Dogg presented in the *MTV* programme, the singer's Stockholm apartment appeared pleasantly modest. In Cenac's report, this persiflage of the materialistic 'bling culture' of American hip hop thus stands as a synecdoche for a comprehensive critique of politics that is solely aimed at the fundamental right of the individual to realize 'the American dream'. At the same time, Cenac questions the American concept of freedom, which is based on a minimal state, and whose political implementation has often been referred to as 'American Exceptionalism', particularly in neo-conservative discourse (Ceaser 2012). In the radical rhetoric of

1 Cenac's report broadcasted in two parts on 21 and 22 April 2009, and can be viewed on the website of the show: http://www.thedailyshow.com/watch/tue-april-21-2009/the-stockholm-syndrome-pt--1; http://www.thedailyshow.com/watch/wed-april-22-2009/the-stockholm-syndrome-pt--2 (05.06.2013).

2 Cavuto is a *Fox Business Network* anchor and commentator; O'Reilly is a television host and political commentator on *Fox News Channel*.

3 The O'Reilly quote from 2009 is integrated in the trailer of Wyatt Cenac's satire.

the Tea Party and *Fox News*, Sweden operates as a counter-model to this idea of society. This is why a critique of the American self-conception of exceptionalism can be raised through a satirical report from Stockholm.

It may seem surprising that Sweden qualifies as such an antipode. In terms of popular and consumer culture, Sweden seems to resemble the United States in many ways; just think of the shopping malls on the outskirts of the provincial cities, which Sweden had before most European countries (Schrödl 2009). Or consider the so-called *raggare* – Swedish hot rodders – and their tuned Cadillacs and Buicks, cruising the streets of Varberg, Västerås and Umeå nightly, a subculture inspired by American rockabilly. However, despite some cultural similarities, Sweden and the Nordic countries occupy an exceptional position, which is almost diametrically opposed to the American model of society, especially when it comes to individual security granted by social policies or a notion of modernity measured by the degree of secularization and freedom from taboos. Often taken for the whole Nordic region, Sweden in parts of American political discourse thus serves as a category of distinction highlighting America's alleged uniqueness. It is constructed as an alterity, fulfilling the function of a coequal, yet unfree 'Other'. It is here, that Homi Bhabha's dictum 'almost the same but not quite' (Bhabha 2004: 122) rings true. In his remarks on mimicry, whereby he originally means a subversive empowerment strategy applied by colonized societies, Bhabha argues, that it is the remaining difference in a process of outward convergence, that has the potential to cause the at times menacing disconcertment, which is the precondition for the construction of alterity and thus also of identity, a nexus we are familiar with since Edward Said's *Orientalism* (1978). It seems as if the oppositional self-conceptions of exceptionalism in America and in the Nordic countries were interdependent.

Europe's Next Top Model

The self-conception of 'Nordic exceptionalism', according to which 'the best of all worlds are located in the north'[4] (Henningsen 2011: 6), and which leads to a 'conviction of political, cultural and moral superiority' (9), is encouraged by a largely positive hetero-image of the Nordic societies. Apart from the discourse of American neo-conservatives outlined above, the Nordic countries enjoy a commendable reputation, precisely because they are regarded as a unique place, 'where the negative aspects of modernization are effectively obviated by government measures' (Rühling 2007: 249). This international fascination reverberates in the region, as it reinforces the sense of its own chosenness (Werler 2007), which is an integral part of any exceptional identity position. Nordic media's penchant for extensively addressing any international attention to news

4 All translations from German, Danish, Swedish and Norwegian by Ebbe Volquardsen.

and stories from home contributes to this process and helps to consolidate the self-conception of 'Nordic exceptionalism' (Hjort 2005: 54).

James W. Ceaser (2012) has pointed to the inflationary recent use of the concept 'American exceptionalism'. However, neither the people who use it, nor academic scholarship would have been able, according to Ceaser, to supply a definition of the term and its history. The same could be noted about the Nordic counterpart, which also remains vague as an analytical category.[5] Freedom from prejudice, tolerance, solidarity and equality: the roots of these values, often linked to the idea of 'Nordic exceptionalism' (Browning 2007; Kofoed and Simonsen 2007), may go further back than to the consolidation of the Scandinavian welfare state systems in the postwar period – in the Danish case, for instance, to the peasant cooperative movement of the late nineteenth century and to the free-spirited Lutheranism of theologian N.F.S. Grundtvig (Østergaard 1991; Mouritsen 2006). However, the Nordic countries, especially Sweden, first acquired their international reputation as models worthy of imitation, when they, during the Cold War era, revealed a successful middle way between socialism and capitalism, characterized by a universal and individualistic welfare policy.[6] Moreover, through their substantial commitment to international peace policy and 'development aid' in the 'Third World', the Nordic countries could stand out from the rest of conflict-laden Europe and consider themselves as a peace-loving and reasonable entity, which – despite Denmark and Norway's NATO membership – has often been perceived to act outside the military blocs (Browning 2007).

After comprehensive social reforms, which have led to a gradual deviation from the ideal type of the social democratic welfare state (Esping-Andersen 1990), and due to the emergence of internal conflicts over immigration issues and the integration of Muslims into the Nordic societies (Gad 2011), the question of a 'decline of exceptionalism' has been raised in recent years (Browning 2007). However, this does not seem to have harmed the positive hetero-image of the Nordic societies and the fascination associated with them. While Southern Europe, in particular, is suffering from the international crisis of the financial markets, the British *Economist* in February 2013 devotes a cover story to the Nordic countries, in which they once more are declared 'the next supermodel'.[7] True, the current financial crisis has also left its mark on Denmark, Sweden, and especially Iceland (see Rice and Loftsdóttir's chapters). Therefore, the renaissance of the Nordic countries' model status, rather than by the region's actual economic performance, appears to be guided by a shift in the political coordinate system, which is leaving the old east–west binary, from Cold War times, in favour of a new European north–south divide. German literary scholar Dieter Richter describes the recent

5 See Loftsdóttir and Jensen 2012b for an overview over different uses of the concept 'Nordic Exceptionalism' in recent scholarship.

6 See Trägårdh 2012 for a recent account to the features of the model of the Scandinavian welfare state.

7 *The Economist*, 2–8 February 2013.

change of coordinates on Europe's mental map as follows: 'Whereas the evil until the fall of the Berlin Wall lurked in the east, it now threatens from the south. And whereas the Germans until 1989 regarded themselves parts of the free west, they now locate themselves on the cross of the mental compass rose in the increasingly strong north' (Richter 2012: 47).[8]

In times of crisis, the north seems to become attractive. Separatist Scots already consider themselves members of that Scandinavian club, the *Nordic Council*, an affiliation, which they derive from Highlanders and Northern Islanders once sharing the Old-Norse language (Theils 2011). Others revive the socio-economic model of the north, to which – so it says on the cover of *The Economist* – the whole world should pay attention. Moreover, infected by 'Scandi fever' (Kingsley 2012), millions of Britons and large proportions of the liberal American middle class are keenly following the Danish TV series *Borgen* about the fictitious social-liberal Prime Minister, Birgitte Nyborg. The Copenhagen Dream Factory is inviting its international audience to 'a journey into a hyper-modern society, in which women have the power, men take care of the children, and where an abortion can be treated as a sideline without the entire episode having to stand under the banner of guilt' (Thorsen 2013). As to America, it seems, as if a polarized attitude towards the Nordic countries was symptomatic of the frequently ascertained division of society into two irreconcilable political camps. For some, the region functions as a utopian place of yearning for alternate conceptions of modernity. For others, it evokes connotations with governmental limitations of freedom, and thus memories of totalitarian systems from Cold War times.

However, America's partial rejection of 'the Scandinavian'[9] is more than a manifestation of the crisis ideology of neoliberalism, whose failure is met by its defenders with a defiant disparagement of all those, who already before the start of the crisis had thought to know better. Based on an analysis of the hetero-stereotype of the promiscuous Swede, which until recently has been powerful on both sides of the Atlantic, Stephan Michael Schröder (1996) has illustrated the historical dimensions of ambivalent connotations of the strong Scandinavian image. Schröder interprets the emergence of the stereotype as an expression of an increasingly critical attitude towards the welfare state, the best-known project of Swedish modernity, which from the 1970s at times has been blamed for carrying certain totalitarian traits, for instance in Roland Huntford's (1971) writings. Whereas the image of the sexualized blonde Swede as a *pars pro toto* for emancipatory social policies regarded as 'the Swedish sin' according to Schröder has faded in the wake of the gradual liberalization of European societies, the stereotype persists in

8 It is obviously the West Germans that Richter has in mind when describing the time before 1989.

9 I here use the geographical terms 'Nordic countries' and 'Scandinavia' synonymously, as they usually are not distinguished between in public discourse outside the region. 'Scandinavia' is the more common term, whose image often is constituted by notions of Sweden only.

puritan America and, what is more, has lost little of its discursive link to the model of the Scandinavian welfare state that evokes both criticism *and* fascination. Thus, the lascivious Swede is also ubiquitous in Wyatt Cenac's satirical portrait of the alleged 'socialist nightmare'. However, the image is not used for the portrayal of Sweden as a Sodom and Gomorrah, but is an integral part of a desirable social utopia. Once again, the entertainer holds a mirror up to the materialistic machismo of American popular culture, and at the same time provides evidence of the long-term tenacity of the hetero-stereotype and its functions as analysed by Schröder.

Jonathan Franzen and the UnSwedishness of Freedom

'The West is struck by a veritable obsession with freedom' (Schanz 2012: 6). So begins Danish historian of ideas, Hans-Jørgen Schanz in his short history of the concept of freedom, a notion, which according to him has degenerated into a fetish (7). 'Freedom' also remains a vague category in Jonathan Franzen's novel of the same name, published in 2010. In his two-generation family epic, Franzen narrates no less than a political history of the American nation. Although we, in longer flashbacks, accompany the protagonists, Patty and Walter Berglund, back to their teenage years, *Freedom* is first of all a portrait of the time after the terrorist attacks of 9/11, when George W. Bush was president of the United States, neo-conservatives propagated the radical freedom of the market until its collapse, and America under the slogan 'Enduring Freedom' went to war in Iraq. It is this era Schanz recalls when criticizing the fetishization of the concept of freedom. This is also the time, when American political discourse provides Scandinavia with the above-mentioned connotations, which make it fruitful as a category of distinction. Franzen has also noticed this nexus. While references to Scandinavia remain rare in the nearly 600-page novel, the passages, where they appear, reveal some interesting information about the interdependence of American and Nordic self-conceptions of exceptionalism.

With the character of Walter Berglund, Jonathan Franzen has created a literary ideal of the American 'Volvo liberal', which according to linguist Geoffrey Nunberg is a pejorative label used by conservative opinion makers to disparage the lifestyles of the sophisticated American middle class (Nunberg 2007: 66). In analogy with my earlier findings on the functionalization of 'the Scandinavian' as a category of distinction, Nunberg explains that the pejorative effect of linking the unpretentious brand *Volvo* with a certain lifestyle is due to the car's country of origin, 'socialist' Sweden, and to the 'serendipitous gynecological resonance' (66) of the word.[10] As if it weren't enough that Walter Berglund indeed calls a box-shaped Volvo 240 station wagon his own, he also is a staunch activist against

10 When pronounced the American way, 'Volvo' is almost homophonic with 'vulva'. Nunberg hereby confirms the potency of the nexus between sexualization and criticism of the system, which Schröder (1996) has analysed.

the overpopulation of the world, a committed bird conservationist and one of the first, who in the 1980s preferred the renovation of a Victorian house in decayed downtown St Paul to life in the safe housing estates in the suburbs. When Nunberg talks about liberals, who according to conservative opinion makers are conducted by 'infantile rebelliousness or misplaced sympathy for the downtrodden' (64), Franzen's readers will have no one but Walter Berglund in mind. However, when Walter is giving up his job as a lawyer for *The Nature Conservancy*, and instead is becoming involved with business people from the Bush-Cheney clan, on whose behalf he is intended to enforce the resettlement of the inhabitants of a future coal mining area, and later convert the land into a reserve for the cerulean warbler, it becomes clear, that the 'Volvo liberals' like the little blue songbird belong to an endangered species.

Names often have figurative meaning in Franzen's novel. It is with reference to George W. Bush's notoriously partying twin daughters, when the girl, who one night in New York City seduces Walter's and Patty's son Joey, the only Republican within the family, is called Jenna. And Walter himself? It is, after all, he who until his dubious deal with the coal industry acts as a foil to the Bush-era's exceptional zeitgeist, and in whose mind the flipping of one of the *Volvo*'s dashboard switches can generate 'such a satisfying Swedish click' (Franzen 2010: 5). Of course, his name is chosen deliberately, too. Three quarters of the way through the novel we learn about Walter's grandfather Einar's immigration history, but by then, the almost stereotypical family name Berglund and references to Walter's childhood and youth in Hibbing last out to let the attentive reader know that Walter descends from Swedish immigrants. In that area of northern Minnesota there are more people of Scandinavian background than anywhere else in the United States. According to neo-conservative discourse, freedom makes American civilization stand out from the rest of the world and therefore liberates the United States from the dictates of the international community (Ceaser 2012). Apart from the 'axis of evil' as the ultimate opposite to America, Scandinavia has – as the examples above have shown – served as a category of distinction for this exceptional identity position. Hence, when Franzen makes his protagonist, who struggles with the fetishization of freedom, a Swedish-American, he is consistently guided by the predominant images of cross-cultural hermeneutics.

Much later in the novel, we read about grandfather Einar's emigration from Central Sweden to Minnesota in the early twentieth century. The chapter partially evokes memories of Vilhelm Moberg's 'Emigrant series' (1949–59). However, whereas the Swedish emigrants in Moberg's books are fleeing bad harvests, famine and the oppressive restraints of the powerful state church, Einar Berglund's emigration is motivated by a personal problem with his mother, who is giving all her maternal love to Einar's younger brother. It thus sounds like an ironic comment on the current debates, proclaiming Sweden America's unfree Other, when it says in the novel: 'America, for Einar was the land of unSwedish freedom, the place of wide-open spaces where a son still could imagine he was special' (Franzen 2010: 444). The notion of chosenness is inherent in any self-conception of exceptionalism – be it the American or Nordic. In Franzen's work however, this notion is turned into a caricature in the same paragraph. After a short description of Einar's humble career, it says: 'But nothing disturbs the feeling of specialness like the presence of other human beings feeling identically special' (444). In short, the exceptional as a group identity already inheres crisis. It does not suit for the consolidation of an 'imagined community', which according to Benedict Anderson 'is the hallmark of modern nations' (Anderson 2006: 36).

Finally, there is Walter's college friend and eternal rival in love, Richard Katz, who becomes a successful rock musician, and as the reckless 'cool guy' of the story stands in opposition to the sensible and slightly boring 'good guy', Walter. While Walter is starting his new job as the coal industry's bird conservationist, we meet Richard in a Turkish hotel room watching a Danish art film and 'in his utter boredom … taking 5,000 euros of Danish government arts funding up his nose' (Franzen 2010: 191). Whereas arts and culture in the United States are predominately financed by private funds, the generosity of government arts funding in Denmark is probably without equal. The receipt of such a grant, which in American discourse to some might seem as an illegitimate governmental intervention into the freedom of art, while others may envy the Danes their generous cultural policy, is for the artist in Franzen's panorama of characters merely a welcome opportunity to invest in a few lines of cocaine. Here, the Bush-era's political charging of 'the Scandinavian' as a category of distinction once more undergoes an ironic twist. I will now leave post-9/11 America and examine how self-conceptions of exceptionalism at the same time are discussed, criticized and revaluated in the Nordic countries.

'Nordic Exceptionalism' in Crisis

'Nordic exceptionalism' is based on the assumption of a unique Scandinavian model of society. Apart from the social democratic welfare state, this model is characterized by societal openness, tolerance, and freedom from prejudice, a hetero-stereotype, which largely coincides with the countries' own national and regional self-images (Koefoed and Simonsen 2007; Habel 2009; Henningsen 2011). Yet in Northern Europe itself, the self-conception of exceptionalism has for some years been the subject of critical debates (Browning 2007; Palmberg 2009; Loftsdóttir and Jensen 2012a). This is not least due to some striking recent events that have unsettled the image of the Nordic countries as peaceful and neutral observers of world affairs. In 2011, self-proclaimed crusader Anders Behring Breivik out of anti-Islamic motives shot and killed 77 mainly young people on the island of Utøya and in Oslo. According to his ideology, the victims embodied a threat to Norwegian society, as they were advocates of immigration-friendly policies. In the spring of 2013, riots in Stockholm's suburbs awakened memories of the war-like scenes in the *banlieus* of Paris a few years before and raised doubts about Sweden's integration policy, which often has been praised as exemplary (see also Hübinette's chapter about whiteness as a way of understanding the Swedish reaction to the crisis of multiculturalism). The violent reactions to the Mohammed cartoons published by the Danish newspaper *Jyllands-Posten* in 2005 aroused international attention and made hitherto inconspicuous Denmark – like the United States after 9/11 – enter a state of national insecurity.

It is particularly these conflicts caused by ongoing social change towards greater cultural heterogeneity, which challenge the Nordic self-conception of exceptionalism. Cultural scientists have therefore in recent years examined the narrative of ethnical and cultural homogeneity, which the national identities of the Nordic countries are based on, and in this context turned their attention towards the region's earlier histories of intervention and encounter in Africa, Asia, America and the North Atlantic (Keskinen et al. 2009; Jensen 2012; Loftsdóttir and Jensen 2012a; Naum and Nordin 2013). The topic both covers the revaluation of the varying colonial histories of the countries and their self-conceptions 'as champions of minority rights and mediators in global politics' (Fur 2013: 18). Having been the only greater colonial power among the Nordic countries, especially in Denmark, the recent interest in historical interventions outside the country's territorial borders extends beyond academia and has for some years been a frequent topic in literature, film and the visual arts. Kim Leine's Greenland novels *Kalak* (2007) and *Profeterne i evighedsfjorden* (2012) for a long time topped the Danish bestseller lists, and journalist Alex Frank Larsen in his reality TV programme *Slavernes slægt* and a monograph of the same name (Larsen 2008) searched for ancestors of Danes descending from West Indian slaves.[11] Conceptual artist Kristian von Hornsleth with his *Hornsleth Village Project Uganda 2007* made a particularly provocative contribution to the critical negotiation of colonialism, and finally, author Jakob Ejersbo in his trilogy (2009) on Nordic aid workers in East Africa, parodied the exceptional self-image of Scandinavians' altruistic commitment to the elimination of the inequalities of globalization.[12] To this list of recent literary, cinematic and artistic works, addressing Scandinavia's historical and contemporary interventions in other parts of the world, one could add the award-winning feature films *Efter Brylluppet* (2005) and *Hævnen* (2010) by Danish director Susanne Bier. As in Ejersbo's books, it is not a direct colonial encounter that Bier's films revolve around. Her issue is Scandinavian 'development aid' in the 'Third World', a topos which has significantly contributed to the construction of the Nordic

11 Today's US Virgin Islands in the Caribbean were a Danish colony until 1917. See Marselis 2008 for a critical analysis of Larsen's TV programme and the project.

12 Hornsleth paid all the residents of a Ugandan village for adopting his own family name, and then photographed the villagers holding up their changed ID cards. The art project and its controversial reception are analysed in Ørjasæter 2011. Jakob Ejersbo's so-called 'Africa Trilogy' (2009) consists of the novels *Eksil* and *Liberty* and the novella collection *Revolution*. See Körber 2011, and Thisted 2011 for readings of the trilogy from a postcolonial perspective.

self-conception of exceptionalism (see also Ystanes' chapter on tourism in Guatemala and how this relates to a Norwegian perspective).

Scandinavian Interventions

Maria Eriksson Baaz (2001) has argued that Scandinavian 'development aid' is characterized by an anti-imperialistic identity, finding expression in the frequent portrayal of Scandinavian 'aid workers' as less paternalistic and more respectful towards the recipients. Hereby, Scandinavians distance themselves from other countries' 'development aid projects' and insinuate that neo-colonial interests guide these. Such a self-image, resting on a notion of ethical and moral superiority, falls into line with a strong narrative about Scandinavia's alleged non-participation in colonialism (Baaz 2001; Palmberg 2009; Öhman 2010; Fur 2013), and is in part based on some prominent political positioning during Cold War. Whereas American and European involvement in Africa has been interpreted as a competition between the blocs, a developmental race, in which the main aim of the West was to prevent the poverty-stricken new states of sub-Saharan Africa from affiliating with communism (Büschel 2009), the Nordic countries, especially Sweden, took a third position. Under Prime Minister Olof Palme, the country distanced itself from European expansionism and allied instead with the decolonization movements of Southern Africa, which Sweden, Denmark and Norway supported with significant financial benefits (Sellström 1999; Morgenstierne 2003). Ever since Palme's clear positioning against apartheid and also since the Congo crisis, during which Swedish UN Secretary-General Dag Hammarskjöld mediated,[13] the Nordic countries' sovereign Africa politics has played a significant role in the construction of an altruistic and anti-imperialist self-conception in Scandinavia. In analogy with the above-discussed role of 'the Scandinavian' as a category of distinction for the notion of 'American exceptionalism', the genesis of an imagined 'Nordic exceptionalism' partially is an outcome of Scandinavia's historical distancing from America's global leadership and the West's self-interest-driven 'Third World' politics.

The theme of well-intentioned Nordic intervention in the crisis areas of the world is a strong element in Susanne Bier's work. In her romantic comedy *Den Eneste Ene* (*The One and Only*; 1999), a Danish couple adopts a girl from Burkina Faso, who after the sudden accidental death of the adoptive mother helps the father to find a new love. The drama film *Brødre* (*Brothers*; 2004) is set in Copenhagen and Afghanistan, where Bier for the first time employs the stylistic device of parallel montage, which she later extends in *Efter Brylluppet* and *Hævnen*. 'Bier

13 Dag Hammerskjöld was killed in a plane crash over Northern Rhodesia, now Zambia, while mediating in the Congo in 1961. The circumstances of the crash are still an unsolved mystery and subject to various speculations and conspiracy theories (Williams 2011).

puts the wealth and presumed happiness of Denmark in perspective through the poverty and violence of a Third World country', writes film critic Louise Kidde Sauntved (2011: 27) about this particular practice, which has to be reckoned typical of Bier's work. Yet, eventual ambitions to meet the crises of the world with peaceful conflict solutions are in *Brødre* a thing of the past. Denmark is at war in Afghanistan, and the plot develops around the psychological and moral sufferings of Danish officer Michael, who, after being taken as a war prisoner by the Taliban, is forced to kill a fellow prisoner and never finds a way back to a decent life. *Brødre* can therefore be classified as a typical anti-war film, a genre, which often addresses the psychological power of destruction in warfare.

In Bier's later films *Efter Brylluppet* and *Hævnen*, the peaceful intervention of Scandinavians in 'developing countries' is a focus. *Efter Brylluppet* is alternately set in Denmark and India. The protagonist Jacob Pedersen, played by Mads Mikkelsen, is the head of a children's home in Mumbai. In order to save the financially troubled institution from closing, Jacob travels to Copenhagen, where the rich Swedish businessman Jörgen Hansson (Rolf Lassgård) offers the prospect of a generous donation for the orphanage. It is in the Danish capital and on the estate of the Hansson family outside of the city, that the action takes place. Parallel cuts to India remain rare, but the hectic urban landscape of Mumbai forms a strong contrast to the scenes taking place in rich, green and placid North Zealand. In addition to the extreme close-ups of the characters' faces, the contrasting of two landscapes, appearing contrary in both a visual and an associative way, is the primary aesthetic feature of the film.

With Rolf Lassgård, internationally known for his role as Inspector Wallander in the film versions of Henning Mankell's crime novels, Danish Susanne Bier has cast a Swedish actor for one of the leading roles in *Efter Brylluppet*. The same holds true for *Hævnen*, starring Swedish actor, Mikael Persbrandt. Danish and Swedish are alternately spoken in both films. Although integrating actors from other Nordic countries is not an unusual practice in modern Scandinavian film productions, casting the Swedish actors in Bier's case helps to emphasize the Pan-Scandinavian character of the topoi negotiated in the films: 'development aid', altruism and morality, all of which are associated with the Nordic self-conception of exceptionalism. The protagonist in *Hævnen* is Swedish Anton, who is working as a 'doctor without borders' in an African refugee camp, and who after a brief amorous escapade has recently separated from his Danish wife. Although the scenes of the drama are not explicitly denominated, the Sudanese crisis region Darfur comes to mind in the African scenes. As to the Danish part, people familiar with the region quickly recognize the provincial town Rudkøbing on the island of Langeland. It is here that Anton and his family live. The temporal dispersion between the African and the Danish course of action is more balanced in *Hævnen* than between the Indian and the Danish in *Efter Brylluppet*. In the latter film, the action mainly takes place in Denmark. However, the opening scenes of the films feature some striking similarities. Both films begin in the Global South, which the European cinema audience connotes as foreign, exotic, and in all respects being a striking image of the 'Other'. We meet the protagonists Jacob and Anton, both engaged in 'development aid', and both sitting on the back of pickup trucks, accompanied by their respective group of cheering Indian or African children. Jacob and Anton are revered as heroes at their work places. The scenes thus reproduce a common image of fictional and non-fictional representations of white 'aid workers' in the countries of the 'Third World'. Firstly, I will discuss *Efter Brylluppet* in more detail, and then *Hævnen*, which in 2011 won the Academy Award for Best Foreign Language Film.

After the Wedding

The soundscape precedes any image. In the opening titles, hooting cars acoustically prepare the viewer for the expected scenery. Then, from the aerial perspective, the camera gradually zooms in on the slums of the Indian city, where the first scenes of *Efter Brylluppet* take place. At street level, the view simultaneously reaches the metaphorical bottom of society, where there are beggars and invalids, reliant on provisional prostheses. Jacob Pedersen is supplying scantily clad children with a modest meal. The staging of his place of work as a chaotic space is highlighted by bright colours and nervous hand-held camera work, reminiscent of Lars Von Trier's *Dogme* concept. Soon after, the viewer learns of Jacob's upcoming Copenhagen travel and becomes acquainted with the Indian orphan boy, Pramod, whom Jacob is taking care of as a kind of foster son. Jacob promises to be back from Denmark on time in order to celebrate Pramod's birthday.

The night before his departure, Jacob lies awake. The viewer can briefly look into his mind and see the hand of a white woman gently stroking his body. We will later understand that Jacob was thinking of his former lover, Helene; she is the reason why he does not want to return to Denmark. The locations of the next scenes, Kastrup airport, bathed in bluish light, and the luxurious Copenhagen hotel room, equipped with functionalist Scandinavian design, underline the staging of the busy Indian cityscape as the ultimate 'Other' of an organized and functional Scandinavia. In this world dominated by prosperity, Jacob initially is a foreigner. We learn that he has broken all ties with his Danish past and so has neither friends nor family in Copenhagen. To emphasize his alienation, the scenes, where Jacob is clumsily getting familiar with the luxury amenities of the hotel room, in which billionaire Jörgen has accommodated his guest, are accompanied by Indian sitar music.

Gradually, we learn of Jörgen's project, which forms the core of the film's plot. When we are alone with the rich patriarch, we are supplied with a slight advance in knowledge with respect to the other characters. The room at his estate, to which Jörgen likes to adjourn, is decorated with hunting trophies from all over the world and therefore – in contrast to Jacob's humanitarianism – represents the colonial side of Western intervention in the Global South. Against the backdrop of their Scandinavian context, these scenes bring Karen Blixen's partially autobiographical stories about big-game hunting in East Africa to the scene, which serve as an intertext. The scenes in the private retreat of the entrepreneur are interrupted by still images of symbols of *vanitas* like seared plants and a dead fox, foreshadowing Jörgen's approaching death. As the story progresses, we learn that Jörgen is suffering from cancer, and understand that the reason for inviting Jacob to Copenhagen has little to do with the will to support Indian orphans. Jörgen wants Jacob to attend the wedding of his adopted daughter Anna, whose biological father is, in fact Jacob. Jörgen has long-since been married to Jacob's former lover Helene, and his plan is to install Jacob as the new head of the family before facing his inevitable death. Several times, Jörgen delays Jacob's departure to India. Jacob breaks his promise and cannot return for the birthday of his foster son. In the meantime, he gradually learns to appreciate his 'Danish family'.

The problem of 'development aid relationships' becomes apparent in the conflicting interests of the donor and the recipient, writes Maria Eriksson Baaz (2001: 165). However, the fundamental asymmetry of power, which characterizes such relationships, would lead to the receiver adjusting to the interests of the donor. This also happens in the case of Jörgen and Jacob, who eventually meets the conditions of the donor, and permanently settles in Copenhagen, where he, supported by his daughter Anna, is going to manage a multi-million dollar fund to benefit Indian orphans. What at first glance fits into the usual patterns of neo-colonial 'development aid relations' now seems to conceal ambivalences. During Jacob's attempts to renew the relationship with Helene, the mother of his adult daughter, we hear about his former alcohol and drug abuse. Against the backdrop of the erratic lifestyle of the young Jacob, his commitment in India suddenly no longer appears in the light of exceptional altruism, but rather seems to embody a form of selfish escapism. Escaping into regions connoted as primitive, combined with the hope for undergoing a kind of catharsis, is a common trope in literary colonial discourse (Volquardsen 2014). Disclosing the pathological traits of this practice, *Efter Brylluppet* thus conforms to numerous contemporary works by Scandinavian artists, which critically reevaluate the narratives spun around cultural encounters that long-since have been contributing to the construction of a self-conception of exceptionalism.[14]

In a Better World?

Hævnen means 'the revenge', a theme which occupies a central position in Bier's 2010 drama film. However, to the international audience the film was presented under the title *In a Better World*, which – especially in the context of the familiar technique of contrastively juxtaposing two landscapes by means of parallel montage – gives reason to expect a critical and ironic negotiation of the exceptional image of a Scandinavian 'regime of goodness' (Tvedt 2003). The scenery of the

14 See Volquardsen 2014 for a similar reading of Kim Leine's novel *Kalak*.

probably Sudanese refugee camp and the sparsely equipped infirmary, where the first scenes take place, may from the point of view of the European film audience evoke similar associations of otherness as the Indian cityscape initially shown in *Efter Brylluppet*. However, by adroitly applying the technique of sliding parallel cuts, Bier succeeds in establishing an aesthetic connection between the two settings in Africa and Denmark. Unlike in her older films *Efter Brylluppet* and *Brødre*, the two contrarily connoted landscapes do not stand in opposition to each other. Instead, associations of proximity and similarity are generated. First, Anton is presented in his role as a doctor in the refugee camp, where he has to fight against the atrocities of a local warlord, who sexually abuses young women and then slashes open their genitals. Then the action continues in Denmark. The camera zooms in on the hilly African landscape, where suddenly two *Vestas* windmills come up on the horizon. Finally, the editing technique transforms even the parched desert soil into fertile Danish farmland. We are on the island of Langeland. Two seemingly contradictory places formally merge with one another: here the African civil war zone marked by violence, chaos and anarchy, there the peaceful Danish island landscape surrounded by blue sea and interspersed with tastefully furnished houses.

'White men are saving brown women from brown men', writes Gayatri Spivak (1994: 93) in her essay 'Can the Subaltern Speak?', describing the relationship between colonizers and colonized. Her dictum can also be applied to post-colonial situations. Spivak argues that Eurocentristic discourse's vehement rejection of the patriarchal practices associated with the Global South leads to the woman of the south being incapacitated for a second time. She thus comes to the conclusion to negate the question posed in the title of her text; the subaltern remains silent. What in Spivak's essay is to be understood metaphorically, is practised quite tangibly in *Hævnen*. The Swedish doctor saves African women from the consequences of a black tyrant's irrational violence. Thus, the film initially falls into line with stereotypical colonial patterns of representation, within which an enlightened European 'Self', whose burden is to civilize the alleged savages, opposes a barbarous African 'Other'. In the Danish scenes, Anton is depicted as a pacifist and a loving father, who by his virile appearance combined with traits regarded as feminine, embodies a gender model often reckoned exceptionally Scandinavian. He visually stands in opposition to the African mass murderer. The ugly wound, which a lost eye has left in the face of the warlord, contrasts with the Swedish doctor's bright blue eyes. However, I argue that it is precisely these long-lived patterns of representation that are challenged in the film. The topos of irrational violence, in colonial discourse firmly linked to the south, undergoes in *Hævnen*, what Arjun Appadurai (2008) calls deterritorialization, and which according to him is the hallmark of globalized modernity. The effect of merging landscapes generated by sliding parallel montages supports this process of deterritorialization on an aesthetic level.

The English film title *In a Better World* allows several interpretations. On the one hand, it raises the question, whether the one scene of the drama, placid

Rudkøbing, compared with the second setting, the African country harassed by civil war, indeed is a better place, marked by ethical and moral superiority. On the other hand, it refers to the desires and thoughts of a second main character, the Danish pupil, Christian. Christian's mother, whom the boy obviously has had a closer relationship to than to his father, has recently died from cancer. In any experience of injustice, Christian, devastated by the grief, swears to take revenge. When he notices that his new school friend Elias, Anton's son, is bullied and humiliated, he uses physical violence against the offender. When Anton, during a stroll through town with the boys, is beaten by an infamous local ruffian, and due to his peaceful nature refuses to put up a fight, Christian forges a plan to avenge Anton by blowing up the thug's car. When playing in an old barn, Christian and Elias had previously discovered dynamite.

The plan nearly ends in a disaster when Elias narrowly escapes death. What is more, the revenge of Rudkøbing happens at the very time when Anton, back in Africa, is breaking with his pacifist principles. One day, the notorious murderer, who with his militia is terrorizing the region around the camp, has to make use of Anton's medical assistance. This is given despite the surprise and displeasure of the African assistants. However, when yet another raped women is brought to the infirmary and soon dies from her injuries, the African warlord expresses nothing else than scorn, ridicule and necrophiliac desires. Anton, enraged, leaves the disarmed tyrant to the justice of the angry mob in the camp, where he is lynched. Questions about the legitimacy of revenge, the meaningfulness of pacifism and the existence of an ethical and moral superiority of the north over the south remain unanswered throughout the film; they become the subject matter for intense debate instead. Emotionally troubled by his acceptance of a person's death, Anton does not find time to listen to his son Elias's concerns in faraway Denmark. Hence, he cannot thwart Christian's plan of revenge. This coincidence challenges protagonist Anton's hero image established in the course of the film, and questions the existence of a better (side of the) world referred to in the English film title. The division of the world into good and evil, familiar and exotic, rational and irrational, which Edward Said (1978) attested to Western knowledge production, appears obsolete.

In the credits of the film, we finally are presented a series of still images displaying different landscapes, which could be anywhere in the world. It is with these images that Susanne Bier ultimately breaks with her practice of juxtaposing contrarily connoted regions, which she established in *Brødre* and kept up in *Efter Brylluppet*. The aesthetical realization of deterritorialization, which leads to that certain cultural or social practices no longer are tied to a fixed location (Appadurai 2008), is thereby completed by the end of the film.

Conclusion

'Africa, it seems is becoming a global condition. Or at least, Africa as *imagined* in Euro-America', write John and Jean Comaroff (2012: 125), a dictum, which appears suitable as a possible interpretation of the film *Hævnen*. Euro-American discourse has since colonial times connected the irrational use of violence with the geographical entity of Africa. In the film, however, irrational violence is simultaneously used in the Sudan and in Denmark. Is Denmark evolving towards Africa, as the title of the Comaroffs' essay suggests? At least the aesthetic effect of merging landscapes employed by Susanne Bier is indicating that. Of course, a slap in the face by a Danish provincial town thug can hardly be compared with an African warlord's mutilation of women. Yet, both actions – combined with the act of revenge – can potentially lead to a fatal end. Elias barely survives, as the offender's car goes into the air just a few feet in front of his face.

The Comaroffs argue that the nations of the Northern hemisphere in times of financial crisis, increasing ethnic conflicts and unstable labour markets, are gradually becoming reminiscent of Africa – both in positive and problematic ways (Comaroff and Comaroff 2012). The theory describes the alleged paradox, that the world in the age of globalization at the same time is becoming more homo- *and* more heterogeneous. Homogeneous, because the societies of the world – in the north and in the south – at an increasing rate share common risks, conflicts and challenges, and thus are becoming more similar to each other. Heterogeneous, since such a development is largely due to the migration of people, ideas and goods, which make the particular societies more diverse. Self-conceptions of exceptionalism, be they of an American, a Nordic or a third kind, are contrary to such a development. Yet, it seems as if exceptionalist identity positions were going through a revival, every time the increasing entanglement and interconnection of the world is primarily seen as a globalization of conflict and risk.

In the wake of growing social and cultural diversity, primarily caused by immigration, Scandinavians have recently been discussing perceptions of Danishness, Swedishness and Norwegianness intensely, and in this context at times reinforced self-conceptions of exceptionalism, which let the countries appear ethically and morally superior and at the same time placed a high degree of normativity pressure on all outsiders. It is especially literature, film and the visual arts that have addressed the inconsistency of this discourse, which soon turns out to be of an intolerant kind. In my analysis, Susanne Bier's films *Efter Brylluppet* and *Hævnen* have served as such examples for contemporary artistic works that focus on cultural encounters and the narratives spun around them and thus evoke a critical discussion of the Nordic self-conception of exceptionalism. The first part of the chapter has unfolded a similar picture with regard to America. In the United States, marked by growing poverty and a chronic fear of terrorism, the perception of crisis like in the Nordic countries seems to evoke an increased need for highlighting the alleged uniqueness of the 'Self'. Moreover, the American self-conception of exceptionalism has shown to be dependent on a category of distinction. Reviving

America's traditional skepticism towards Scandinavia, Sweden – as the epitome of the region – momentarily seems to hold the position of such an alterity. In this sense Sweden is regarded as America's coequal but unfree 'Other'. However, the concept of freedom is internally disputed in the United States. In the eyes of some, freedom has degenerated into a fetish or been abandoned in favour of anxious 'securiocracy'. This is why the political charging of 'the Scandinavian' in neo-conservative discourse is challenged by a critical negotiation in literature and popular culture. Examples were Wyatt Cenac's satirical travelogue from Stockholm, and Jonathan Franzen's novel *Freedom*. However, both sides of crisis-ridden post-9/11 America's representation of 'the Scandinavian' – the discursive construction of the region as a category of distinction and the parody of this phenomenon – appear to contribute to the manifestation of 'Nordic exceptionalism' as an American hetero-stereotype, whereas the Scandinavian self-conception of exceptionalism gradually seems to blur.

Works Cited

Anderson, Benedict (2006 [1983]) *Imagined Communities: Reflections on the Origin and Spread of Nationalism.* London and New York: Verso.

Appadurai, Arjun (2008 [1996]) *Modernity at Large: Cultural Dimensions of Globalization.* Minneapolis and London: Minnesota University Press.

Baaz, Maria Eriksson (2001), 'Bistanden och partnerskapets problematik', in McEachrane, Michael and Louis Faye (eds) *Sverige och de Andra: Postkoloniala Perspektiv.* Stockholm: Bokförlaget Natur och Kultur, 159–86.

Bauman, Zygmunt (2000) *Liquid Modernity.* Cambridge: Polity Press.

Beck, Ulrich (2008) *Weltrisikogesellschaft: Auf der Suche nach der verlorenen Sicherheit.* Frankfurt am Main: Suhrkamp.

Bhabha, Homi K. (2004 [1994]) *The Location of Culture.* London and New York: Routledge.

Browning, Christopher S. (2007) 'Branding Nordicity. Models, Identity and the Decline of Exceptionalism'. *Cooperation and Conflict* 42 (1), 27–51.

Büschel, Hubertus (2009) 'In Afrika helfen. Akteure westdeutscher "Entwicklungshilfe" und ostdeutscher "Solidarität" 1955–1975', in Kruke, Anja (ed.) *Dekolonisation: Prozesse und Verflechtungen 1945–1990.* Bonn: Dietz, 333–65.

Ceaser, James W. (2012) 'The Origins and Character of American Exceptionalism'. *American Political Thought*, 1 (1), 3–27.

Comaroff, Jean and John L. Comaroff (2012) 'Theory from the South: Or, how Euro-America is Evolving Toward Africa'. *Anthropological Forum*, 22 (2), 113–31.

Esping-Andersen, Gøsta (1990) *The Three Worlds of Welfare Capitalism.* Princeton, NJ: Princeton University Press.

Franzen, Jonathan (2010) *Freedom.* New York: Farrar, Straus and Giroux.

Fur, Gunlög (2013) 'Colonialism and Swedish History: Unthinkable Connections?', in Naum, Magdalena and Jonas M. Nordin (eds) *Scandinavian Colonialism and the Rise of Modernity: Small Agents in a Global Arena.* New York: Springer, 17–35.

Gad, Ulrik Pram (2011) 'Peace, welfare, culture. Muslims as a security problem in Danish integration discourse', in *NORDEUROPA forum*, 21 (1), 41–72.

Habel, Ylva (2009) 'Whiteness Swedish style', in Stephens, Kolade (ed.) *Afrikansksvenska röster.* Malmö: Notis, 90–119.

Henningsen, Bernd (2011) *Ting und Polis oder die Vorbildlichkeit der politischen Ordnung des Nordens*, Öffentliche Vorlesungen 165. Berlin: Humboldt-Universität zu Berlin.

Hjort, Mette (2005) *Small Nation, Global Cinema: The New Danish Cinema.* Minneapolis and London: University of Minnesota Press.

Huntford, Roland (1971) *The New Totalitarians.* London: Allen Lane.

Jensen, Lars (2012) *Danmark: Rigsfællesskab, tropekolonier og den postkoloniale arv.* København: Hans Reitzels Forlag.

Keskinen, Suvi et al. (eds) (2009) *Complying with Colonialism: Gender, Race, and Ethnicity in the Nordic Region.* Farnham and Burlington: Ashgate.

Kingsley, Patrick (2012) *How to be Danish: A Short Introduction to the State of Denmark.* London: Short Books Ltd.

Koefoed, Lasse and Kirsten Simonsen (2007) 'The Price of Goodness: Everyday Nationalist Narratives in Denmark'. *Antipode* 39 (2), 310–30.

Körber, Lill-Ann (2011) 'Den svenske verdensorden på West Kili. At være hvid i Afrika hos Jakob Ejersbo'. *Kritik*, 199, 71–80.

Larsen, Alex Frank (2008) *Slavernes slægt.* København: DR Multimedie.

Loftsdóttir, Kristín and Lars Jensen (eds) (2012a) *Whiteness and Postcolonialism in the Nordic Region: Exceptionalism, Migrant Others and National Identities.* Farnham: Ashgate.

— and — (2012b) 'Nordic Exceptionalism and the Nordic "Others"', in Loftsdóttir, Kristín and Lars Jensen (eds) *Whiteness and Postcolonialism in the Nordic Region: Exceptionalism, Migrant Others and National Identities.* Farnham: Ashgate, 1–11.

Marselis, Randi (2008) 'Descendants of Slaves: The articulation of mixed racial ancestry in a Danish television documentary series'. *European Journal of Cultural Studies*, 11 (4), 447–69.

Morgenstierne, Christopher Munthe (2003) *Denmark and National Liberation in Southern Africa.* Uppsala: Nordiska Afrikainstitutet.

Mouritsen, Per (2006) 'The particular universalism of a Nordic civic nation. Common values, state religion and Islam in Danish political culture', in Modood, Tariq et al. (eds) *Multiculturalism, Muslims and Citizenship: A European Approach.* London and New York: Routledge, 70–93.

Naum, Magdalena and Jonas M. Nordin (eds) (2013) *Scandinavian Colonialism and the Rise of Modernity: Small Agents in a Global Arena.* New York: Springer.

Nunberg, Geoffrey (2007) *Talking Right: How Conservatives Turned Liberalism into a Tax-Raising, Latte-Drinking, Sushi-Eating, Volvo-Driving, New York Times-Reading, Body-Piercing, Hollywood-Loving, Left-Wing Freak Show.* New York: Public Affairs.

Öhman, May-Britt (2010) '"Sweden helps". Efforts to Formulate the White Man's Burden for the Wealthy and Modern Swede', in Jensen, Lars et al. (eds) *Nordic Colonial Mind. Kult* (7). Roskilde: Roskilde University, 122–42.

Ørjasæter, Kristin (2011) 'Art, Aid and Negotiated Identity. The Family Pictures of Hornsleth Village Project Uganda', in Thomsen, Bodil Marie Stavning and Kristin Ørjasæter (eds) *Globalizing Art: Negotiating Place, Identity and Nation in Contemporary Nordic Art.* Aarhus: Aarhus University Press, 227–43.

Østergaard, Uffe (1991) 'Peasants and Danes. The Danish National Identity and Political Culture'. *Comparative Studies in Society and History*, 34, 3–27.

Palmberg, Mai (2009) 'The Nordic Colonial Mind', in Keskinen, Suvi et al. (eds.) *Complying with Colonialism: Gender, Race, and Ethnicity in the Nordic Region.* Farnham: Ashgate, 35–50.

Richter, Dieter (2012) 'Alles eine Frage der Klimazone'. *Die Zeit*, 14 June, 47.

Rühling, Lutz (2007) 'Swedes', in Beller, Manfred and Joep Leerssen (eds) *Imagology: The Cultural Construction and Literary Representation of National Characters.* Amsterdam and New York: Rodopi, 248–50.

Said, Edward (2003 [1978]) *Orientalism.* London: Penguin.

Sauntved, Louise Kidde (2011) 'The Catastrophic Tales and Booming Career of Susanne Bier'. *Film Comment*, 47 (2), 24–7.

Schanz, Hans-Jørgen (2012) *Frihed*, Tænkepauser (1). Aarhus: Aarhus Universitetsforlag.

Schröder, Stephan Michael (1996) *Mehr Spaß mit Schwedinnen? Funktionen eines deutschen Heterostereotyps*, Arbeitspapiere Gemeinschaften (3). Berlin: Nordeuropa-Institut.

Schrödl, Daniel (2009) 'Insel(s)hopping. Alltag in schwedischen Einkaufszentren'. *Norrøna*, 43, 74–82.

Sellström, Tor (1999/2002) *Sweden and National Liberation in Southern Africa*, 2 vols. Uppsala: Nordiska Afrikainstitutet.

Spivak, Gayatri Chakravorty (1994) 'Can the Subaltern Speak?', in Chrisman, Laura and Patrick Williams (eds) *Colonial Discourse and Post-Colonial Theory: A Reader*. New York: Columbia University Press, 66–111.

Theils, Lone (2011) 'Skotterne vil være skandinaver'. *Politiken*, 11 December.

Thisted, Kirsten (2011) 'For en "écriture anticoloniale". Kulturel oversættelse og litterære kodeskift i Ejersbos Afrikatrilogi'. *Kritik*, 199, 89–98.

Thorsen, Nils (2013) 'International "Borgen"-feber. Det er moderne at dyrke Danmark'. *Politiken*, 6 January.

Trägårdh, Lars (2012) 'Mellem liberalisme og socialisme. Om det særlige ved den nordiske model'. *Kritik*, 206, 40–50.

Tvedt, Terje (2003) *Utviklingshjelp, utenrikspolitikk og makt: Den norske modellen.* Oslo: Gyldendal.

Volquardsen, Ebbe (2014) 'Old and New Trends in Danish-Greenlandic Migration Literature', in Körber, Lill-Ann and Ebbe Volquardsen (eds) *The Postcolonial North Atlantic: Greenland, Iceland and the Faroe Islands*. Berliner Beiträge zur Skandinavistik (20). Berlin: Nordeuropa-Institut.

Werler, Tobias (2007) 'Wenn aus Gerechtigkeit Vorzüglichkeit wird. (Chancen-) Gleichheit und Schulbildung in Skandinavien', in Dose, Inken et al. *Vorbildfunktion vs. Entsorgungspädagogik? Schulpolitik und Bildung in Skandinavien und Deutschland.* Leipzig and Berlin: Edition Kirchhof and Franke, 39–64.

Williams, Susan (2011) *Who Killed Dag Hammarskjöld? The UN, the Cold War and White Supremacy in Africa.* Manchester: Hurst and Co.

Chapter 3
'Now is Necessity': Icelandic Charity during the Crisis Years

James G. Rice

Introduction

This chapter focuses on the implications of 'crisis', and 'The Crisis', for charities' clients. The emphasis of this discussion is on discursive production – spoken word, print and images – regarding material aid charities and their recipients in the mainstream Icelandic media over the years 2007–12.[1] While specifically examining the period before, during and after the autumn 2008 economic crisis, my interest does not concern what charities *do* in a practical sense (a subject already explored in a two-year ethnographic study of a material aid charity in Iceland (Rice 2007)), but centres on how charities are framed discursively. Media communications relating to charities exhibited certain patterns regarding the portrayal of their clients and their work. However, media attitudes shifted dramatically during the crisis of 2008 when portrayals of charitable practices devoted to assisting only the most marginalized sectors of Icelandic society took on a collective, nationalistic aura.

Charity was re-positioned as serving a nation-in-crisis, quite unlike the earlier focus on the *usual* clients of charity, such as elderly and disabled people. The intention of this discussion is not merely to document how charities were represented in the media, but to delineate such discursive representations as productive. These discourses have an effect on how phenomena are perceived and explained, which in turn impacts on how people are situated in economic, political and socio-cultural positions. For the most marginalized members of society, these discursive practices in effect *normalized* these sectors of the population as the expected clientele of charity, and in turn normalized the structural inequities they had to contend with, as well as the expected charitable response to addressing these issues. Media accounts of the work of charities are not innocent in the sense of being an objective statement, even if such objectivity were possible, but are intended to convey knowledge, shape opinion and encourage action on the part of a wide array of social actors. As the philosopher Michel Foucault contends, 'it is in discourse that power and knowledge are joined together' (Foucault 1980: 101).

---

1 This fieldwork component of this research was supported by the Social Sciences and Humanities Research Council of Canada Doctoral Fellowship and a part of media analysis by The Icelandic Centre for Research (Rannís: grant number 130426-052).

While the shock and the worst effects of the 2008 crisis gradually receded in Iceland, the media accounts of charity, mostly returned to their pre-crisis form to focus once again on single mothers, senior citizens, disability pensioners and other sectors of society often portrayed as vulnerable and favoured by charitable donors and volunteers. But it was not all business as usual in the sphere of Icelandic charity. Charities, especially in the greater Reykjavík area – the main urban centre in the country – were confronted by significant numbers of migrant labourers. These people were primarily from Poland and Lithuania and had sought work in Iceland during the growth years, and who had lost their jobs during the crisis. Such 'foreigners (*útlendingar*)' formed a large part of the post-crisis clients and were gradually incorporated into the practices and discourses of charity and which entered into debates in the public arena about ongoing changes in the larger society.

However, the rapidity and the extent to which charity discourses changed during the crisis of 2008 was surprising, prompting me to undertake a detailed survey of charitable discourses as the crisis unfolded. This survey informs the following analysis. The dramatic shift from a focus on marginalized people to that of the nation at large, combined with a sharp critique of the state and the banking sector, led me to question my earlier findings on charity, which held that charity acts as a force for the *status quo*. Yet these changes, in response to crisis, were not lasting. As I monitored the discursive output concerning charity, the traditional categories of vulnerable populations began to re-emerge by 2012, although with a continued focus on unemployment and foreign labourers.

While I argue that the practices of charity largely serve to maintain the existing order of structural inequalities, a close examination of charity discourses in Iceland during the crisis years also revealed a degree of malleability which does not sit well with the notion of the *status quo*. Cultural norms in relation to understanding poverty are maintained primarily through portraying poverty as something that afflicts only delimited sectors of society, and through showing inequality as a natural feature of society, with charity as an appropriate response – the last supports of the formal assistance system. However, this is perhaps best not interpreted as an example of discursive discontinuity either, or as representative of some kind of sudden break or shift in how inequality is understood in contemporary Iceland, engendered as the result of a sudden and dramatic crisis. Rather, this phenomenon is something like the anthropologist Henrik Vigh's (2008) understanding of 'chronicity': a notion of crisis as endemic for some and episodic for others (see also Tikka and Sumiala and Jensen's chapters on crisis as transitional and crisis as permanent). The notion of chronicity captures the charity situation. Marginalized sectors of the population continue to remain marginalized before, during and after such crises, whereas for others a crisis represents an unusual break or discontinuity, even if such crises may be predictable and the expected outcomes of the capitalist order. The longitudinal analysis of the Icelandic crisis years through the perspective of charity discourses offered here provide some insights into one of the mechanisms through which the normative order of things is re-asserted after a time of crisis. And, in keeping with the focus of this edited volume, provide insights into the different power dynamics and subjectivities located within Iceland, the Nordic countries and beyond (Loftsdóttir and Jensen, Introduction, this volume).

The Mother of All Crises

The term 'Crisis', as remarked by Marxist critic Raymond Williams in his classic *Keywords*, 'has of course been extended to any difficulty as well as any turning point' (Williams 1983[1976]: 85). 'Crisis' has been repeatedly invoked to describe the events that engulfed Iceland and which led to the collapse of its financial sector in 2008 – the contextual focus of this chapter. While it is beyond the scope of this chapter to discuss in detail the causes of the economic collapse in Iceland,[2] it is within its ambit to discuss its ramifications as they affected charity recipients. This notion of crisis as a sudden and dramatic rupture, turning point or discontinuity with the normative state of affairs is an appropriate fit for the general shock and surprise felt by many who lived through these times in Iceland, myself included. The Iceland I first encountered in 2002, during a pre-fieldwork visit, was experiencing unprecedented growth as the result of the liberalization of its economy, with negligible levels of unemployment. The notion of poverty (*fátækt*) was something left behind in the past of Iceland's former status as an underdeveloped Danish colony on Europe's periphery. In contemporary times, poverty was perceived as an individual phenomenon, an outcome of personal circumstances rather than structural economic or political factors, with charity playing a supportive role to help those who 'could not make ends meet', or at least this is how it was largely portrayed to me by charity officials. As such, I viewed the vehement critiques of the capitalist order that emerged in 2008 in Iceland with a measure of cynicism, considering that poverty, un- or underemployment and marginalization was something many charity clients had had to contend with for years, if not their entire lives. It seemed that a 'crisis' is only a crisis when it affects the affluent. From a Marxist perspective, such crises that arise are the expected result of capitalist production and its inherent contradictions and inequities, and not primarily linked to individual circumstances. If anything, such crises are a necessary stage in the process of the structural transformation of the existing socio-economic order. The transformative potential of crisis is not overlooked by the defenders of the *status quo* either, as the anthropologist and geographer David Harvey argues (2005). He contends that the primary function of state intervention into the economy has long been 'to control crisis and devaluation in ways that permit accumulation by dispossession to occur without sparking a general collapse or popular revolt' (Harvey 2005: 163). Yet the particular crisis of 2008 had given Harvey pause in terms of its scale, scope and implications. He referred to the 2008 financial crisis in *The Enigma of Capital* (2010) as the 'mother of all crises,' but continued his argument stating that this crisis 'must also be seen as the culmination of a pattern of financial crises that had become more frequent and deeper over the years' (Harvey 2010: 6). As such, the notion of 'crisis' contains within it elements

2 For a more detailed overview of the causes of the financial meltdown in Iceland, see Loftsdóttir, Chapter 9, this volume. Also Loftsdóttir (2012).

of structural transformation and change, but also of continuity in regard to the forces that seek to maintain the status quo.

In order to illuminate the implications of this 'mother of all crises' and its intersection with charity discourses in Iceland, I collected and analysed all of the reportage in the mainstream Icelandic print media over the years 2007–12 using the search string '*Mæðrastyrksnefnd*' (Mothers' Support Committee). Mæðrastyrksnefnd is the material aid charity with which I conducted a two-year ethnographic fieldwork study for my PhD in anthropology (Rice 2007). The charity is one of the oldest and institutionalized local charities in Iceland, having formed in 1928 as the focal point for a number of women's organizations in Reykjavík with the explicit goal of helping marginalized women and their children with material aid, together with legal assistance. In my experience of the contemporary philanthropic context, rarely was the issue of charity discussed in the mainstream Icelandic media that did not include a reference to Mæðrastyrksnefnd. Additionally, discussions of charity, or of Mæðrastyrksnefnd itself, often included a reference to the other major organizations that provided this kind of assistance, such as *Hjálparstarf kirkjunnar* (Icelandic Church Aid) and *Fjölskylduhjálp Íslands* (Iceland's Family Help). Officials from all three of these organizations were often consulted whenever the issues of poverty or charity were raised in the media. The media sometimes included other organizations, such as the Icelandic branches of the Red Cross and the Salvation Army. I was familiar with the discursive media output concerning charities in Iceland during the time of my fieldwork, but I did not engage in a methodical study of this matter.

In order to analyse the quantitative and qualitative dimensions of the charity discourse in Iceland immediately before, during and after the crisis, I collected all examples that discussed, explicitly or tangentially, Mæðrastyrksnefnd and the other major material aid charities over the years 2007–12. I focused primarily on the three major Icelandic national newspapers – *Morgunblaðið*, *Fréttablaðið,* and *DV*. This search alone produced approximately 500 stories on a range of matters, such as calls for assistance, the insights of charity officials on various social issues, reports on notable donations, opinion pieces, and editorials. I also included in the analysis the few relevant articles from other sources as they appeared in my search, such as from the now defunct *24 Stundir* newspaper, as well as the occasional piece from the business paper *Viðskiptablaðið*, the rural oriented *Bændablaðið*, and a small number of radio and television programmes which were aired by the national broadcast services *RÚV*. All examples of these media occurrences were charted and analysed according to date of publication in order to understand the temporal patterns of reportage. The content was then analysed, including both the text and accompanying images, from which analytical themes were extracted. What follows next is a detailing of my analysis of this reportage which I have organized into three sections: *What Crisis?*, which details the media reportage on charities leading up to the crisis; *A Crisis for All*, which analyses the sudden shift that occurred in 2008 to that of a nation in crisis; and *A Crisis for Some*, which explores the re-emergence of the pre-crisis charitable discourses over the years 2011 and 2012, and which emphasizes charity as the domain of delimited marginalized populations.

What Crisis?

The collection of material aid charities that I encountered in Reykjavík over the years 2004 through to 2006 during my dissertation research (Rice 2007) comprised a 'charity complex' which involved a wide range of interested parties, from municipal to state governments, businesses, religious institutions, political parties, advocacy and grassroots organizations, schools to individuals from the public. I argued that these combined efforts at mobilizing charitable activities to address structural inequalities, at best, mitigated some of the short-term effects of poverty; in the long-term, such charitable assistance was not capable of addressing the kinds of substantive transformations needed to challenge structural inequality. In effect, though perhaps not intent, these charitable endeavours served to preserve the socio-economic *status quo* concerning poverty by directing resources and media attention toward low-level material relief activities that were often bereft of the necessary activist work needed to draw attention to the root causes of such structural inequalities. Any notion of 'crisis' was absent from the discursive representation of charities, either in the words of my research participants or observable in media accounts. A few short years later and the word 'crisis' (*kreppa*) would become omnipresent in spoken and written discourse in Iceland.

What was apparent in these media accounts during my fieldwork was an overwhelming focus on the donors, which usually consisted of a flattering portrayal of the donors and a description of what was given. The text was often accompanied by photos of charity officials shaking hands with the donor and accepting over-sized novelty cheques or an example of the goods in question. When the clients were discussed, it was generally done so in reference to the demographic categories they represented which followed how such charities delimited their clientele. The most predominant were disability pensioners (*öryrkjar*), single mothers and senior citizens. In empirical terms, this made sense in regard to disability pensioners who accounted for roughly half of the clientele of Mæðrastyrksnefnd at the time. However, during the time of my research seniors only accounted for a slim minority of their clientele; there were numerically more students and unemployed seeking help at this charity yet these categories received much less attention in media accounts. Other local charities reported some differences in their numbers, but their demographic categories and the way in which they reported on their work were strikingly similar.

Charitable discourses and practices tend to exhibit a degree of conservatism and continuity, as the demographic categories that comprised the 'worthy' and 'unworthy' poor that guided charity work on the European mainland have existed for centuries (Jütte 1994; Lindberg 1993). These notions of the worthy poor appeared to govern Icelandic charitable practices, to varying degrees, once such material aid charities began to appear in the country in the late nineteenth and early twentieth centuries (Hákonardóttir 2000; Rice 2007). Yet such discourses are also to an extent malleable and responsive to changes in the larger society. The traditional 'worthy' or 'sick poor' categories were still present in various ways during the time of my ethnographic study of Icelandic charity over the years 2004 to 2006. What had historically been a charitable focus on widows, orphans and the sick was realized in contemporary Iceland as a focus instead on single mothers, disability pensioners and seniors; yet the mindset which insisted on sorting the clients according to perceptions of need and worthiness persisted, even if the specific categories changed for a number of complex reasons. For example, for a number of years a debate about men as charity clients was ongoing in which the predominantly 'feminized' charity discourses shifted to incorporate marginalized men in Iceland (Rice 2009), though this expansion of charity categories does not necessarily translate to a critique of the larger socio-economic order that produces poverty and marginalization.

The media representations of charitable work during the pre-crisis years in Iceland overwhelmingly made the basic reference to these demographic categories among their clientele but with very little critical analysis of why charities' assistance was needed. Rather than emphasizing common structural factors people in these categories often shared – such as low income, low education and training, high costs of living and taxation, meagre social supports, or physical, social, or economic exclusion from society – these categories were treated as if their designation was evidence enough to warrant charitable assistance without any need for further inquiry. It appeared that the primary discursive task of charities was not to expose the underlying factors that contributed to structural poverty but to ensure a steady flow of support to redistribute aid to their clients. If anything, the more traditional charities preferred to work quietly in the background rather than seeming too brazen by requesting support, or appearing to criticize the government. For example, Mæðrastyrksnefnd explicitly referred to this silence in a newspaper article: 'it has not been Mæðrastyrksnefnd's way in the past 76 years it has been operating to publicize its work. That is why you hear so little from the committee. They work silently.' Further, the author of the article had clearly tread very carefully when explicating the reasons their clientele sought their assistance: 'Temporary difficulties are often the reason for these visits which the clients manage to get a grip on, but unfortunately many also have very difficult situations for different reasons' (*Morgunblaðið* 2004: 41). Such an analysis, in my interpretation, highlights the temporality of the clients' situations and which implies that these situations will be resolved, or at least alleviated, with the aid of charity. The rather ambiguous reference to the longer-term clientele is accurate in the sense of implying the complexity of the issues at hand, but it hardly points to causality.

These media representations did not invoke any sense of crisis. The closest reference which approximated any sense of crisis or even urgency was the often articulated variants of the phrase 'more need than ever before'. This phrase was included in the title or sub-headers of a number of articles (e.g. '*Fleiri þarfnast aðstoðar fyrir páskana en áður*' [*Morgunblaðið* 2005: 52]; '*Sífellt fleiri leita sér aðstoðar*' [*Morgunblaðið* 2006: 11]).[3] However, the theme of 'more need than ever before' was nothing new in the discourse of Icelandic charities. Having done some exploratory research on the media discussions of charity in Iceland when Mæðrastyrksnefnd formed in the 1920s for my dissertation work, I was often struck with a sense of déjà vu when I engaged in the later survey of contemporary charity discourses undertaken for this chapter. For example, one article on the work of this particular charity from 1932 could easily have been written in 2005, with the only difference at all being some rather dated language: 'This time the need is more than ever before, and that is why the mothers' support committee counts on distinguished townspeople to help as they have done so before' (*Morgunblaðið* 1932: 3). Vague references to 'more need than ever before' without exploring why, or references to working silently in the background are hardly conducive to mounting a critique of the larger socio-economic order necessary to pressure for change.

However, it would be unfair to state that Icelandic charities totally ignored structural factors; rather, they would make reference to general issues such as 'low wages,' or describe the phenomenon within an individualized, and de-politicized, 'people who cannot make ends meet' (*Fréttablaðið* 2004: 6) framework. Nor would it be fair to say that these charity practices and discourses remained frozen and unresponsive. Mæðrastyrksnefnd's historic focus on widows, single mothers and their children was being rethought during my fieldwork. The Icelandic Church Aid had been working with Mæðrastyrksnefnd by offering to assist with the increasing numbers of single men – often with serious mental health and substance abuse issues – and I took part in numerous private debates with the staff of Mæðrastyrksnefnd who wanted to retain their historic focus and others who wanted their organization to be more attuned to the contemporary context. This discussion was also informed by the fact that joint parent custody arrangements were increasingly common in Iceland, rendering the notion of 'single mother' more complex than it had been in the past and bringing greater attention to the prior invisibility of single fathers. This was reflected in the greater willingness of local area charities to assist men and discuss these issues openly in the media. For example, the chairperson of another charity, Fjölskylduhjálp Íslands (Iceland's Family Help), argued that men in difficult situations 'are becoming more visible in society … [b]efore Fjölskylduhjálp these men had nowhere to go' (*Morgunblaðið* 2005: 52).

Again, this expansion of the charitable categories illustrates some of the tensions observable in charitable discourse between ongoing social changes and with the general conservatism of the charitable system in Iceland. This was particularly evident in the widespread silence about the issue of immigration from charities in media accounts in pre-crisis Iceland. For much of its history, Iceland

3 'More need assistance for Easter than before'; 'Increasingly more seek assistance.'

has not been a destination for significant immigration prior to the late twentieth century due to its relative remoteness and limited economic opportunities. This rapidly changed with the modernization of the Icelandic economy and which resulted in, among other things, a relatively new phenomenon of labour migration to Iceland. Also in the wider Nordic context this makes Iceland a latecomer as a migrant destination. By the year 2000, foreign nationals comprised 3 per cent of the national population and trebled to 9 per cent during Iceland's boom years. Labour migrants were largely attracted by the availability of work in the fish processing industries, and later, in the service sector and construction industries (Wojtyńska, Skaptadóttir and Ólafs 2011: 7–8). Despite the often heated internal debates of local charities, the issue of the increasing number of immigrant clientele at these charities was, for the most part, muted in charity discourses, with the exception of the Icelandic Red Cross. The Icelandic Red Cross has long been concerned and quite vocal about the issues facing immigrants in Iceland. Whenever I spoke with the staff of Mæðrastyrksnefnd about this issue, it was apparent that they were both uneasy and uncertain as to what to make of these recent societal changes, but the increasing number of immigrants among their clientele was not perceived as a crisis. Rather, the presence of recent immigrants at local charities was met with bewilderment and a measure of suspicion. The notion of Iceland being a homogeneous society was invoked by the charity workers I spoke with to explain the hesitancy of many towards embracing a notion of a multicultural Iceland, and the 'fear of the other' to explain their suspicion about immigrant clients.[4] Immigrants at Mæðrastyrksnefnd, for example, during this time were generally described by the staff to me as 'Asian women', or a collection of national labels that were freely interchangeable ('Thais', 'Filipinos', 'Vietnamese') but which did, to an extent, reflect the gendered and national patterns of labour migration to Iceland in the late 1990s (Skaptadóttir 2010). Such immigrants were most certainly seen as hardworking, yet perhaps also as a temporary (and disposable) labour pool whose long-term link to Iceland was questionable.

The preference for describing charities as assisting the 'classic' categories of single mothers, disabled people and seniors predominantly characterized the discursive media output on charities in the years leading up to the crisis of 2008. Some attention shifted to the issue of men and immigrants in the years marking the end of my fieldwork in 2006. This shift in focus continued into 2007, but the discursive representation of the clients of charity nevertheless appeared to be selective. The majority of the discursive output of charities during pre-crisis Iceland tended to be muted, somewhat uncritical and acted as a force for the *status quo* – soliciting charity donations rather than advocating political agitation. Even in the more openly critical accounts, there is a sense that the authors and the reading public are somehow distinct from those who are struggling and who form the target group of charitable endeavours. In reports the donors were presented

4 See also Hübinette (Chapter 4, this volume) concerning the case of Swedish multiculturalism.

as 'us' whereas the people who sought charitable assistance were 'those people,' perhaps best summarized in Icelandic with the negative connotation associated with the phrase '*þetta fólk*' (those people); those who are not like us. For example, in one newspaper editorial concerning charities (*Morgunblaðið* 2007: 26), references are made to Iceland's wealth and prosperity and high-status ranking in various international comparisons and indicators, but that poverty nevertheless exists. The problem is presented not as one of a lack of wealth in Iceland, but of an unequal distribution of this wealth.[5] Yet at the same time, Icelanders are lauded as generous when it comes to such charitable collections, and the public are reminded not to forget, especially around the holidays, those who cannot afford to celebrate holidays, such as Christmas. In such accounts, the reference to the unequal distribution of wealth is laudable yet the critique remains blunted; the readers are not informed as to why unequal distribution exists and what can be done about it beyond giving to charity. Further, the act of reminding readers 'not to forget' suggests that this is something that could be forgotten; in other words, it is a problem that afflicts only a minority of the population and not the nation as a whole. What remains unarticulated was any sense that there was a crisis in Iceland concerning the number of people who regularly sought charitable assistance. Of course, an exception from this assertion is the 'more need than ever before' discourse. But as I argue above, this may be questionable as a 'crisis' given that this seemed to have been the *de facto* position of this particular charity for the last 80 years, though it is, perhaps, useful as a tool to encourage donors. Nevertheless, there were indications discoverable in these discourses that Iceland was changing and that things were not as well as they appeared to be; such concerns would turn to alarm with the economic collapse of 2008.

A Crisis for All

The media output of charities in the years leading up to the crisis, even for the first half of 2008, mirrored longstanding practices: a flurry of media attention to charities around the holidays of Easter and Christmas, with a general silence otherwise beyond isolated calls for donations; depictions of the clientele as a set of categories that were seen as resonating most favourably with the donating public, even though these categories did not always best reflect the empirical reality of the clients' demographics; and a general lack of a sense of crisis or urgency about structural inequality. However, as 'The Crisis' emerged and then deepened in the autumn of 2008, there was a distinct and notable shift in the discursive production of charities.

On the one hand, there were more stories about an increase of people seeking assistance at local charities. This was not surprising in and of itself, yet I had rarely

---

5 'Ekki fer á milli mála að það eru miklir peningar í umferð í íslensku samfélagi, en þeim er misskipt' (*Morgunblaðið* 2007: 26).

seen stories like these on the front pages of local papers. Such stories started to appear in late 2008 (e.g. *Fréttablaðið* 2008: 1). These stories also differed in that there was indeed a significant, rapid and demonstrable increase, with charities reporting that they were assisting two to three times the amount of clientele than normal prior to the crisis. Another front page story in *Morgunblaðið* displayed a photograph of the shelving at Mæðrastyrksnefnd full of bags of food waiting to be donated with the caption: '*Hundruð matarpoka bíða úthlutuna*' (Hundreds of foodbags waiting to be distributed) (*Morgunblaðið* 2008a: 1). As the crisis deepened, the discourse of charity officials shifted to emphasize families and the unemployed, or both in tandem as one charity official commented: 'Families have increased; we have had, among others, coming to us couples who are both unemployed with four or five children.' In this same article, a comment was also made about the increased number of foreigners (*Fréttablaðið* 2009: 10). References were of course still made in regard to disability pensioners and seniors, but the emphasis had notably shifted into that of a crisis that was affecting wide swathes of the population rather than small, delimited groups.

I expected local charities to follow past practices and run advertisements or stories in the local papers around the holidays to solicit for donors and volunteers. Yet I noticed that in 2008, inserted into one of the usual ads placed in the papers for the Christmas drive for Mæðrastyrksnefnd, was the phrase: '*Oft var þörf en nú er nauðsyn*' (Often was need but now is necessity) (*Morgunblaðið* 2008b: 12). The sentiments are curious in that it is implied that prior to the crisis there was 'need' but now this has become a 'necessity', either due to the dramatically increased number of clientele or the changing demographics of the clientele. One of the more startling articles in this regard was a two-page spread on the work of Mæðrastyrksnefnd in December of 2008 (*Morgunblaðið* 2008c: 26–7). A sub-header within the article referred to the new faces prominent among the applicants seeking food ('*Ný andlit áberandi í hópi umsækjenda um mat*'). Within the article, a charity official starts with the usual recitation of the traditional charity recipients – disability pensioners, seniors, single parents – but then commented that now the 'clients are from all classes from society' ('*umsækjendur úr öllum stéttum þjóðfélagsins*'). Rarely did I previously encounter direct references to the issue of economic class in Icelandic society, aside from a small handful of critical scholars. This charity official continued that the recipients of charity now encompassed both the working and professional classes: 'Now we are seeing many people who are out of work. Today, for example, we saw some women who were working in banks, but most of the new clients are those who were working in the construction industry', referring to the latter as primarily 'foreign men' (ibid.).

The discourse of charity officials appeared to be structured to bridge a gap between retaining the emphasis on the traditional clientele with an inclusion of the recently unemployed from all walks of life. Charity was no longer focused on the small and marginalized minority but on a crisis that concerned the nation as a whole. This sentiment was made very clear in the discourse about the donors that appeared in the media. One pattern that emerged in 2008 that was markedly different prior to the crisis was a reference to donations made to local charities in the name of 'togetherness' (*samkennd*) and 'standing together' (*standa saman*). Such sentiments were absent prior to the crisis, as the donor discourse was phrased in terms of 'helping those who have little' and so forth, which had created a clear demarcation between donor and client. Such distinctions were collapsed under the new crisis-era charity discourse in which anyone, presumably, could find themselves standing in a charity queue. For example, one article recounted the donation by a designer of tablecloths done in the style of the Icelandic flag. The donor referred to the donation as being 'done in the spirit of the day in Iceland, to stand together and show togetherness'[6] (*Morgunblaðið* 2008d: 4). Another donor commented that people in the country seem to be in harmony and are standing back to back during the crisis[7] (*Morgunblaðið* 2008e: 16). In another article, the crew of a fishing trawler donated their travel fund to the charity Mæðrastyrksnefnd. The captain referred to the act as one of showing 'solidarity' (*samstaða*) and how terrible it would be to use the travel fund for the crew to go on a vacation when so many people have it so bad (*Morgunblaðið* 2008f: 4). Another group of individuals decided to take up a travelling collection for the charity using a model ship that they built as a prop. The ship is referred to as a 'national clipper' (*þjóðarskútu*) with obvious nationalistic references to Iceland's nautical history – the model is replete with an Icelandic flag. In a story about their work with this travelling collection ship, a 'symbol of unity' (*sameiningartákn*), they also praise the staff of Mæðrastyrksnefnd, referring to them as the 'real heroes of Iceland'[8] (*Morgunblaðið* 2008g: 4). I interpreted these sentiments as an indirect swipe at the previous 'heroes of Iceland' before the crisis, the much praised 'outvasion Vikings' (*útrásarvíkingar*) or 'business Vikings' who were perceived as the primary cause of both Iceland's boom years as well as the subsequent crisis.

The intention here is not to belittle the sentiments expressed by these donors. However, it is to raise questions about the shift in the charitable discourses to the communal and nationalistic sentiments that were absent from such discourses prior to the collapse. One may ask where these sentiments of 'solidarity' and 'unity' were prior to 2008, and if they are lacking, what does this mean for how the general public views the traditional recipients of charities? In my discussions with the clients of Mæðrastyrksnefnd prior to the crisis of 2008, I often thought of their lives as they described them to me as one long non-ending series of crises endured in the struggle with poverty. These crises included: dealing with health or impairment issues and all of their disabling effects, the issues of violence, mental health and substance abuse that afflicted the clients or their families, and the indignity of having to rely on charity. Yet from the perspectives of charities and the

6 'Þetta er í þeim anda sem hefur verið á Íslandi undanfarið, að standa saman og sýna samkennd.'

7 'Fólkið í landinu virðist samstiga um að snúa bökum saman í kreppunni.'

8 'Þetta er sameiningartákn og er þannig hugsað að þessar konur séu raunverulegar hetjur Íslands.'

donors, there remained a gulf between those who gave and those who receive. The routine crises of the long-term clients were apparently not as significant as 'The Crisis', presumably because of the issue of scale but also because the issues of chronic debt and impoverishment were now a concern of the working class and the more affluent classes rather than the usual 'underclass' during times of stability. However, this nationalistic focus on charity as a symbolic of collective unity was not to last. As the crisis unfolded and ran its course, the period of recovery that appeared to follow witnessed a return to similar charitable discourses as in the pre-crisis years, albeit with a lingering focus on structural unemployment and anxieties about coming to terms with Iceland's status as a multicultural society.

A Crisis for Some

As the crisis of 2008 ran its course and signs of recovery began to appear, there was again another shift in the discursive output of charities. There was, of course, continuity in the form of articles in the usual framework of growing needs and difficulties making ends meet (e.g. *Fréttablaðið* 2010a: 10). However, by 2011 the *status quo* concerning the demographics of the clientele was reasserting itself, as there were discourses articulated that would not have been out of place in 2004, with the reference to increasing numbers of disability pensioners, seniors, single mothers and large families. The headlines of articles about charity, often linked to the traditional Christmas allocation, referred to 'more elderly and disabled' ('*Fleiri aldraðir og öryrkjar*', *Morgunblaðið* 2011a), or 'large families and disabled people seeking assistance' ('*Stórar fjölskyldur og öryrkjar leita aðstoðar*', *Morgunblaðið* 2011b), with one charity official asserting that among the large families and seniors seeking assistance there were 'more Icelanders than before' (*Morgunblaðið* 2011c) in reference to the change (or the reversion) among the national or quasi-ethnic demographics of the clients. All of these discourses sought to, in a manner of speaking, domesticate and tame poverty in the context of post-crisis Iceland by situating it as something experienced by a minority of delimited sectors of the population. This discursive formation of charity appeared quite similar to the pre-crisis forms and was markedly different from the crisis era discourses of only a few short years before. However, it would not be accurate to say that the pre- and post discourses were identical. As I have argued, charitable discourses, while displaying a certain tendency towards conservatism, are nevertheless always to an extent malleable and there would be no reason for the discourses of 2011 and 2012 to have remained in-stasis, even if the 2008 crisis did not occur. There remained, for example, a discernible level of uncertainty and anxiety regarding Iceland's economic situation and the effects of government cutbacks on marginalized people (e.g. *Fréttablaðið* 2011: 6). Nonetheless the rapidity and extent to which this discursive output retreated back to a focus on the traditional clients was surprising, even if this did include a begrudging acceptance of immigrant clients.

The regulation of foreign labour had changed during the boom years as Icelandic law was brought into greater accordance with EEA/EFTA regulations. From 2002, work permits needed to be granted to non-EEA migrants, whereas citizens of EEA/EFTA nations have the legal right to reside and work in Iceland. As such, residents of EEA/EFTA countries had a much easier time seeking work and residing in Iceland. A combination of these developments and EU expansion resulted in Polish and Lithuanian nationals accounting for the majority of foreign nationals in Iceland by 2011 (Wojtyńska, Skaptadóttir and Ólafs 2011: 8). As such, the discourse of 'Asian women' that I had been used to morphed into one concerning 'foreign', primarily Polish, 'men'. A significant proportion of these Polish labour migrants were males working in the construction industry. As the result of the crisis, the unemployment rate of foreign nationals was double that of Icelandic citizens. Some 42 per cent of these were working in the construction sector which was particularly hard-hit as construction projects ground to a halt (ibid.) and whose presence was increasingly noted by Reykjavík area charities. One result of this is that the presence of these foreign labourers at local Reykjavík charities spurred questions about immigration, unemployment, and the shifting national/cultural demographics.

Charitable organizations supportive of immigrants, such as the Icelandic Red Cross, continued to be vocal in their support of assisting immigrants and advocated for a vision of a multicultural Iceland. However another charity, Fjölskylduhjálp Íslands (Iceland's Family Help), followed a decidedly different path. During the spring of 2010, this charity decided to prioritize 'Icelandic' clients, as well as creating a separate waiting line for foreign nationals. It was reported on the front page of the national newspaper *Fréttablaðið* (*Fréttablaðið* 25 March, 2010b: 1–2), which stated: 'Icelanders are a priority for Fjölskylduhjálp: Fjölskylduhjálp Íslands placed foreigners in one queue and Icelanders in another. The manager says that many foreigners show up in large groups in the lines and some Icelanders have given up waiting.' The manager defended the practice, arguing that the foreign nationals, primarily young Polish men, have a 'different line culture' than Icelanders; some will show up early in the day and allow other men who show up later to queue jump. As a result, older Icelanders who 'toiled their whole lives' as well as young mothers with babes on their arms leave in frustration without receiving assistance. The reference to the traditional charitable categories in order to elicit sympathy was not surprising. Yet what was significant about this was the general public condemnation of these practices. It appeared that this charity misjudged public attitudes about unemployed foreign nationals seeking help when so many Icelandic citizens were also out of work, as they too were the clear victims of the crisis. The following day, an article appeared entitled: 'Fjölskylduhjálp harshly criticised' (*Fréttablaðið* 26 March, 2010c: 6). The city's social welfare services held a meeting with the charity to ensure that this would not happen again. The municipal council of Reykjavík and its human rights board also contributed to the discussion adding that such practices will not be tolerated. The matter was taken up on a national level, as the Minister for Social Affairs stated in parliament that any practices which discriminated between people based on their backgrounds were not acceptable. There was, in addition, little support forthcoming from other local charities. The charitable arm of the Lutheran Church argued that this practice was a violation of the Icelandic Constitution itself. Other Reykjavík area charities made efforts to distance themselves from these views and practices.

This example is illustrative of the malleability of the discursive formation that revolves around charity, yet the issue at stake in post-crisis Iceland concerning immigrants increasingly appeared to be whether or not they 'belonged' as the clients of local area charities (perhaps with a sub-text as to whether or not they belonged in Iceland altogether), rather than an examination of the causes of why people needed the help of charities in the first place. Given my familiarity with Icelandic charities and the discursive output concerning charities in Iceland over the last decade, it would not be surprising at all to see immigrants, or 'new Icelanders' (*nýir Íslendingar*), come to form one more category in the types that form a charity's clients. The structural reasons as to why they need this assistance remain veiled behind these discursive practices.

Conclusion

The anthropologist Henrik Vigh (2008) notes that the term 'crisis' is often perceived quite differently depending upon one's situation. For the majority of people from the wealthier and more privileged parts of the world, a crisis is an unusual and rather unfortunate or traumatic event or series of events which are most likely temporary in nature. Yet as Vigh rightly points out, 'for many people around the world – the chronically ill, the structurally violated, socially marginalised and poor – the world is not characterised by peace, prosperity and order but by the presence and possibility of conflict, poverty and disorder' (Vigh 2008: 7) (see also Ystanes (Chapter 7) and Ranta-Tyrkkö (Chapter 6), this volume). Many of the charity clients I encountered in 2004–2006 were not struggling with temporary difficulties as implied in the term 'crisis'. The discourse which circulated around charity in Iceland refrained from political critique of the socio-economic order in favour of presenting a descriptive, rather than analytical, portrayal of poverty as something that afflicted delimited groups of the population in a decontextualized, framework of people struggling as the result of personal circumstances. These circumstances dramatically shifted to become a national problem with the crisis of 2008 and charity re-positioned itself as responsive to a collective crisis that engulfed all of Iceland, which often entailed a pointed critique of the structural factors underlying the collapse. Yet such a perspective was not to last, as the emphasis within such charitable discourses re-asserted the role of charities as assisting vulnerable populations and other 'victims' of unfortunate circumstances.

The important role that these discourses played – though care should be taken not to over-emphasize their importance – offers insights into the workings of the discursive mechanisms that act to preserve the *status quo*. There are reasons, many beyond the scope of this discussion, for the return of a centre-right national government in Iceland in 2013. Such a government is perceived by some as being the architects behind the liberalization of the Icelandic economy, especially the liberalization of the financial sector, which played a key role in the 2008 crisis. While the election of a government associated with the collapse bewildered foreign observers, from the perspective inside Iceland it was less surprising. While doing this survey of charity discourses over the course of 2011 and 2012, the sense of *déjà vu* was overwhelming. In many ways, as charities returned to focusing on disability pensioners and single mothers, it felt like nothing had changed and lessons were not being learned. I had already been sceptical of the overly optimistic visions of a new Iceland that would supposedly emerge from the ashes of the crisis. Moreover, I was troubled to see that charities were discussed as they had been during 2004. When the new centre-right government was elected in 2013, it appeared to me as a symbol that the process was now complete: Icelanders, it seemed, wanted to return to the 'good years' and chose to conveniently forget that those 'good years' were a mirage in the first place. They also chose to conveniently forget the Marxist adage that crises are the normative component of an unstable order, and that whatever prosperity envisioned would be short-lived.

Yet discourses concerning charity are not a force for the *status quo* in a comprehensive sense. The re-thinking of the exclusion of men as charity clients occurred as the result of a number of factors in response to changes in the larger society. The focus on immigrants unemployed as the result of the crisis did not appear to lead to calls for their expulsion. On the contrary, one charity's attempt to marginalize 'foreign' clients was met with societal and governmental condemnation, and the discourse of other charities reflected this shift towards an increasing perception of Iceland as a multicultural society. These charitable discourses provide a window into the mechanism of how discursive formations can act as a force for the maintenance of the order of things, but also how they can also act as a force for change.

Works Cited

Foucault, Michel (1980) *The History of Sexuality. Volume 1: An Introduction.* Robert Hurely, trans. New York: Vintage Books.

— *Fréttablaðið* (2004) 'Fólk sem nær ekki endum saman.' 22 December, 6.

— (2008) 'Fleiri leita sér aðstoðar'. 18 October, 1.

— (2009) 'Þúsund fengu mataraðstoð'. 3 February, 10.

— (2010a) 'Hjálparþurfi fólki fjölgar'. 17 November, 10.

— (2010b) 'Íslendingar í forgang hjá Fjölskylduhjálp'. 25 March, 1–2.

— (2010c) 'Fjölskylduhjálpin gagnrýnd harkalega'. 26 March, 6.

— (2011) 'Stjórnvöld skera nálægt beini'. 7 December, 6.

Hákonardóttir, Inga Huld (2000) 'Philanthropy, Politics, Religion and Women in Iceland before the Modern Social Welfare System, 1895–1935', in Markkola, Pirjo (ed.) *Gender and Vocation: Women, Religion and Social Change in the Nordic Countries, 1830–1940*. Helsinki: SKS, 177–210.

Harvey, David (2005) *A Brief History of Neoliberalism*. Oxford: Oxford University Press.

— (2010) *The Enigma of Capital: And the Crises of Capitalism*. Oxford: Oxford University Press.

Jütte, Robert (1994) *Poverty and Deviance in Early Modern Europe*. Cambridge: Cambridge University Press.

Lindberg, Carter (1993) *Beyond Charity: Reformation Initiatives for the Poor*. Minneapolis: Fortress Press.

Loftsdóttir, Kristín (2012) 'Colonialism at the Margins: Politics of Difference in Europe as Seen through Two Icelandic Crises'. *Identities: Global Studies in Culture and Power* 19 (5), 597–615.

Morgunblaðið (1932) 'Mæðrastyrksnefndin', 21 December, 3.

— (2004) 'Af hverju heyrist svona lítið'. 13 November, 41.

— (2005) 'Fleiri þarfnast aðstoðar fyrir páskana en áður'. 22 March, 52.

— (2006) 'Sífellt fleiri leita sér aðstoðar'. 12 April, 11.

— (2007) 'Í landi allsnægtanna'. 30 November, 26.

— (2008a) 'Hundruð matarpoka bíða úthlutunar'. 4 December, 1.

— (2008b) 'Jólasöfnun'. 27 November, 12.

— (2008c) 'Það vilja allir hjálpa og gefa'. 4 December, 26–7.

— (2008d) 'Nytsamlegar gjafir áberandi'. 13 November, 4.

— (2008e) 'Mæðraljós í myrkrinu'. 13 November, 16.

— (2008f) 'Gáfu Mæðrastyrksnefnd ferðasjóðinn'. 27 November, 4.

— (2008g) 'Geta tekið þátt í smíði þjóðarskútu'. 28 November, 4.

— (2011a) 'Fleiri aldraðir og öryrkjar'. 1 December, http://www.mbl.is/frettir/innlent/2011/12/01/fleiri_aldradir_og_oryrkjar/.

— (2011b) 'Stórar fjölskyldur og öryrkjar leita aðstoðar'. 14 April, http://www.mbl.is/frettir/innlent/2011/04/14/storar_fjolskyldur_og_oryrkjar_leita_adstodar/.

— (2011c) 'Þrjú hundruð fjölskyldur leituðu eftir neyðaraðstoð í gær'. 29 December, 2.

Rice, James G. (2007) *The charity complex: an ethnography of a material aid agency in Reykjavík, Iceland*. PhD Dissertation. St John's: Memorial University of Newfoundland.

— (2009) 'We only help women with children here': Male Clients at an Icelandic Material Aid Charity. *Norma: Nordic Journal for Masculinity Studies* 4 (2), 169–82.

Skaptadóttir, Unnur Dís (2010) 'Integration and Transnational Practices of Filipinos in Iceland'. *E-migrinter* 5, 36–45.

Vigh, Henrik (2008) 'Crisis and Chronicity: Anthropological Perspectives on Continuous Conflict and Decline'. *Ethnos* 73 (1), 5–24.

Williams, Raymond. (1983[1976]) *Keywords: A Vocabulary of Culture and Society*. New York: Oxford University Press.

Wojtyńska, Anna, Unnur Dís Skaptadóttir and Helga Ólafs (2011) *The Participation of Immigrants in Civil Society and Labour Market in the Economic Recession*. Reykjavík: Faculty of Social and Human Sciences, University of Iceland.

Chapter 4
Racial Stereotypes and Swedish Antiracism: A Swedish Crisis of Multiculturalism?

Tobias Hübinette

Introduction: Racial Scandals in a Swedish Context

The so-called 'crisis of multiculturalism' is but one of many crises as the editors Kristín Loftsdóttir and Lars Jensen point out in the first chapter of this book, and in the Swedish case the economic crisis has hardly hit Sweden at all. With regards to the environmental crisis the nation prides itself in being one of the most sustainable and eco-friendly countries in the world, and concerning issues of migration and diversity, the self-image of Swedes as well as the image of Sweden in the world is still that the country and its people is firmly antiracist. However since 2011, numerous public debates have taken place in Sweden regarding the presence and use of different racial stereotypes across a range of media. Seen collectively, they can be viewed as challenging Sweden's self-image as the world's most antiracist country – and they can also be conceptualized as the Swedish version of the 'crisis of multiculturalism', which within the Swedish context becomes an antiracism in crisis rather than a crisis of multiculturalism, although there are certainly similarities between them. These debates are either caused by a race scandal, that is for example when a politician or a celebrity is 'caught' saying something demeaning about migrants and minorities, or by someone criticizing a certain representation for being racist despite claims that it is antiracist or at least non-racist (see, for example, Eriksson Henrik 2011 and Lundberg 2011, 2012).

In the spring of 2011, a race scandal erupted at the elite Lund University when a group of white students in blackface, chained and half-naked, performed a slave auction at a dinner party having a jungle theme (Eriksson Gustaf 2011). A media debate ensued, with many white Swedish voices defending the students' behaviour as an expression of a non-racist liberated humour, which is especially common among university students. Several non-white Swedes however pointed out that such an event could only take place in a country which refuses to regard itself as racist. The slave auction scandal at Lund University was reported not only nationally but also in many other countries. It led the American politician Reverend Jesse Jackson to write to the Swedish Minister of Education asking that the Swedish school system place the topic of slavery, and Sweden's participation in it, on the curriculum, while the European Network Against Racism (ENAR) sharply condemned the incident at one of Northern Europe's most prestigious universities in a letter to Birgitta Ohlsson, Sweden's Minister for EU Affairs (Centre against Racism 2011). In other words, the whole affair became embarrassing, and Reverend Jackson was subsequently invited by Lund University to give a public lecture on the new multiracial Sweden and the new diverse Europe, with the clear message that such racial stereotypes cannot be tolerated.

Despite this message, in the autumn of 2011, the slave auction debate was followed by a heated public discussion over a stereotypical image of an Asian man used for many years as the logo of a popular chocolate bar. Throughout 2012 more than a dozen public debates concerning racial stereotyping of Africans, Muslims, Jews and other minorities followed. Practically all of these debates resulted in polarized positions along racial lines, just like the debate on the slave auction scandal. Particularly during the course of 2012, a general feeling of the country being in crisis developed as new debates on different racial stereotypes replaced each other seemingly without an end. The critique of racial stereotypes principally comes from Swedes of colour who argue that the presence of such stereotyping in contemporary Sweden hurts and humiliates minorities and hinders the development of a new Swedishness wherein non-white Swedes can be fully included as Swedes and feel at home in Sweden. The defensive perspective is dominated by a majority of Swedes who argue that they cannot see that such stereotypes can be racist in contemporary Sweden, and sometimes also that they need to be preserved for the future as they are a part of the national cultural heritage.

According to opinion polls taken since 2011, approximately 90–95 per cent of respondents defend the use of certain racial representations (see, for example, Sandahl 2011). Many also associate such representations with their own childhood experiences by using sentimental language to describe the pleasure that is associated with some racial stereotypes. Critics, mainly non-white Swedes, are repeatedly accused of espousing censorship eagerness ('censuriver'), aggressiveness ('våldsamhet') and over-sensitiveness ('överkänslighet'), all emotional registers strongly associated with extremism and 'non-Swedishness'. At the same time, the mainly white defenders of racial stereotypes are increasingly accused of being racist and of reproducing racist structures by the mainly non-white critics, something which leads to polarization.

By examining three recent public debates concerning different kinds of racial stereotypes as case studies, this chapter aims to elucidate the needs, desires and the affective energies that are articulated to defend the various racial stereotypes debated within the last years in Sweden, and within the framework of this book's crisis theme – in this case the 'crisis of multiculturalism'. Key questions include: what are the relations between the racial stereotypes, Swedish whiteness and Swedish antiracism? Why do so many white Swedes want to use and defend racial stereotypes in spite of the critique coming from Swedes of colour who explicitly express that they feel offended and humiliated by them? What is at stake and what is felt to be under attack, and how can this crisis be conceptualized and analysed? How is it possible to understand why so many white Swedes, including highly educated, leftist, liberal and self-identifying antiracists, want to defend and preserve racial stereotypes in the name of antiracism? Is it a matter of an old-fashioned colonial type of racism, as many critics of the racial stereotypes claim when they label the defenders of racial stereotypes as downright racist? Why do these debates develop similarly with comparable dynamics, and why do they almost always end in a destructive deadlock situation, traumatizing both parties and polarizing the country as a whole? And for whom is this a crisis, and how can this crisis be analysed within the framework of the 'crisis of multiculturalism'?

At the end, I argue that all these public debates concerning racial stereotypes can be analysed as a particular form of a Swedish multiculturalism in crisis, and which in the Swedish case is about an antiracism in crisis. Such an analysis does not mean that I condone antiracism as a political movement and as an ideological standpoint, and that I want to essentialize Swedish antiracism, and I am also aware that although hegemonic antiracism in Sweden means a colour-blind antiracism, there are also oppositional voices and actors. This chapter also aims at understanding antiracism as a position that can be deployed and articulated for many different purposes, and with Swedish antiracism and its current crisis as the case study, and it is therefore also a contribution to the emerging field of the study of white antiracism in Western countries. Finally, as a Korean adoptee I acknowledge that I have been active within several debates on different racial stereotypes, particularly when it comes to speaking out against Asian stereotypes, so this chapter speaks of personal experience (Hübinette and Räterlinck 2012; Hübinette and Tigervall 2011).

Swedish Antiracism and Swedish Whiteness

While the concept of antiracism is evidently the core national ethos of contemporary Sweden *par excellence*, meaning that being Swedish is putatively equivalent with being antiracist, it also becomes clear according to studies of the Swedish antiracist movement that antiracism in Sweden is principally a white business, contrary to the situation in the English-speaking world where the minorities themselves have been in the forefront as the primary actors, for example in the American civil rights movements and in the creation of the academic fields in the US of ethnic, postcolonial and critical race and whiteness studies (Jämte 2013; Malmsten 2007; Omi and Winant 1994).

Another fundamental difference is that Swedish antiracism is heavily invested in colour blindness as its hegemonic ideology, and which again makes it different from the situation in the English-speaking world (Hübinette, Hörnfeldt, Farahani and René León Rosales 2012). This official colour-blind antiracism comes from the conviction that race is not a relevant category in Swedish society, and is symbolized by the historically unique parliamentary decision of 2001 to abolish the word race in all law texts and official documents and which all parties agreed upon (Hübinette and Lundström 2011). Thus, Sweden became the first country in the world to remove the word race itself from its language – something which truly must be seen as the most radical colour-blind performative speech act ever in modern history, to allude to Sara Ahmed's (2006) analysis of white antiracism and its futile understanding of racism as something which can be done away with once and for all and left behind by the way of antiracist legislation and rhetoric. The removal of the word has also lead to it being more and more difficult to speak about racism and racists and label something as being racist, as everything that has to do with race is almost always connected to essentialism, biologism and National Socialism.

Outside of Sweden, and perhaps symptomatically in the English-speaking world, research on white antiracism and on state and elite antiracism has been conducted as part of the emergence of critical race and whiteness studies ever since the 1990s (Doane and Bonilla-Silva 2003; Hartigan 2000; Frankenberg 1993; Fuji Johnson and Enomoto 2007; Hage 1998; Lentin 2011; O'Brien 2009). Inspired by the masculinity studies theorist Raewyn Connell's concept of hegemonic masculinity and borrowing from Amanda Lewis' (2004) idea of hegemonic whiteness, the American Sociologist Matthew Hughey (2010, 2012) has developed an analysis of a white racial identity in the US context based on his study on activists in a white nationalist organization and in a white antiracist organization. He argues that beyond the obvious antagonistic ideological positions, they both share the same white narratives, white perspectives and white privileges, and which taken together ultimately reproduce white supremacy in the USA regardless if it takes place within a racist or an antiracist political framework.

This argument engages with the concept of hegemonic whiteness, and borrows from critical studies on white antiracism in the English-speaking world. I regard the idea of antiracism to be the core value of hegemonic whiteness in Sweden. It is therefore valid to discuss white hegemonic antiracism within the Swedish context. By this I mean that antiracism and whiteness usually proceed together, and that white Swedes regard themselves as being automatically antiracists and non-racist simply by being Swedes. Further, Swedes also expect to be regarded as antiracists by non-Swedes. This self-perception is something which several scholars have studied and written about previously, and which can also be found in the other Nordic countries in the form of what is known as a specific Nordic exceptionalism (Habel 2008, 2012; Loftsdóttir and Jensen 2012; Palmberg 2009; Pred 2000; Pripp and Öhlander 2008).

Multicultural Sweden and the Crisis of Multiculturalism

Sweden is a country which sees itself as inherently antiracist, and this is in accord with its global image since its governments supported anticolonial and democratic struggles, movements, leaders and dissidents in the post-war period and throughout the Cold War. It is self-perception which Sweden also shares with the other Nordic countries, as is evident in Ebbe Volquardsen's contribution to this book. This antiracist Sweden, is perhaps best epitomized by the legendary Social Democratic

Prime Minister, Olof Palme, whose life ended in 1986 when he was shot by an unknown assailant. Palme had taken a firm, radical and active stand against racial segregation in the US, against the apartheid regime in Southern Africa and against Western interference and military interventions in the Third World regardless of whether the perpetrators were British, French, Portuguese, American or Russian, and whether the *coup d'états* and the atrocities happened in Chile or Argentina, South Korea or Vietnam, Angola or the Congo (Bjereld 1992).

Anti-fascist, anticolonial, and antiracist policies were placed on the national and international agenda by the Social Democrats who governed between the years 1932–76, 1982–91 and 1994–2006, and with renowned Foreign Ministers like Östen Undén, Torsten Nilsson and Anna Lindh, whose ethos became synonymous with the Swedish model, and with the Swedish welfare state, Swedish neutrality and Swedish peacekeeping. For example, Sweden became and still is the largest donor country per head to the postcolonial world since the 1960s (Eriksson Baaz 2002; Öhman 2007). Swedish researchers like Gunnar Myrdal and Gunnar Dahlberg have played a crucial and active part in UNESCO's work on the reconceptualization of race, and in countering racism after the Holocaust and at the beginning of the decolonization process. This necessary work helped instigate the newly founded organization's first statement on race in 1950 and resulted in the UN International Convention on the Elimination of All Forms of Racial Discrimination (ICERD) (Andersson 2011).

Sweden is also proportionally, without competition, the largest receiver of Third World children for adoption, as well as of refugees, migrants and spouses from the postcolonial world. Remarkably this still is the case at the time of writing, and this policy has resulted in a non-white population of around 12–14 per cent of the total population – a proportion which is almost doubled in the bigger cities as well as among the birth cohorts below 18 years old (Hübinette 2012). Furthermore, it is also probable that Swedes have interracial relationships to a far greater extent than is the case in any other Nordic country. In 2011 as many as 131,048 individuals had been born in Sweden with one parent born in Sweden and one parent born in either Africa, Asia or South America, while the equivalent number of individuals who had been born in Sweden with two parents from one of these three continents stood at 167,264 (Hübinette 2012). This means that Sweden is outstanding among the Nordic countries in terms of having invested in the creation of a society marked by diversity and by interracial relationships already at an early stage. These diversity statistics also make it difficult to compare Sweden to the other Nordic countries and their urban spaces, where the proportions of migrants and minorities are much lower than in Sweden.

Due to Sweden's unique relationship to the former colonies, to people of colour during the post-war period, as being the leading Western voice for decolonization and third world liberation, and its still unthreatened top position as the proportionally most significant haven for refugees and migrants in the West, the idea of antiracism has become a crucial part of national identity. As a result, Sweden always heads international lists and comparisons as having the most progressive migration and integration policies, and as having the most radical anti-discrimination legislation in the world, and also as having the most solidly antiracist population in the world who self-identify as tolerant and as being against racism and discrimination. There are several recent rankings and reports that show that the proportion of Swedes who are categorized as being intolerant and as having a negative attitude towards diversity and migration is said to be a world record low 4.9 per cent or even lower than that (for such comparisons and statistics, see Huddleston, Niessen, Ni Chaoimh and White 2011 and Mella, Palm and Bromark 2011).

This is also something which the Swedish government, official Sweden and many ordinary Swedes proudly reiterate, and the idea of antiracist Sweden also transcends the left and right division, resulting in the somewhat curious declaration from Sweden's far right party, the Sweden Democrats (SD), that they are antiracist. Antiracism has become a cherished part of the nation's self-image. Antiracist Sweden is also marketed and branded abroad, for example, through diplomacy and development aid, and has become the international image of the country, not least in the non-Western world.

Recently, however, the earlier positive rhetoric on diversity has also changed in Sweden just like in most other Western countries due to a combination of a shrinking welfare system at a time of rapid neo-liberalization of the economy and a general feeling of being under siege of globalization (see the chapters of Kristín Loftsdóttir, Minttu Tikka and Johanna Sumiala, James G. Rice and Satu Ranta-Tyrkkö for how this siege of globalization affects other Nordic countries). The 'crisis of multiculturalism' has on the other hand not been as pronounced for example in the UK, Germany, France, the Netherlands and the other Nordic countries, where anti-immigration and particularly anti-Moslem rhetoric nowadays is being voiced not just by the far right but by liberal elites (Lentin and Titley 2011). The current Liberal Swedish Prime Minister Fredrik Reinfeldt has for instance never spoken out against a multiculturalist society, and he has continuously defended Swedish antiracism and Sweden's current migration policy, and severely and repeatedly criticized the Sweden Democrats for being intolerant and xenophobic to the extent that its leader Jimmie Åkesson has accused the Prime Minister of espousing 'pure hate' against his party (Åkesson 2013). In other words, Sweden still stands out as a country which still explicitly wants to see itself as being multicultural.

Racial Stereotypes under Attack

Public debates concerning racial words, expressions and representations have also taken place and do erupt occasionally also in the other Nordic countries (see for example Rastas 2012 and Rossi 2009). Sometimes, such debates spill over to another Nordic country. An example of this which highlights how Sweden is seen as being almost ridiculously antiracist by a neighbouring country was the discussion that followed the removal of some film clips in Walt Disney's film *Santa's Workshop* from 1932, and which also came to affect Denmark. In December 2012 the public service company Swedish Television announced that the American mother company had decided to remove some stereotypical film clips in *Santa's Workshop* – among them an African American girl portrayed as a so-called picaninny figure (Lindh 2012). *Santa's Workshop* has been screened on the main Swedish television channel during Christmas Eve ever since 1960 as part of Disney's programme *Donald Duck's Christmas Eve*, and a similar programme titled *Disney's Christmas Show* has also for many years been screened in Denmark. The announcement created an uproar in Sweden among the general public, mainly concerning the removal of the picaninny girl, and a poll showed that 96 per cent of the population was against Disney's decision to remove the Picaninny girl (Nelson 2012). In Denmark, however, the event was reported as a typical expression of Swedish 'politically correct censorship' even if it was an American decision from the beginning which Swedish Television only complied with, and as the Danish screening was not affected by the removal of the film clips, a spokesperson for the public service company Danish Broadcasting Corporation, Jakob Stegelmann, could proudly tell the Danish media that 'we are screening the politically incorrect version from 1932 – no censored versions here' (Harder 2012).

Another example of a debate that involved another Nordic country was the discussion following the Finnish video diary titled *Tervetuloa Suomeen* (Welcome to Finland), which was co-financed by the Finnish and Swedish film institutes, and which was a part of a Nordic Culture Fund film project called Doxwise Nordic with participating youngsters in all the Nordic countries filming their own lives. One of the Finnish contributions was this film, in which a group of white Finnish male youngsters mock and harass a hunger-striking Afghan refugee outside the Finnish parliament by drinking beer and eating pork and by making use of racializing words and expressions. When the film was released on the Internet in October 2012, particularly Swedish antiracists pointed out that it endorsed a racist mentality and language, while the Finnish film editor of the Doxwise project, Liisa Juntunen, however did not agree with the criticism and defended the publication of the film by saying that 'one cannot edit the reality' (Tiberg and Starbrink 2012). In other words, both the debate on *Santa's Workshop* and the *Tervetuloa Suomeen* discussion, are good examples of when other Nordic countries' image of Sweden as a radical antiracist and 'politically correct country' is highlighted.

I will now summarise three public discussions on racial stereotypes that have taken place in Sweden recently. There are well over a dozen race scandals and subsequent debates on racialized images and expressions to choose among only since the spring of 2011's Lund University slave auction. The three debates I discuss below have in common that they are related to visual culture and to the spheres of art and culture, and that they, just like the slave auction event, received media attention outside of Sweden. In the age of transnationalism when particularly visual culture knows no national borders, and when the mass phenomenon of viral memes is an everyday Internet practice, race scandals are often caused by visual stereotypes, and they are usually connected to the cultural industry in a broader sense.

The first debate that I have chosen to look upon concerned the Finnish candy company Fazer and its chocolate bar *Kina* (China) which until the summer of 2012 made use of a stereotypical head of an Asian wearing a 'coolie hat' as its logo, and similar logos of so-called 'Chinamen' exist also in other Nordic countries. The chocolate bar is popular in Sweden and has existed since 1961, and is usually known as *kinapuffar* (China pops) in colloquial speech, and as a brand name sometimes also as *Kina Gul* (China Yellow). In September 2011 Patrik Lundberg (2011), an adopted Korean man who is a journalist, published a newspaper column about the everyday racism that he is exposed to as an Asian man in Sweden with mostly white Swedes mocking and making fun of his appearance by pointing, shouting and laughing at him intermittently in public. In the article, he also pointed out that this logo and similar visual images and representations of Asians in contemporary Sweden might play a part in and explain this treatment by making it socially acceptable.

Lundberg's column immediately became viral in social media and on the Internet as it probably was interpreted as an attack on a beloved Swedish candy, which generations of Swedes have eaten and therefore are very fond of. The article was met with an explosion of mainly white voices in newspapers, on television and radio, and above all in digital media protesting against his claim that Asians are exposed to everyday racism (Hübinette and Tigervall 2011; Lundberg 2012). His critics argued that he exaggerated or even lied about his experiences of being exposed to racism, and that on the contrary a majority of Swedes like and even embrace Asians perhaps more than any other minority in the country – for example Swedish men marry Asian women and Swedish women adopt Asian children. Above all, people protested against Lundberg's argument that Fazer's Kina logo is a racial stereotype and this became even more pronounced as the company Fazer stated that they would change the logo and only keep the so-called coolie hat without any head. Through this focus on the logo itself the topic that Lundberg wanted to raise, namely the socially accepted everyday racism against Asians in public spaces, disappeared from the discussion and instead something of a public uprising against the 'political correctness' of both Lundberg and Fazer erupted.

While *kinapuffgate* (China pop-gate) continued, (as it has been satirically baptized by the defenders of the logo), the public service company Swedish Television arranged and screened a debate programme about the logo and commissioned SIFO, Sweden's most respected agency within the area of opinion and social research, to conduct an opinion survey which established that 97 per cent of the informants disagreed that the logo could be offensive to anyone in Sweden when asked if they agreed that the logo was stereotypical (Sandahl 2011). This is in spite of the fact that undoubtedly the most common socially accepted and culturally institutionalized racialized stereotype in contemporary Sweden is the image of the Asian man, who is usually portrayed as being despicable and ugly or nerdy and ridiculous, and who may be found in a range of media including;

on stage, in film, as a character in books or as an illustration in a newspaper or in a magazine (Hübinette and Tigervall 2011). The continuous prevalence of this image of Asian men shows that certain visual stereotypes deriving from the colonial period and its colonial archive are still maintained and are cherished by the vast majority as they have become so naturalized and normalized.

The second debate took place in 2012 and concerned the artist Makode Linde and his art, and who for a time became world famous overnight. This happened when his blackface cake was eaten by the Swedish Minister of Culture, Lena Adelsohn Liljeroth, at the Swedish Museum of Modern Art in April 2012, when the Swedish Artists' National Organization celebrated its 75th anniversary. The minister had been invited and was asked to cut the first piece of a cake designed for the occasion by Linde who is an artist of mixed origin, and who is known for his blackface or golliwog art, which he himself calls 'Afromantics'. The cake depicted a nude African woman and attached to the cake was the artist's own head in blackface. As the minister cut into the cake the artist screamed, and the Minister smiled, giggled and laughed and so did the almost wholly white audience consisting of artists, many of them famous in Sweden. The event was widely circulated as a race scandal on the Internet and through YouTube as a film clip.

Some days later, the National Association of African Swedes called the event a racist spectacle and asked for the minister's resignation, and thereafter the debate erupted (Karlsson 2012). In the ensuing debate the Swedish Artists' National Organization and a more or less completely unanimous Swedish media defended the artist and his blackface cake as being radically antiracist. The overarching argument coming from almost solely white voices was that Linde is using a racialized stereotype and manipulates it so that it can be used in an antiracist way (Momodou 2012). However, the National Association of African Swedes was alone as an organization criticizing the event, Linde and his art, with the sole exception of the Antiracist Academy, an association of antiracist researchers in Sweden. Some weeks after the event, Linde invited the public to a performance at a gallery in downtown Stockholm where he painted anyone who wanted in blackface. The performance was co-organized by Linde's friend, Alexander Bard, a gay icon and pop artist in Sweden, and famous for openly defending his right to use the Swedish N-word as long as his 'brother', most probably meaning Linde, refers to himself that way (Eriksson Henrik 2011).

The cake event and the subsequent performance became Linde's breakthrough on the art scene, both in Sweden and globally, and the prices of his blackface art works increased dramatically. After the event, although he is only a little over 30 years old, he held a retrospective exhibition at an art gallery in Stockholm where literally thousands of his blackface art pieces were for sale. Linde became the beloved favourite of the white cultural and academic establishment and was praised as one of the most radical antiracists in the country. The largest circulating Swedish newspaper liberal *Dagens Nyheter* published several long articles and interviews with Linde and about his blackface art and nominated him for *Dagens Nyheter*'s cultural prize, while describing the cake and the artist as being 'deeply antiracist', and so did the magazine *Expo* which is without any competition Sweden's leading and most established antiracist voice (Hübinette and Räterlinck 2012). When Swedes of colour, most of them of African origin, criticized Linde, and his art, for spreading and reproducing stereotypes of Africans, and for lacking any social and political connection to other black Swedes, as well as for endorsing white racist humour, they were called 'extremists' and 'censorship supporters' or simply accused of not understanding art at all, and the debate became known as *tårtgate* (cakegate).

A third debate which raged in Sweden in 2012, and which possibly was the most aggravated and also aggressive one as children were in the focus, concerned the illustrator and artist Stina Wirsén and one of her characters from her children's books. Wirsén's children's books have for many years been respected and popular, particularly among educated leftist and liberal-minded Swedes who see themselves as militant antiracists – this also may explain why she received so much support from this demographic group in the debate. In September 2012, Wirsén's animated film for small children, *Liten Skär och alla små Brokiga* (Little Pink and the Motley Crew), premiered at several Folkets bio cinemas (People's cinema – a network of leftist cinemas) around the country, with the world-famous actor Stellan Skarsgård as one of its voices – it included some of her children's book characters.

The film contained four characters depicting one white girl, Little Pink, and three children of colour of whom one represents a black girl, Lilla Hjärtat (Little Heart), and who closely resembles the US American racial stereotype of a black child known as a picaninny. Lilla Hjärtat is wild and uncontrollable in the film, she even tries to eat one of the other children, a character which seemingly is supposed to be an adopted Asian boy named Bosse, and who is portrayed as being weak, sensitive and feminine. Already before the premier, as the picaninny-like character Lilla Hjärtat was depicted on the film poster, mainly Swedes with an African origin began to criticize Wirsén and her film on Facebook and on the Internet by pointing out how hurtful such a stereotype is to black people (see, for example, Touray 2012).

Soon the media picked up the critique on Facebook, and thereafter the debate on Stina Wirsén's character Lilla Hjärtat started in the public sphere, and became particularly heated as it concerned children's culture questioning what the needs and perspectives of children may look like. While Wirsén and her supporters defended the character by saying that children of colour in Sweden need to be more represented in children's culture in general to be able to reflect themselves and feel included, Swedes with an African origin and parents with black children instead pointed out that children of colour will not be able to discover themselves in a stereotype even if the intention is explicitly antiracist (Polite 2012a). Wirsén was heavily supported by the white dominated cultural elite of Sweden, especially within the media and the art world, and her critics were said to be 'aggressively violent' by the chief editor of *Dagens Nyheter*'s cultural section, Björn Wiman, who also lamented the withdrawal of the character from the film poster which was one consequence of the debate, by using a Swedish proverb which says that something disappears as 'if removing all sugar from the soft drink' ('om allt socker tas bort ur saften') (Wiman 2012).

Margareta Rönnberg, a film scholar within the study of children's culture has published a monograph analysing the whole debate, and arguing that Lilla Hjärtat is not a racial stereotype but signifies an animal, possibly a mole, when children interpret the character Lilla Hjärtat (Rönnberg 2013). In her book, Rönnberg even calls this adult-centred attitude 'adultonormativity', and condemns Wirsén's critics not just for being exaggerating extremists, but also as adults who do not take into account children's own interpretations. Finally, at the end of the debate, when Wirsén announced that she would stop drawing the character Lilla Hjärtat in new books due to the criticism, it turned out that the Swedish Institute (which is a part of Sweden's Ministry of Foreign Affairs and the equivalent of the British Council and the Goethe Institute) was cooperating with Wirsén outside Sweden. The institute had used some of her stereotypical characters printed on products targeted for children in Japan and in other countries as part of its design project called 'Sweden in style', as a way of branding Sweden as a multicultural and antiracist country (Polite 2012b).

Conclusion: A Nation in Crisis

Swedish antiracism differs from other forms of antiracism, for example, from antiracism in the US, which Matthew Hughey (2010, 2012), John Hartigan, (2000), Eileen O´Brien (2009) among others have studied. When returning to the notion of antiracism being the core national ethos of Sweden and the perceived essence of Swedishness, and of antiracism constituting Swedish hegemonic whiteness in contemporary Sweden, it is important to note that difference. In the US and in the English-speaking world in general, including in countries like Canada and Australia, there is a history of colonialism, genocide and slavery, and of the civil rights and social movements that were led by the minorities themselves, white antiracism emerges within these contexts from a position of guilt and apology and from a conviction of white privilege. Unlike Swedish society, these societies therefore must actively strive for altering the power relations between their majority population and their minorities (see, for example, McGonegal 2009). At the same time, it is true that white antiracists in the US may sometimes also unintentionally strengthen and reproduce racist structures as well as essentializing whiteness itself (Eichstedt 2001; Marty 1999). Furthermore, white antiracism may on the surface seem to fight for the same cause in the English-speaking world as in Sweden. However, there are several fundamental differences that have to be taken into account.

To begin, in a country where upwards of 95 per cent of the population perceive themselves as being antiracist or even non-racist, and where antiracism is as taken for granted and as naturalized within the national psyche as being, for example, for democracy and against dictatorship, and which the vast majority of all Swedes without doubt also are, it is not easy either to discuss issues related to race or experiences of everyday racism at all in the public sphere, and it has become more difficult after the 2001 abolishment of the word *race* itself from Swedish language (Huddleston, Niessen, Ni Chaoimh and White 2011; Mella, Palm and Bromark 2011). Contrary to the sense of postcolonial and post-civil rights guilt which is very much the basis for antiracism in the English-speaking world, dominant Swedish antiracism does not relate to Sweden as having played a part in colonialism, and racism is mainly connected to other countries such as the US, Germany and South Africa.

Further, as Swedishness is intertwined with whiteness to the extent that it is almost impossible to distinguish between them, antiracism becomes a part of a chain of equivalence. According to the logics of discourse analysis: Swedishness is whiteness and Swedishness is antiracism, and in the end all white Swedes are antiracists (Hübinette and Lundström 2011). Consequently, as non-whites are not seen as Swedish and are not allowed to become fully Swedes, it also becomes impossible for them to occupy the position of antiracists, at least on the same 'advanced' level as white Swedes. Instead, at best they can become minority subjects who fight prejudices within their own group such as sexism and homophobia, and at worst they are seen as intolerant and narrow-minded because they are minorities and limited by their 'culture'. In the very worst case they are just seen as being inherently aggressive, violent and atavistically fanatical. The outcome is that minority Swedes cannot be antiracists to the same extent as majority Swedes – it is a privileged white position, which mainly and almost only white Swedes can occupy and speak and act from.

This understanding of hegemonic Swedish whiteness makes it possible to read the recent public discussions on racial stereotypes from a perspective which does not just see the defenders as being simply old-fashioned colonial-style racists or looks upon the critics as being nothing but aggressive minority extremists. Instead, I find it both more constructive, as well as more valid to analyse the majority defence of racial stereotypes as a majority defence of Swedish antiracism itself, and in the end as a defence of the ideal of antiracist Sweden and of Sweden itself. I also find it more constructive to understand the critique of the stereotypes coming from Swedes of colour as a claim to be included within a Swedishness which until now has excluded them due to the hegemonic Swedish whiteness which equalizes Swedishness, whiteness and antiracism. This analysis may help to explain both why so many white Swedes desperately cling to some of these stereotypes, as well as the equally desperate frustration that is expressed by Swedes of colour when they want majority Swedes to understand that the very same stereotypes that they defend and fight to preserve are hurtful and demeaning to them.

In other words, I contend that the recent escalation of debates concerning racial stereotypes in language and visual culture, and the inability of white Swedes to recognize their privileges and entitlements and to give up their claims to authority and their management of the public sphere, can be understood as antiracism in crisis. It represents a people that cannot assimilate and accommodate an increasingly diverse and multiracial Sweden. In this vein, there are similarities to debates on racial stereotypes in other Nordic countries, such as the one that followed the republication of the children's rhyme 'The Ten Little Negros' in Iceland in 2007, and which Kristín Loftsdóttir (2013) analyses as an attempt to dehistoricize and disconnect Icelandic whiteness from a racist history.

Furthermore, it can also be maintained that this might be the specific Swedish version of the pan-European so-called crisis of multiculturalism (see the introduction to this book), although it is again important to remind the reader that no leading Swedish politician has spoken out against either diversity, multiculturalism or immigration, given the specificity of Swedish whiteness and Swedish antiracism. By contrast, these Swedish debates on racial stereotypes and their outcomes return to the same roots as the perceived crises of multiculturalism in other European countries, in the sense that they are not about a crisis involving the minorities themselves but a fundamental crisis on an existential level regarding the self-representation of the white majority society itself. The crisis of multiculturalism is therefore on a deeper level a crisis of whiteness. In the Swedish case it may therefore be possible to say that the Swedish version of a crisis of multiculturalism is about the start of the breaking down of the master narrative of Sweden and of the Swedes as the most antiracist country and people in the world.

In the future, to be able to break up the deadlock situation regarding the contesting views on racial stereotypes in Sweden which produces so many destructive emotions and which risk exacerbating the antagonism between the majority population and the minorities even more, it is therefore crucial to deconstruct the current hegemonic Swedish whiteness and the self-image of antiracist Sweden. It is also necessary to open up for a new Swedishness which includes Swedes of colour as well, and which also makes it possible for them to be able to speak from a position as antiracists, and which does not render them designations like aggressive extremists and aggravated censorship supporters. However, for this to happen majority Swedes must relinquish their fear of losing control over the discourse on and interpretation of racial stereotypes, which ultimately can be translated as a fear of losing a particular antiracist Swedishness which has bestowed them with the power and the monopoly to decide both what racism is and what it looks like and what antiracism is and means in contemporary Sweden. The 15 or so public debates on racial stereotypes that have raged in Sweden from 2011, and which have divided the country and created a public atmosphere of frustration and distrust, as well as of rage and hate, are not just symptoms of an antiracism and a nation in crisis. The aftermath of these debates is also the beginning of the dismantling of a hegemonic Swedish whiteness which is out-dated and not fit for the new multiracial Sweden. These are the first steps towards the construction of a new antiracism and a new Swedishness which in both cases are separate from being solely a white business.

Works Cited

Ahmed, Sara (2006) 'The Non-performativity of Anti-racism'. *Meridians: Feminism, Race, Transnationalism* 7 (1), 104–26.

Åkesson, Jimmie (2013) *Satis polito*. Sölvesborg: Asp and Lycke.

Andersson, Axel (2011) 'UNESCO och rasfrågan' [UNESCO and the race issue]. *Glänta* 19 (2), 89–97.

Bjereld, Ulf (1992) *Kritiker eller medlare? Sveriges utrikespolitiska roller 1945–1990* [Critics or mediators? Sweden's foreign policy roles 1945–1990]. Stockholm: Nerenius and Santerus förlag.

Centre against racism (2011) *Årsrapport 2011* [Annual report 2011]. Stockholm: Centre against racism.

Doane, Ashley W. and Eduardo Bonilla-Silva (eds) (2003) *White Out. The Continuing Significance of Racism*. New York: Routledge.

Eichstedt, Jennifer L. (2001) 'Problematic White Identities and a Search for Racial Justice'. *Sociological Forum* 16 (3), 445–70.

Eriksson, Gustaf (2011) 'Sminkade sig svarta – sedan såldes de på "auktion"' [They used make-up as Blacks – then they were sold at an 'auction']. *Lundagård* 18–4–2011.

Eriksson, Henrik (2011) 'Bards påhopp på skådespelaren: "Neger neger neger" [Bard's attack on the actor: 'Negro negro negro']. *Nyheter 24* 2011-12-15: http://nyheter24.se/nyheter/inrikes/637860-bards-pahopp-pa-skadespelaren-neger-neger-neger.

Eriksson Baaz, Maria (2002) *The White Wo/man's Burden in the Age of Partnership. A Postcolonial Reading of Identity in Development Aid*. Göteborg University: Department of Peace and Development Research.

Frankenberg, Ruth (1993) *White Women, Race Matters: The Social Construction of Whiteness*. London: Routledge.

Fuji Johnson, Genevieve and Randy Enomoto (eds) (2007) *Race, Racialization and Anti-racism in Canada and Beyond*. Toronto: University of Toronto Press.

Hage, Ghassan (1998) *White Nation: Fantasies of White Supremacy in a Multicultural Society*. Annandale: Pluto Press.

Habel, Ylva (2008) 'Whiteness Swedish Style'. *Slut* 2, 41–51.

— (2012) 'Rörelser och schatteringar inom kritiska vithetsstudier' [Movements and shades within critical whiteness studies], in Hübinette, Tobias, Helena Hörnfeldt, Fataneh Farahani and René León Rosales (eds), *Om ras och vithet i det samtida Sverige* [On race and whiteness in contemporary Sweden], 45–82. Botkyrka: Multicultural Centre.

Harder, Thomas (2012) 'Disney fjerner sort duke fra juletegnefilm' [Disney removes black doll from animated Christmas film]. *Ekstra Bladet* 21-12-2012.

Hartigan, John (2000) 'Object Lessons in Whiteness: Antiracism and the Study of White Folks.' *Identities* 7 (3), 373–406.

Huddleston, Thomas, Jan Niessen, Eadaoin Ni Chaoimh and Emilie White (2011) *Migration Integration Policy Index III*. Brussels: British Council and Migration Policy Group.

Hübinette, Tobias (2012) *Den svenska utländsk bakgrund-befolkningen den 31 december 2011* [The Swedish foreign background-population 31 December 2011]. Botkyrka: Multicultural Centre.

— and Catrin Lundström (2011) 'Sweden after the Recent Election: The Double-binding Power of Swedish Whiteness through the Mourning of the Loss of "Old Sweden" and the Passing of "Good Sweden"'. *NORA – Nordic Journal of Feminist and Gender Research* 19 (1), 42–52.

— and Carina Tigervall (2011) '"Japanese, Japanese, Japanese ...". Representations of East Asians in Contemporary Swedish Visual Culture'. In Eide, Elisabeth and Kaarina Nikunen (eds) *Media in Motion. Cultural Complexity and Migration in the Nordic Region*. Farnham: Ashgate, 125–43.

—, Helena Hörnfeldt, Fataneh Farahani and René León Rosales (2012) 'Om ras och vithet i det samtida Sverige. Inledning' [On race and whiteness in contemporary Sweden. Introduction], in Hübinette, Tobias, Helena Hörnfeldt, Fataneh Farahani and René León Rosales (eds) *Om ras och vithet i det samtida Sverige* [On race and whiteness in contemporary Sweden], 11–36. Botkyrka: Multicultural Centre.

— and Lennart E.H. Räterlinck (2012) 'Makode Lindes konst förstärker vit rashumor' [Makode Linde's art reproduces white race humour]. *SVT Debatt* 2012-06-12: http://debatt.svt.se/2012/06/15/24073.

Hughey, Matthew W. (2010) 'The (Dis)similarities of White Racial Identities: The Conceptual Framework of "Hegemonic Whiteness"'. *Ethnic and Racial Studies* 33 (8), 1289–1309.

— (2012) *White Bound: Nationalists, Antiracists, and the Shared Meanings of Race*. Stanford: Stanford University Press.

Jämte, Jan (2013) *Antirasismens många ansikten* [The many faces of antiracism]. Umeå University: Department of Political Science.

Karlsson, Pär (2012) 'Afrosvenskar kräver ministerns avgång' [African Swedes demand the resignation of the minister]. *Aftonbladet* 17-04-2012.

Lentin, Alana (2011) 'What Happens to Anti-racism when we are Post Race?' *Feminist Legal Studies* 19 (2), 159–68.

— and Gavan Titley (2011) *The Crises of Multiculturalism. Racism in a Neoliberal Age*. London: Zed Books.

Lewis, Amanda (2004) 'What Group? Studying Whites and Whiteness in the Era of Colorblindness'. *Sociological Theory* 22 (4), 623–46.

Lindh, Sara (2012) 'Disney klipper i Kalle Ankas jul' [Disney edits in Donald Duck's Christmas]. *Expressen* 14-12-2012.

Loftsdóttir, Kristín (2013) 'Republishing "The Ten Little Negros": Exploring Nationalism and "Whiteness" in Iceland'. *Ethnicities* 13 (3), 295–315.

— and Lars Jensen (eds) (2012) *Whiteness and Postcolonialism in the Nordic Region. Exceptionalism, Migrant Others and National Identities*. Farnham: Ashgate.

Lundberg, Patrik (2011) 'Ni sliter själen ur mig' [You are ripping my soul out]. *Helsingborgs Dagblad* 13-09-2011.

— (2012) *Gul utanpå* [Yellow on the outside]. Stockholm: Rabén and Sjögren..

Malmsten, Jenny (2007) *Den föreningsdrivna antirasismen i Sverige – antirasism i rörelse*. [Organisation driven antiracism in Sweden – antiracism on the move]. Malmö University College: International migration and ethnic relations.

Marty, Debian (1999) 'White antiracist rhetoric as apologia: Wendell Berry's *The hidden wound*', in Nakayama, Thomas K. and Judith N. Martin (eds) *Whiteness: The Communication of Social Identity*, 51–68. Thousand Oaks: Sage.

McGonegal, Julie (2009) *Imagining Justice. The Politics of Postcolonial Forgiveness and Reconciliation*. Montreal: McGill-Queen's University Press.

Mella, Orlando, Irving Palm and Kristina Bromark (2011) *Mångfaldsbarometern 2011* [Diversity barometer 2011]. Uppsala University: Department of Sociology.

Momodou, Jallow (2012) 'Sweden: The Country Where Racism is Just a Joke'. *The Guardian* 18-04-2012.

Nelson, Oscar (2012) 'Disney: "Kan förstå det nostalgiska värdet"' [Disney: 'Can understand the nostalgic value']. *Aftonbladet* 14-12-2012.

O'Brien, Eileen (2009) 'From Antiracism to Antiracisms'. *Sociology Compass* 3 (3), 510–12.

Öhman, May-Britt (2007) *Taming Exotic Beauties. Swedish Hydropower Constructions in Tanzania in the Era of Development Assistance, 1960s–1990s*. Royal Institute of Technology: Department of History of Science and Technology.

Omi, Michael and Howard Winant (1994) *Racial Formation in the United States: From the 1960s to the 1990s*. New York: Routledge.

Palmberg, Mai (2009) 'The Nordic colonial mind', in Keskinen, Suvi, Salla Tuori, Sari Irni and Diana Mulinari (eds) *Complying with Colonialism. Gender, Race and Ethnicity in the Nordic Region*. Farnham: Ashgate, 36–50.

Polite, Oivvio (2012a) 'Se till mig som liten är' [Look at me who little is]. *Expressen* 26–9–2012.

— (2012b) 'Brokiga är business' [Motley is business]. *Expressen* 26–10–2012.

Pred, Alan (2000) *Even in Sweden. Racisms, Racialized Spaces, and the Popular Geographical Imagination*. Berkeley: University of California Press.

Pripp, Oscar and Magnus Öhlander (2008) *Fallet Nogger black: Antirasismens gränser* [The case of Nogger black: The limits of antiracism]. Stockholm: Agora.

Rastas, Anna (2012) 'Reading history through Finnish exceptionalism', in Loftsdóttir, Kristín and Lars Jensen (eds) *Whiteness and Postcolonialism in the Nordic Region. Exceptionalism, Migrant Others and National Identities*. Farnham: Ashgate, 89–103.

Rönnberg, Margareta (2013) *'Lilla hjärtat är en mullvad.' – 'Nä, pengvin!' En studie av kontroversen kring Stina Wirséns filmfigur* ['Little Heart is a mole.' –

'No, penguin!' A study of the controversy surrounding Stina Wirsén's film character]. Visby: Filmförlaget.

Rossi, Leena-Maija (2009) 'Licorice boys and female coffee beans: Representations of colonial complicity in Finnish visual culture', in Keskinen, Suvi, Salla Tuori, Sari Irni and Diana Mulinari (eds) *Complying with Colonialism. Gender, Race and Ethnicity in the Nordic Region*. Farnham: Ashgate, 119–35.

Sandahl, Ronnie (2011) 'Helig rasism i form av chokladpuffar' [Holy racism in the form of chocolate pops]. *Sandah* 03.10.2011.

Tiberg, Cecilia and Beppe Starbrink (2012) 'Filminstitutet: Det är chockerande"' [Film institute: 'It is shocking']. *SVT.se* 02.11.2012: http://www.svt.se/kultur/film/rasistisk-video-vacker-upprordhet.

Touray, Fatou (2012) 'Barnfilm med rasistisk nidbild av svarta' [Children's film with racist stereotype of blacks]. *The Gambia* 07-09-2012: http://thegambia.nu/2012/09/07/barnfilm-med-rasistisk-nidbild-av-svarta.

Wiman, Björn (2012) 'Vad blir det kvar av konsten om allt socker tas bort ur saften?' [What is left of art if all sugar is removed from the soft drink]. *Dagens Nyheter* 30.09.2012.

Chapter 5
Dancing on the Fissures: Alternative Senses of Crisis in the Faroe Islands

Kimberly Cannady

The 18-island archipelago of the Faroe Islands stretches across the North Atlantic roughly halfway between Iceland and Norway. The population, almost 50,000 inhabitants, are governed by the Danish constitutional monarchy and, for the most part, enjoy a uniformly high quality of life. Unlike their Icelandic neighbours to the north, the Faroe Islands weathered the recent European economic crisis. While global climate change has had an impact on the Islands, environmental crises have not risen to the level found in Greenland where traditional ways of life are directly threatened by global warming. Yet the ongoing marginalization of the Faroe Islands, as enacted through Danish hegemonic policies, has created an atmosphere of perpetual political and economic insecurity. In the midst of this insecurity, Faroese have conscientiously fostered a sense of cultural security through the narratives and performance practice of dance and music. This artistic expression helps articulate powerful differences between the Faroese and the Danes.

The larger Nordic region is comprised of some of the most politically stable nations in the world, but it is also a site of uneasy political relations. These include global concerns regarding indigenous rights and decolonization. In the Faroe Islands there is a lingering sense of dependency on Denmark, culturally, economically and politically, after centuries of hegemonic relations. Significant financial subsidies from the Danish state currently preclude independence, compound a long-drawn-out colonialism, and overshadow a demonstrable desire for independence. The Faroe Islands are also implicated in a pan-European crisis of multiculturalism. The Faroese themselves are a minority ethnic group within the larger nation-state framework of Denmark, while at the same time increased immigration to the Islands is further diversifying the population. Notably, the Faroe Islands are home to an endemic crisis of political and cultural legitimacy rooted in historical narratives and in contemporary interactions with Denmark, and the larger European Union. This chapter explores how Faroese narratives of difference from Denmark, through the arts, have fostered a sense of continuity and empowerment despite a legacy of marginalization. In addition to economic concerns, the archipelago faces significant depopulation of native Faroe Islanders, notwithstanding the increasing immigration. This depopulation is an outcome of weak higher education infrastructure, combined with limited employment opportunities – a situation with parallels to other economically challenged areas of Europe. Depopulation of the Islands is expected to continue at a rate of 20 per cent over the next 40 years with further decline to follow. With over 20,000 Faroese individuals already residing in Denmark, the majority of the new outward migrants are expected to settle there as well.

The longevity of crisis in the Faroe Islands correlates with Henrik Vigh's description of the potential for those experiencing endemic crisis to experience long-term 'existential incoherence' (Vigh 2008: 9). Taking into account the history of the Islands, a sense of this existential incoherence permeates the social fabric. Yet in tandem with these political and economic concerns, the Faroe Islands thrive culturally with music making, dance, theatre, and the visual arts. In what follows, I explore contemporary music making and dance in the Faroe Islands as modern cultural practices that work to forge a sense of continuity and cohesion among Faroese people, for those in the Islands and for those already living abroad. The arts in the Faroe Islands have had a close relationship with the drive for self-determination and sovereignty, as I will discuss in relation to the formalization of the Faroese language in the nineteenth century, as well as forming a key component of national narratives that underpin empowering Faroese self-understanding.

This chapter offers a study of enabling articulations of identity and art in the context of crisis in the Faroe Islands; my writing is grounded in ethnomusicological theory and methodology, including extensive fieldwork throughout the North Atlantic region. I focus on the relationship between a particular type of Faroese dance and crisis as a response, in part, to Susan Reynolds Whyte's call for research on the topic of chronic crisis, 'that recognizes specific causes and patterns of oppression, and particular ways of managing despair, ensuring a modicum of security, and maintaining hope in an uncertain situation' (Whyte 2008: 99). Indigenous balladry and chain dancing, known as the Faroese dance, help to mediate crisis through the accompanying narratives of cultural longevity and through the physical practice of the dance.

I draw on my experience with dancing and balladry in the Faroe Islands, Iceland and Denmark during the period of fieldwork for my doctorate over 2011 and 2012. Between July and September of 2012 I researched specifically in Tórshavn, the capital of the Faroe Islands, attending musical performances across traditional, popular and classical genres. I interviewed musicians, educators and politicians and, attended the Faroese Summer Institute hosted by the University of the Faroe Islands, where I studied the Faroese language and other aspects of the society together with other students from across North America and Europe. As part of this programme, we were taught the history of the chain dance and accompanying balladry and participated in an evening of chain dancing and singing with local musicians. Outside of this institutional setting, I participated in evenings of chain dancing and singing at celebrations, festivals, and other gatherings in both the Faroe Islands and Denmark.

A more focused description of these practices appears below, but it is worth stating that the Faroese dance consists of dancers creating a closed circle that has been likened to a self-contained universe with the dancers turning their backs on the chaos of the outside world (Jackson 1991: 16). The dance accompanies a ballad, and is in the form of a chain made by linking hands with the person to the left and to the right and then alternatively taking two steps to the left and one step to the right in time with a ballad being sung. Instead of dancing in one big circle, the group moves in a serpentine manner so that dancers come face to face with each other throughout the movements. The physical aspects of the dance, as well as the narratives that surround it, contribute to the dance's role as a vital marker of continuity in contemporary Faroese society.

The Faroese dance, when seen as a contemporary practice, is a dynamic expression of agency. Yet there is a tendency to excavate for its historical roots and view it as a 'preserved' historical practice that had long died out elsewhere. For example in his work, *Faroe: The Emergence of a Nation*, John F. West wrote:

> The Faroese ring dance has preserved into modern times a medieval ballad tradition of great interest, centuries after it has perished everywhere else. It is believed to be related to the line dance, which originated in French courtly circles in the 13th century and over the next 200 years spread all over Europe. (West 1973: 41)

West concludes that, 'the isolation imposed by distance and by commercial monopoly thus preserved in Faroe a cultural pattern that had long since become extinct elsewhere' (West 1973: 44). Here it is important to tease out the extent to which language of preservation and extinction work to render the Faroese as somehow more traditional or rooted in the past than contemporaries elsewhere, as this discourse is directly linked to the pseudo-colonial relationship between the Faroe Islands and Denmark. Johannes Fabian noted that colonizers frequently imposed alternative space and time to the colonized, whether by actually trying to remove the colonized bodies from a shared space in the context of the United States and Australia, dividing and allocating space between colonizers and colonized as in South Africa, or 'with the help of various devices of sequencing and distancing one assigns to the conquered populations a *different* time' (Fabian 1983: 30). In this writing I tease out how such narratives enable the Faroese to construct empowering notions of cultural longevity and agency, while resisting the idea that contemporary cultural practices in the Faroe Islands render islanders as overtly tradition-bound or pre-modern.

Dance in particular, and the arts in general, provide for cultural longevity and agency; these are vital notions for the Faroese, due to a history of subordination under the Danish crown, and ongoing concerns of sovereignty and minority rights. As a dependent territory of Denmark, but neither a member of the European Union nor the Schengen Zone, the Faroe Islands are precariously positioned. Their situation has strong parallels with Greenland, in the efforts to secure viable pathways towards full sovereignty (for more information see Jensen's chapter on Greenland in this collection). However, while Greenlanders fuel their drive for political self-determination with the search for minerals and other natural resources, such as natural gas and oil, Faroese attempts to increase economic revenue from their main natural resource, fish, have been met with great resistance from the international community. As of late 2013, the Islands are in conflict with the European Union and a group of nations known as the Coast States that includes the European Union, Russia, Norway, Iceland (and the Faroes themselves) over fishing quotas. In late August 2013 the Islands declared that they would triple their quota of herring and mackerel catches, up from the lowest share among Coast State members at 5 per cent. The European Union then enacted punitive measures against the Islands by instituting fierce trade sanctions against them (Jolly 2013, B6). With fish and fish products comprising 95 per cent of all export from the Faroe Islands these sanctions will debilitate the Faroese economy while creating an even tenser political atmosphere.

While focused on the specifics of the Faroe Islands, this work engages with ethnomusicological research examining the fundamental role of the arts in populations experiencing endemic crises. Laura Adams, in writing about theatre in Uzbekistan, notes the vital role that participation in theatrical events played in fostering a post-communist sense of normalcy (Adams 2005: 336). Ethnomusicologists, in particular, have written about the relationships between music, dance and colonial forms of cultural control and crisis (see Askew 2002; Guilbault, 2007; Irving 2010). Not only do the arts contribute to fostering senses of continuity and stability in cases of crisis, scholars including, Orchardson-Mazrui researching with the Mijikenda in Eastern Africa, argue that the importance of ritual practices and performances becomes more strongly manifested during times of crisis (Orchardson-Mazrui 1998: 86). Thus the performing arts can provide platforms of agency, empowering expressions of identity, and community building for populations that have experienced political and cultural oppression.

A Crisis of Legitimacy – Some Background

The ongoing relationship between the Faroe Islands and Denmark represents a political and economic quagmire that begins has deep roots in the history of the Islands. The exact date of the first settlement in the Faroe Islands is contested, but sources suggest that Irish monks settled around 700 CE with Norse colonists arriving around 825 CE (Arge 1991: 101). Scant documentation exists of the first few hundred years on the Islands, though sources suggest that initial Norse settlement was fuelled by a desire to escape tyrannical rule in medieval Norway. While substantiation of such claims is difficult, they provide background to frequently evoked narratives of the strength and endurance of the strong-willed Faroese facing oppressive foreign rulers. As the centuries progressed, the Faroe Islands, along with Iceland and Greenland, were brought into union under the

Danish crown. Karen Oslund, in writing about these North Atlantic relations, argues that, 'Much of Faroese history, from the thirteenth century on, can be understood in terms of its relationship with Denmark and a relationship with Europe that was largely mediated through Danish interpretations of the Faroes' (Oslund 2011: 124). This mediation of the Faroe Islands through Danish interpretations had large-scale implications throughout Faroese society.

Other scholars have narrowed in on the inextricable link between Faroese-Danish relations and political and linguistic issues in the Faroe Islands (Knudsen 2010: 128). Language policy in the Faroe Islands was a clear site of institutionalized 'Danification' of the Faroese. This was reinforced with the introduction of compulsory schooling in Danish and the ultimate goal to enforce Danish as the national language of the Faroe Islands in the nineteenth century (Knudsen 2010: 129). By this time, the Faroese language had already taken on the status of a 'low' spoken variety, with Danish a formalized written 'high' variety. The subordination of Faroese to Danish only officially ended in 1938 when the two languages were recognized as equal by the Danish government. Nonetheless, efforts to develop an orthography for the Faroese language remain an ongoing project. Despite the desire to separate Danish and Faroese cultural elements, particularly through language, scholars have noted that in the efforts to assert a Faroese linguistic identity separate from Denmark, the Faroese have essentially turned to Icelandic as their new model (Oslund 2011; Knudsen 2010; Nauerby 1996).

While vast inroads have been made in Faroese language politics, Faroese economics remains tied to Denmark. After a period of private individuals holding trading rights over the Islands, starting in 1709 and ending in 1856, the Danish crown held an absolute monopoly over trade in the Faroe Islands. The sole commercial establishment in the Faroe Islands was the royal monopoly's warehouse in Tórshavn. Their exports were almost entirely comprised of wool and woollen goods and products from fishing, fowling, limited agriculture, and whale hunting. Wylie points out that there was no Faroese middle class during this time; there were a few tenant farmers with the rest of the population kept at poor living standards due to the iron fist of the Danish monopoly (Wylie 1993: 378). At the same time, the Danish crown owned over half of the land in the Islands, and extracted significant taxes from the inhabitants (West 1973: 13).

In addition to being the seat of the trade monopoly and royal power, Copenhagen served as the primary site of education for any Faroese individuals, as well as Icelanders and Greenlanders, seeking a university education in the nineteenth and twentieth centuries (Loftsdóttir 2012: 60; Jensen 2012: 111). The presence of Faroese students in Copenhagen during the nineteenth century, when Denmark itself underwent a pronounced national awakening, directly influenced a subsequent national awakening in the Islands. These Faroese students worked to apply the same ideals of the Danish national awakening to their own homelands. Thus the late nineteenth century brought increased efforts to foster senses of political and cultural cohesion to the Faroe Islands. At the forefront of many of these efforts was a growing desire to differentiate themselves politically and culturally from the Danish realm. Such efforts to establish differentiation in otherwise relatively similar populations are central to understanding the larger Nordic realm (Wylie 1981: 9).

Another site of 'Danification' in the Faroe Islands came with an 1828 law regulating the use of family names within the Danish realm. Up until this point it was common in both Denmark and in the Faroe Islands for individuals to hold patronymic last names and in the case of the Faroe Islands, last names also indicated the actual location of where a family came from in the Islands. The 1828 law mandated that all last names within the Danish realm end in '-sen', effectively obliterating the local naming practices in the Faroe Islands.[1] It was not until 1992 that the Faroese home-rule government was given the right to determine naming laws for people within the Faroe Islands. In Denmark proper, a 2005 law finally reintroduced the possibility of using patronymic last names. This law also mandates that Denmark's Ministry of Integration can work together with the Faroe Islands to approve names that abide by Faroese naming law.

Desire for separation from Denmark finally came to a head in 1946 when the Faroese held a referendum and voted for independence from Denmark and the Danish government ignored this vote (Debes 1995: 63). Two years later, the Faroe Islands were instead granted home rule and incorporated as an *amt* or county. Malan Marnersdóttir, academic and activist, characterizes this refusal by Denmark to acknowledge the vote for independence as 'utterly frustrating' in her essay, 'Construction and Deconstruction of the Faroese Nation'. She further argues that, '[t]hese events have since become a traumatic feature of Faroese politics. Due to these facts, the national consciousness is high regardless of one's opinion about Faroese sovereignty' (Marnersdóttir 2007: 152). The desire for independence is significant in the Islands, but a sizable portion of the population remains in favour of staying in the Danish realm. Regardless of which side of the debate individuals are on, there is a general consensus that the Islanders should be free to choose.

The Faroe Islands continue as a peripheral area within the Danish realm, teetering between pushing for independence and remaining with Denmark. One of the main obstacles towards independence is the significant financial subsidy given to the Faroe Islands each year by the Danish state. The Danish government has said that the Faroe Islands would be free to break from the kingdom, but that the subsidy would quickly end. For now, at least, the Faroese government has not seen this as a viable route as they would need significantly more time to properly 'de-colonize' and disassociate from the Danish funding. As such, the financial crisis of the Faroe Islands is directly linked to the political crisis of dependency on Denmark.

1 This is also an example of how the absolute rule of the Danish crown, which lasted until 1848, also worked to control and repress individuals living in Denmark proper.

Continuous Dancing

Due in part to the nature of Danish hegemony throughout modern Faroese history, cultural heritage in the Faroe Islands tends to be viewed as precious and fragile. The Minister for Education, Research and Culture in the Faroe Islands remains invested in the preservation and maintenance of Faroese 'cultural heritage' as a key link between past, present and future generations. This emphasis on connecting generations reflects Whyte's argument that 'one of the basic ways in which people everywhere, including those in chronic crisis, experience time is through the relationships between generations' (Whyte 2008: 99). Relationships between generations in the Faroe Islands are partly shaped by actual texts of the ballads, which for so long formed a key component of Faroese oral tradition. While the lyrics themselves sometimes served as pseudo-genealogies, the narrative value surrounding the history of balladry and dance in the Islands also create connections between generations.

The majority of texts addressing cultural heritage and the politics of tradition in the Faroe Islands focus on language, to which song and dance are inherently connected. Jens Christian Svabo, one of the Faroese students in Copenhagen during the mid-eighteenth century, transcribed some of the Faroese ballads and created an early prototype for the reconstruction of written Faroese. V.U. Hammershaimb was also active in collecting and transcribing the oral ballads of the Faroese. Hammershaimb's 1891 publication *Færøsk Anthologi* contained texts of multiple ballads as well as a second edition of his previously published Faroese grammar (Clausen 2006: 197). The Faroese ballads continued to be at the forefront of the transition of Faroese from an oral language to a written language, both for their linguistic value and the performance practices associated with singing the ballads, including the Faroese dance. Of all the different genres of oral poetry documented in the Faroe Islands, the heroic poems are the most commonly performed (Wylie 1981: 70).

The cultivation of uniquely Faroese modes of expression continue to play a major role in forging senses of cohesion within the Faroe Islands. I experienced a great diversity of musical expression in the Islands over a three-month period in the Islands during the summer of 2012. The most striking participatory music and dance performance occurred just after midnight on 30 July when over 20,000 people filled the main square of Tórshavn. This evening concluded Ólavsøka (the Faroese summer festival), and people from all over the country joined together for an evening of song and dance. We sang from small songbooks published for the evening, with a few individuals leading the group through each song over a PA system. Immediately after the last song, a chain of dancers formed as people linked hands and started taking two steps to the left and one step to the right in rhythmic unison. A lone voice broadcast over the crowd sang the verse of the evening's first ballad with the public joining in for each chorus. The chain of dancers quickly grew as nearly everyone participated and began the annual chain dance through the town centre that would last until the early morning. Many adults, children and even a few dogs, were dressed in the Faroese national costume, while many other participants were not dressed in this manner at all.

The Faroese chain dance is a decidedly contemporary practice that fosters senses of cohesiveness in a chronically fragmented society. The dance and the accompanying balladry (*kvæði*) combined are perceived as 'the most precious Faroese musical inheritance ... that make the Faroe Islands exceptional in the world' (Tórshavnar Kommuna 2000: 31). In what follows, I wish to extract 'oral poetry' from within literary studies and discuss the ballads and related dancing as sites of music making. This focus on the performing arts within the Faroese context provides insight into how people engage with creative expression in the face of long-term instability. Further, it highlights the discourse surrounding cultural heritage and tradition in such societies.

Chain dancing and the related ballads, along with the Faroese language, are common markers used to depict the Faroe Islands as home to a population closely tied to medieval peasantry, even in the twentieth and twenty-first centuries. In a 1960 report about a then-recent recording expedition to the Faroe Islands, Matts Arnberg wrote:

> The most important part of the material we collected is the Faroe walking dance, the only survival in the northern countries of the chain dance of the Middle Ages, which has for many generations been the favourite popular entertainment of the Faroe people. In spite of very great difficulties the people of these islands have stuck to their heritage of old nordic culture, a heritage brought over from Norway and further developed according to the demands of their way of life. Here we find a real, living peasant culture, which has for a long time almost disappeared from the other northern countries. (Arnberg 1960: 82)

The language choice – in which Arnberg claims to have found a 'real, living peasant culture' that has disappeared in other locations – risks positioning the Faroe Islands as pre-modern holdout on the fringes of Europe.

This emphasis on the historical roots of the dance works to reinforce a sense of legitimacy for otherwise marginalized cultural practices. Richard Wolfram, among others, has written about the pan-European nature of chain dancing dating back to the Bronze Age. Wolfram also highlights a common understanding that the chain dance as practised in the Faroe Islands originated in medieval France (Wolfram 1956: 33). But Wolfram argues that this idea is born out of a lack of evidence of the dance in the Faroe Islands prior to around the fourteenth century, instead of actual evidence connecting the Faroese and medieval French practices. A historical approach to the study of dance and music in the Faroe Islands has its place in academic study, but as noted earlier, recognizing the contemporary nature of dance practices in the Faroe Islands is also essential.

The actual dance style and balladry create an embodied sense of continuity and cohesion for those participating. As described earlier in this chapter, the dance is performed by a group of people holding hands to form a closed loop. Everyone in the group then moves in unison, repeatedly taking two steps to the left followed by one step to the right, while being led by a *skipari* (leader, more literally translated as skipper or captain). The *skipari* takes the lead in singing ballads that range in subject matter from heroic tales to satirical commentary. He or she typically sings each of the verses and then leads the entire group in the singing of the chorus. Most of the *kvæði* (ballads) have multiple variations, and it is the job of the *skipari* to select which version will be sung and to determine the tempo and style. *Kvæði* are almost always in repetitive verse-chorus format, enabling the group to pick up the chorus with ease. This is a highly participatory performance practice, meaning that nearly everybody in the vicinity of the dance joins in.

The nature of the Faroese dance allows for groups as small as ten with almost no limit on its size, apart from the physical constraints of the site of performance. The dancers can typically squeeze into a relatively small space by forming a twisting chain-like shape, instead of one large circle. This movement guarantees close contact with the rest of the dancers. As the dancers snake in and out, they will at one point or another come face to face with each of the other dancers. Depending on where the dance is being performed, and in which context, the dancers are forced to acknowledge and quite literally to face everyone else in attendance. This can, to some degree, forge a sense of cohesion among the group.

During my time in the Faroe Islands, I experienced the chain dance in multiple settings and contexts. In addition to the final hours of Ólavsøka, I also participated in a chain dance during a wedding celebration for two well-known Faroese musicians, as well as in courses and activities held for foreigners studying the Faroese language at the university. (It is also possible during the summertime for tourists to learn about the dance and participate in one as part of a tourist package, although I did not experience this.) There are also regularly scheduled dance evenings at the Nordic House in Tórshavn and other locations across the Islands. Wylie previously argued that the Faroese dance, 'is one of the few activities in which all Faroese – and only Faroese – may participate fully; foreigners may learn the steps, but are unlikely to learn the words, let alone become *skiparar*' (Wylie 1981: 117). While there are definite language barriers in place for non-Faroese speakers, it is worth noting that I, myself non-Faroese, was always eagerly welcomed into the dance. The Faroese dance, as currently practised, is not exclusionary based on ethnicity or background, which is significant when considering the diversifying population of the Faroe Islands.

The dance is also practised outside of the Faroe Islands. In Copenhagen, a group called *Fótatraðk* meets every other week in the Faroese House. This house, located in Copenhagen's Vesterbro district, serves as a hub of Faroese life, with meeting and rehearsal spaces, and a restaurant and bar. Every other Sunday evening a group of Faroese people gather for about three hours to chain dance and share food. In addition to two separate Faroese choirs based in Copenhagen, this dance society provides an opportunity for Faroese living abroad to meet regularly. When I attended a meeting in April 2012 there were twenty people in attendance, ranging in age from three to their 70s. The dance, along with the Faroese House itself, is a vibrant site of performing Faroeseness, creating cohesion among Faroese living abroad through the physical act of dancing. Notably, people who participate in *Fótatraðk* in the Faroese House do not typically wear the national costume at their informal meetings. Instead the emphasis here tends to be more on socializing and community building.

The Faroese dance is not, however, merely a metaphor for continuity based on performance practice. The dance is steeped in the rhetoric of cultural heritage and the priority placed on 'having roots' in efforts to legitimize marginalized practices and people. Just as Knudsen argued that language policy in the Faroe Islands is predicated on a sense of purism that works to differentiate the Faroese language from Danish (Knudsen 2010: 128), the continued prevalence of chain dance in the Faroe Islands also creates a divide between Faroese practices and Danish practices. Even though these categories are hardly fixed in everyday life, pillars of distinction such as language and art create a sense of difference. In the hands of more powerful groups, such as the Danes, monolithic and narrow articulations of a national culture can take on hegemonic qualities, yet for marginalized minorities, seemingly similar articulations can be a tool of enablement.

The role of performance art in crisis situations also has implications outside of the Nordic context. Postcolonial studies are traditionally dominated by literary studies, but dance and music are also vital aspects of forging cohesion and empowerment in historically subordinated societies. This focus on dance and the related balladry in the Faroe Islands offers a counter model to the more common focus on the novel as a prime nation-building-genre creation (Marnersdóttir 2007: 154). But the dance remains vital not only because people continue to dance, but because of the state-level support directed at the dance. Here issues of government instrumentality and state-level initiatives play a key role, as they do in many other locations around the world. Yet the situation in the Faroe Islands remains distinct from post-colonial models of national culture as explored by Frantz Fanon in his well-known writing on the topic in *The Wretched of the Earth* (2005).

Cultural Heritage

Exactly how participation in performing arts becomes empowering as a site of national expression, particularly for post-colonial communities like the Faroe Islands, extends beyond an ability to create group identity and extends into the realm of cultural heritage. Dancing the Faroese dance in the Faroe Islands, or among Faroese in Denmark, is not necessarily a site of articulating a singular Faroeseness; instead, it is a performance practice that effectively brings diverse people together into one unit. Even some of the Faroese individuals I came to know who steered clear of nationalistic markers such as the traditional costumes, willingly participated in the Faroese dance. I also observed that, while sexual minorities experience legal and social discrimination unseen in other Nordic areas, there seemed to be no taboos on who could participate in the dance along these lines. To borrow from Victor Turner's classic work on *The Ritual Process*, the Faroese dance can be seen as a:

> 'moment in and out of time', and in and out of secular social structure, which reveals, however fleetingly, some recognition (in symbol if not always in language) of a generalized social bond that has ceased to be and has simultaneously yet to be fragmented into a multiplicity of structural ties. (Turner 1969: 68)

This experience leads to what Turner refers to as 'communitas'. Even if only for the length of a dance, a diverse group becomes a cohesive unit. In the case of the massive Ólavsøka chain dance, anyone in the town square would be welcome to join in. However, the power of the Faroese dance is not only found in the actual effects of dancing, but also in the way it intersects historical associations and values determined by the Faroese state, other vested parties, and the participants themselves.

The framework of cultural heritage reinforces the priority for claiming roots and continuity for people around the globe. Laurajane Smith has written about the preoccupation with artifacts and physical items in heritage discourse, noting that the term cultural heritage itself is most often taken to mean the physical, with 'intangible' cultural heritage encompassing areas such as language, performance, music, and dance (Smith 2006: 3). Clearly designating certain items or practices as official cultural heritage is deeply tied to the values and priorities of those doing the designating. Cultural heritage is also tightly connected to the idea of memory, both collective and individual.

For people and societies who have experienced overwhelming political and cultural hegemony, there is potentially significant power in having the freedom to self-determine group values and priorities. For the Faroese, institutional support of the chain dance and balladry, both in terms of education and in financial support from the government, demonstrates the decision to promote and continue to cultivate the dance. But there are also risks associated with cultural heritage discourse for marginalized populations, such as the perception that some groups are more tied to their past or, at worst, actually pre-modern. The government of the Faroe Islands is aware of such risks, and has actively tried to ensure that the dance is taught and performed not as a static relic of the past, but as a modern living practice (Tórshavnar Kommuna 2000: 31). Another potential risk of such cultural heritage discourse is the potential exclusion of those who somehow fall outside of the dominant group in society.

Conclusion

Instead of viewing dance in the Faroe Islands as a relic of an isolated people, it can be read as a powerful site of agency for this society on the cusp of financial, political and cultural crisis. In a study of the relationship between music and culture in contexts of disjuncture and displacement, ethnomusicologist Philip Bohlman notes that music is particularly useful because it simultaneously represents 'a form of expression common to humanity, and as one of the most extreme manifestations of difference' (Bohlman 2011: 31). Bohlman continues in his description of how these manifestations of difference played out in colonial situations with the colonizers often working to limit local musical styles. Clearly articulations of difference and distinction can be a powerful tool for people on both sides of the power equation.

The legacy of cultural 'Danification' in the Faroe Islands as well as ongoing economic and political uncertainty all influence what I have called a crisis of legitimacy. As early as the sixteenth century, the inhabitants of the Faroe Islands were governed not by local leaders, but by the Danish crown in distant Copenhagen. Despite the strong relationship between Denmark and the Faroe Islands, the articulation of a certain 'Faroeseness' as distinct from 'Danishness' rose in importance throughout the nineteenth century. By the end of the nineteenth century, with Denmark experiencing its own national awakening, the Faroese had worked to distinguish their language from spoken and written Danish. At the same time, the continued practice of chain dancing and the accompanying balladry remained key signifiers of a distinct Faroese cultural heritage. This cultural heritage now informs state-level policy-making in the Faroe Islands, and is a vital source of empowering narrative formations. Within the context of crisis, music and dance can serve as vehicles of empowerment through experiences of Turner's concept of 'communitas'. It can also embody powerful collective memory and experience. Inclusion of the performing arts in future studies of crisis could also extend to musical responses to those 'sudden-onset' crises explored elsewhere in this book, including environmental, economic and other cultural elements.

Works Cited

Adams, Laura L. (2005) 'Modernity, Postcolonialism, and Theatrical Form in Uzbekistan'. *Slavic Review* 64 (2), 333–54.

Arge, Símun V. (1991) 'The Landnám in the Faroes'. *Arctic Anthropology* 28 (2), 101–20.

Arnberg, Matts (1960) 'Recording Expedition to the Faroe Islands'. *Journal of the International Folk Music Council* 12, 82–3.

Bohlman, Philip (2011) 'Music and Culture: Historiographies of Disjuncture, Ethnographies of Displacement', in Clayton, Martin, Trevor Herbert and Richard Middleton (eds) *The Cultural Study of Music: A Critical Introduction.* New York: Routledge, 28–39.

Clammer, John (2008) 'Decolonizing the Mind: Schwimmer, Habermas and the Anthropology of Post-Colonialism'. *Anthropologica* 50 (1), 157–68.

Clausen, Marianne (2006) 'Spiritual Songs and Kingo Singing in the Faroe Islands', in Bak, Kirsten Sass and Svend Nielsen (eds) *Spiritual Folk Singing – Nordic and Baltic Protestant Traditions.* Copenhagen: Forlaget Kragen, 197–226.

Debes, Hans Jacob (1995) 'The Formation of a Nation: The Faroe Islands', in Tägil, Sven (ed.) *Ethnicity and Nation Building in the Nordic World.* London: C. Hurst, 63–85.

Dugmore, Andrew J., Christian Keller and Thomas H. McGovern (2007) 'Norse Greenland Settlement: Reflections on Climate Change, Trade, and the Contrasting Fates of Human Settlements in the North Atlantic Islands'. *Arctic Anthropology* 44 (1), 12–36.

Ellefsen, Ann, Svenning Tausen and Sharon Weiss (1996) *Traditional Music in the Faroe Islands.* Tórshavn: Føroya Skúlabókagrunnur.

Fabian, Johannes (1983) *Time and the Other: How Anthropology makes its object.* New York: Columbia University Press.

Fanon, Frantz (2005) *The Wretched of the Earth.* New York: Grove Press.

Jackson, Anthony (1991) *The Faroes: The Faraway Islands.* London: Robert Hale.

Jensen, Lars (2012) 'Danishness as Whiteness in Crisis: Emerging Post-Imperial and Development Aid Anxieties', in Loftsdóttir, Kristin and Lars Jensen (eds) *Whiteness and Postcolonialism in the Nordic Region: Exceptionalism, Migrant Others, and National Identities.* Farnham and Vermont: Ashgate, 105–18.

Jolly, David (2013) 'Europe Set to Impose Sanctions on Faroe Islands Over Herring'. *New York Times*, 20 August, B6.

Knudsen, Karin Jóhanna L. (2010) 'Language Use and Linguistic Nationalism in the Faroe Islands'. *International Journal of Multiculturalism* 7 (2), 128–46.

Loftsdóttir, Kristín (2012) 'Belonging and the Icelandic Others: Situation Icelandic Identity in a Postcolonial Context', in Loftsdóttir, Kristín and Lars Jensen (eds) *Whiteness and Postcolonialism in the Nordic Region: Exceptionalism, Migrant Others, and National Identities*, edited by Kristín Loftsdóttir and Lars Jensen. Farnham and Vermont: Ashgate, 57–72.

Marnersdóttir, Malan (2007) 'Construction and Deconstruction of the Faroese Nation'. *Scandinavian Studies* 79 (2), 151–66.

Mentamálastýrið (2002) *Mentan og menning: Mentanarpolitisk ætlan 2002–2006.* Tórshavn: Mentamálastýrið.

Orchardson-Mazrui, Elizabeth (1998) 'Expressing Power and Status through Aesthetics in Mijikenda Society'. *Journal of African Cultural Studies* 11 (1), 85–102.

Oslund, Karen (2011) *Iceland Imagined: Nature, Culture, and Storytelling in the North Atlantic.* Seattle: University of Washington Press.

Smith, Laurajane (2006) *The Uses of Heritage.* New York: Routledge.

Turner, Victor (1969) *The Ritual Process: Structure and Anti-Structure.* New York: Aldine De Gruyter.

Tórshavnar Kommuna (2000) *Havnin: livandi, kveikjandi, skapandi: Álit um mentan og list í Tórshavnar kommunu.* Tórshavn: Tórshavnar Kommuna.

Vigh, Henrik (2008) 'Crisis and Chronicity: Anthropological Perspectives on Continuous Conflict and Decline'. *Ethnos: Journal of Anthropology* 73 (1), 5–24.

West, John F. (1973) *Faroe: the Emergence of a Nation.* London: C. Hurst.

Whyte, Susan Reynolds (2008) 'Discrimination: Afterthoughts on Crisis and Chronicity'. *Ethnos: Journal of Anthropology* 73 (1), 97–100.

Wolfram, Richard (1956) 'European Song-Dance Forms'. *Journal of the International Folk Music Council* 8, 32–6.

Wylie, Jonathan and David Margolin (1981) *The Ring of Dancers: Images of Faroese Culture.* Philadelphia: University of Pennsylvania Press.

Wylie, Jonathan (1993) 'Too Much of a Good Thing: Crises of Glut in the Faroe Islands and Dominica'. *Comparative Studies in Society and History* 35 (2), 352–89.

Chapter 6
Out of Sight, Out of Mind? The Mining Industry in the Peripheral Regions of Finland and Odisha, Eastern India

Satu Ranta-Tyrkkö

Introduction

Oil, gas and mineral mining remain crucial for maintaining the material basis of modern living standards. However, as resource extraction and industrial production rely on raw materials and an alienated workforce within globally decentralized production, the consequence of their labour – the resultant goods and energy – is taken for granted. Few members of 'the global over-consuming class' (Pasanen and Ulvila 2009: 21–3) would want a mine in their backyard. As Timothy Brennan states, there are recidivist elements within the world economy that are grounded not only on ignorance, but also on consciously chosen blindness and on the suppression of first world material dependencies towards discursively and carefully obscured peripheries, 'zones of invisibility', in the global South (Brennan 2006: 101, 111–12). Rob Nixon (2011: 2, 22, 150–74) refers to a politics of violent invisibility and a psychology of denial that actively produces under- and un-imagined communities, and violence – occurring gradually and out of sight – imposed by the world's *resource omnivores*[1] upon those less privileged. The following discussion is indebted to Brennan and Nixon's writing on these matters.

This chapter analyses the resource crisis by utilizing the notions of periphery, invisibility, and postcoloniality in connection with mineral extraction in Finland and Odisha (formerly Orissa):[2] the first a Nordic state and European Union member, the other, an eastern state within the Republic of India. While the choice of these two locations is empirical – I am a Finn who has occasionally lived in Odisha during the 2000s – Finland and Odisha can also be taken as representatives of the north and the south respectively. In this way this essay connects with Ystanes' chapter on the environmental crisis and tourism in Central America

1 The term was coined by Madhav Gadgil and Ramachandra Guha in *Ecology and Equity: The Use and Abuse of Nature in Contemporary India* (1995).

2 Until 4 November 2011 the official name of the state was Orissa. The Anglicized spelling was changed to better match the pronunciation in the local language Odia – formerly Oria.

and with Jensen's discussion of development and sustainability in Greenland. I reference Raewyn Connell's writing when noting global disparity, alternatively dichotomized as 'west/east', 'developed/underdeveloped', or 'first/third' world, emerging from 'the long-lasting patterns of inequality in power, wealth and cultural influence that grew historically out of European and North American imperialism' (Connell 2007: 212). These categories are ambiguous and relative; enclaves of the South exist in the north and *vice versa.*

Finland's northernness is geopolitical – it also reflects the affluence of contemporary Finnish society. However, the latter has not always been the case. In the beginning of the nineteenth century, Finland was among the poorest countries with high fertility and mortality rates, inefficient agricultural production, and minimal social mobility and economic growth. Modernization came late to Finland in relation to Europe generally (Haapala 2009: 50–51). Despite a history as an eastern county of Sweden until 1809 and thereafter an autonomous grand Duchy of Russia until the Finnish Declaration of Independence in 1917, Finland was never a colony nor, after independence, an imperial power. Even so, Finland has a history that links it to colonialism in the form of numerous colonial relations from trade to missionary work typical of the 1500s to mid-1900s (Löytty 2006: 68–74; Vuorela 2009: 21–2; Ranta-Tyrkkö 2011: 26–31). Moreover, historically the northern part of Finland (as also that of Sweden, see Eriksson 2010: 31–2) has been under internal colonization, which included racism and discrimination towards the indigenous Sami people (Vuorela 2009: 21; Kuokkanen 2007) and ecological colonization in the form of exploitation of its natural resources (Massa 1994: 19–23, 141–272; see also Lehtola 2002: 30–33).

In India, Odisha did not fare well during colonial times or during the first decades of Indian independence. British rule, starting in 1803 under the British East India Company, was marked by severe famines, where the impoverished starved to death in large numbers, simply because they could not afford to buy food (e.g. Kalia 1994: 27). Increasing poverty in Odisha throughout the nineteenth century was linked to high taxation, deficient salaries, and decline of native industries (Acharya 2008: 15–16, 21–2). After India's independence, the tragedy of the state has been that despite 'abundant mineral, forest, hydrologic and other resources' (Mathur 2008: 553), as well as large-scale development projects from the beginning of India's planning era in the early 1950s, Odisha was for decades one of the most destitute states of the country, a south within the south.

This poverty was the result of the state's stagnant economy characterized by a weak industrial base, mass unemployment, abysmally low incomes, and dire distress (Kanungo 2004: 99). Additionally, many interventions undertaken in the name of development, such as dams and steel plants, have been devastating, particularly for the state's significant Adivasi/tribal[3] population (in the 2001 census

3 Adivasi ('original inhabitant') is an umbrella term for a number of ethnic groups considered as the indigenous people of India. Legally, originating from a caste classification made by the British, these groups are known as 'Scheduled Tribes', and according to the

more than eight million people, some 22.1 per cent of Odisha's total population, then approximately 37 million and estimated to have risen to 43 million in 2013). In practice, for the Adivasis 'development' has often meant large-scale displacement, sometimes repeatedly (Mathur 2008: 553–4), and cultural genocide (Padel and Das 2008, 2009). Therefore, Odisha epitomizes a place in which recent economic developments have exacerbated its state of financial, cultural, and environmental crises. A significant section of the state's population inhabits a space where the gulf between development's beneficiaries and its casualties is widening.

As the chapter title and opening paragraphs suggest Odisha and Finland are sites of significant mining activity. In Odisha, geographically the ninth biggest state in India, mining and quarrying has been a rapidly growing sector since the 1980s. According to *The Orissa Review*, published by the Orissa Government (Dash 2007), while 'the state has 16.92 per cent of the total [known in 2007] mineral reserves of India, Odisha's reserves are particularly abundant in chromite (97.37 per cent), nickel (95.10 per cent), graphite (76.67 per cent), bauxite (49.74 per cent), and iron (33.91 per cent) of the total deposits of these metals in India'. During the past few decades, most interest and investment has focused on bauxite-aluminium and iron ore-steel. According to official statistics, the production of bauxite (out of which aluminium is produced) more than doubled between 1994 and 2008 (from 2,148,016 to 4,734,529 tons), and iron ore production increased nearly ten-fold (from 7,988,674 to 77,195,160 tons) (Government of Odisha, Department of Steel and Mines, 2013). By July 2013, the state had 600 mines. Finland's mining boom is more recent, dating to the 2000s. The industry is reemerging after the largely state-owned mining sector consisting of only national companies[4] was neglected during the 1980s, an outcome of low mineral prices and a lack of technological expertise in efficiently concentrating relatively low-ore deposits. The policy was further enhanced by political eagerness to reduce any state ownership of large-scale enterprises.

The recent Finnish mining boom led to the establishment of several new mines. Moreover, from 2008 to 2011 alone, dozens of companies spent more than €250 million on exploration (Uusisuo 2012) and in 2013 to enable ore prospecting as much as 14 per cent of Finland's land mass was under claims processes (Tukes 2013).[5] In 2012, there were 52 mines in Finland. Of these, 12 were metal mines in operation, the Kittilä (Suurikuusikko) Gold Mine and the Talvivaara Mine, extracting nickel and other metals. These are the largest mines of their kind in Europe. The non-metal mines excavate mostly industrial minerals (Tukes 2012; Uusisuo 2012).

2011 census, they constitute over 104 million people, or 8.6 per cent of the total population of India. This makes India the country with the biggest indigenous population in the world.

4 Leading companies included, for example, Myllykoski, Rautaruukki and Outokumpu.

5 While the number is large, nearly one sixth of Finland's land area, mere prospecting seldom leads to mining concessions.

In addition to gold and nickel, Finland also has reserves of iron and uranium. However, although the Talvivaara Mine was recently granted a licence to collect its 'by-product' uranium, the exploitation of uranium remains politically controversial, and is resisted, for example, by the Stop Talvivaara Movement. Despite the long-existing knowledge of uranium deposits in the bedrock there was initially no reference in the company's mining permit applications to uranium. Impediments to mining are indicative of the financial, environmental and management challenges of unwieldy mining projects, rather than the power of the anti-mining movement. Late in 2013 (on 29 November 2013 and 17 December, respectively) the Talvivaara Mining Company applied for a corporate reorganization process, and is at the time of my writing (January 2014) proceeding with reorganization (Talvivaara Mining Company 2014).

Against the global economic pessimism of the late 2000s, it is noteworthy that in both Finland and Odisha the mining industry operates mainly, though not solely, in areas that were (and remain) perceived as peripheral and economically stagnant, i.e. areas considered in a state of unending crisis. It is this liminal status, together with inherent notions of invisibility, and unresolved questions of postcoloniality that engage me. My ethnographic research[6] in Odisha in the early 2000s occurred with the local acting group Natya Chetana, (Theatre for Awareness), whose socially committed work typically deals with issues of structural violence and unmet basic needs.

When touring with the group, I visited several industrial centres considered peripheral because of their location, size and predominantly working-class population. There was noticeable air pollution that the locals said contributes to respiratory diseases that are prevalent in the area,[7] and these relatively small industrial towns in the less densely populated interiors of the state appeared significantly polluted places. The theatre troupe, Natya Chetana, was particularly wary of the mood in these remote towns. I learned that this was because during its early days in 1993 theatre group members had once been severely bashed by members of their audience (despite protests against the assault from some of the other spectators) because their play *Chaita Charita* (the Story of Chaita) was critical of industrial contamination. The incident took place in an area dependent on an aluminium smelter as the main source of employment, and was followed by a debate about the disadvantages and benefits that the smelter caused to the local villagers.

As a Finn researching in Odisha, I found it peculiar that despite the many (and to some extent incomparable) differences between the two places, certain continuing environmental, political, and economic struggles were discussed in similar terms, especially regarding a conflict over resources in northern Finland

6 For example, Ranta-Tyrkkö 2010.

7 These observations and conversations took place in Talcher district, Odisha, in November 2001 when I accompanied Natya Chetana on its tour with the play *Boli* (*Sacrifice*).

and interior parts of Odisha: land, forest and minerals. These were presented as conflicts concerning logging, or the acquisition of land for industrial purposes, and also as struggles for employment and opportunities. Such conflicts involve a number of stakeholders. These include local people, environmentalists, human rights' activists, the state, corporations and their representatives – from politicians to administrators and business moguls. All these stakeholders speak to various ideas about the best procedures and use of the existing resources. The individuals and institutions involved wield differing amounts of political and economic clout. Nor will the opinions of the local people always be undivided. In Finland and Odisha alike, the indigenous peoples' right to land and its produce has remained contested.[8] Moreover, attempts to secure the prerequisites of the continuity of indigenous culture(s) are easily polarized by the need for job creation and economic investments, even on the land that the indigenous communities have traditionally depended on for their sustenance.

Instead of considering the similarity between conflicts over natural resources in Finland and Odisha as coincidence, I accept, following Lena Dominelli (2012: 7) and David Harvey (2011: 184–214), the situation as symptomatic of capitalist relationships between people and the environment. Notwithstanding the differences between the two places, I will examine how the theoretical notions of peripherality, postcoloniality and politics of invisibility can inform understanding of these different contexts with mining industry. In the next section, I address some of the common problems associated with mining industry. Then, I will further explore the parallels and distinctions between Finland and Odisha in relation to mining and its consequences.

The Dirty Business of Mining

Representatives of the mining industry claim the ideas of dirtiness associated with the field utterly outdated. Yet, despite widespread images of extremely

8 The Sami (around 9,000 in Finland) do not have secure land rights in Finland because 90 per cent of the Finnish Sami land belongs to the government. Despite international criticism, Finland has not ratified the International Labour Organization (ILO) Convention No 169, which deals specifically with the rights of indigenous and tribal peoples (UNRIC 2013). While India has not ratified the ILO Convention No 169 either, it had ratified the Convention No 107 (The Indigenous and Tribal Populations Convention) previously in 1958. However, although the Scheduled Tribes have had a special status under the Indian constitution, this has not significantly improved their situation (ILO 2013). The most recent significant shift towards more rights-based approach to Adivasis has been the Scheduled Tribes and Other Traditional Forest Dwellers (Recognition of Forest Rights) Act (2006), passed by the Parliament of India, concerning the right of forest-dwelling communities to land and other resources. While the implementation and interpretation of the act is taking place as part of the continuing land rights contest, it remains to be seen to what extent it will be put into practice.

large, well-planned, technology-intensive modern mines, minerals are still being extracted by artisanal miners, that is, by small-scale or subsistence miners working with hand tools. In many instances, artisanal mining takes place in informal or illegal conditions with rudimentary tools, in the absence of safety regulations and trade unions (Gibson 2011: ix). It often uses women (Lahiri-Dutt 2006: 7; 2011) and children (Lahiri-Dutt 2006: 33–4; see also Majumder 2010 and Harris 2013) as labourers.[9] In India alone, there are an estimated 2,600 active mines (Human Rights Watch 2012: 11). The problem is that for every legal mine there are according to the government's figures, some 30 illegal mines – involving around 80,000 workers.[10] In addition to workers' safety and rights issues large-scale unauthorized quarrying potentially has a number of unplanned, possibly disastrous consequences, starting with changes to, and the pollution of, local water systems. Only legally existing mines have, at least in principle, gone through environmental and social impact assessment processes and are in principle able to be overseen. (This last point is moot given monitoring is practically non-existent due to lack of resources (Human Rights Watch: 11–13).)

There are other characteristics that make the business of mineral extraction dirty. The issues associated with minerals' extraction and use can be portrayed as debts of various, intertwined sorts[11] – ecological, temporal and spatial. These debts are not repaid to the communities where they accrue. Starting with the ecological debt, despite attempts to develop greener technologies mining is known as a polluting form of industry. In addition to the pollution caused during the actual mining and quarrying such as dust and noise, the processes of smelting and refining require vast amounts of energy and toxic chemicals. Accordingly, smelters emit large amounts of greenhouse gases, and their toxic waste is often either released directly into water resources, or stored in ways that makes contamination simply a question of time (e.g. Padel and Das 2009: 338–42, 373–85). In Finland, the sulfate and mineral emissions of the Talvivaara mine have kept polluting the

9 According to the Mines Act, 1952, anyone below 18 cannot be employed in the mines, whereas the Labour Law sets the permissible employment age at 14. However, the states have generally not enforced these laws effectively, and have failed to frame mechanisms to prevent illegal mining and child labour. In some states, like Rajasthan, where I have personally witnessed children working in sandstone mines, many of the child miners, along with adult men and women employed in the sector, fall in the category of bonded labour (Lahiri-Dutt 2006: 6); another practice legally abolished but weakly enforced, essentially a form of employer-slave relationship.

10 *The Human Rights Watch Report* (2012: 13) also claims that '[T]he scale of lawlessness that prevails in India's mining sector is hard to overstate.' There is a widespread problem of government indifference: 'Indian public institutions have broadly failed to oversee and regulate mining firms.' While 'some of these regulatory failures are linked to human rights problems affecting mining communities' …, 'India's government often leaves companies to regulate themselves – a formula that has proven disastrous in India and around the world', *Human Rights Watch Report* 1–5.

11 See Nixon 2011 for a general discussion.

watercourse; there have been several major emissions during the years 2010–13 (e.g. Laita 2013; THL 2012).

While most of the contamination occurs during the actual excavation activity, many mining sites also continue to pollute after their closure (Keeling 2012) through above mentioned storage problems and through radioactive waste in the case of uranium mining, for example. Although acid drainage is a common problem involving the outflow of contaminated water harmful to the environment from abandoned metal and coal mines, radioactive waste represents a particular challenge over time. Therefore, legitimate questions, also connected with the temporal debt of the industry, include, how far can corporate responsibility realistically extend and 'what does "perpetual care" of a contaminated mine site mean in practical terms?' (Keeling 2012). As Nixon argues, the challenge in the midst of contemporary fast-paced politics is to understand and foresee the repercussions of present activities in a range of temporal scales (2011: 2, 11).

Adding to the sense of a debt crisis operating over time, minerals are – within human life-perspective – non-renewable. Extracting mineral resources now means depleting them for future generations. The world's known mineral wealth is being consumed at an increasing rate, which together with projected population growth and the expansion of emerging large economies is likely to bring about a crisis in the supply of many minerals within our lifetimes. For example, the globally existing reserves of zinc, lead, tin and gold are estimated to last approximately another 20 years, and there are many other important minerals whose estimated reserves extend only a decade or two longer. Even if new deposits are found, or if currently unprofitable deposits become profitable, it is unlikely to delay the exhaustion of the resources (Theis and Tomkin 2012: 151, 212–26).

While the affluent consume most of the world's minerals both within nations in the north and overall, the bulk of mineral extraction takes place in the south as well as in the peripheral regions of the north (Theis and Tomkin 2012: 151, 212–26; specifically about aluminum production and consumption see Padel and Das 2009: 682–5, 688–91). Therefore, the spatial aspects of production are intimately linked with the wielding of political and economic power. In general, the effects of natural resources on the welfare of local people appear not to depend so much on the resources themselves but on the social and institutional capacity to manage them. In other words, although natural resources can be a blessing for countries, they may become a curse if governance is poor (Daniele 2011: 567–8; Nixon 2011: 69–70), particularly in contexts of weak regulatory institutions.

Mining is known to be often grossly harmful to vulnerable sections of local populations, such as indigenous people, who often have only customary rights to the land and natural resources they have been dependent on for generations. By contrast, it is lucrative for others. For example politicians may be tempted to utilize their position and insider knowledge for personal financial gain (e.g. Human Rights Watch 2012: 53–5, 'the Case of Janardhana Reddy'). Further, as many minerals are of strategic importance to arms industry, and so to the security interests of large and small states, access to important mineral deposits have been of tactical significance in warfare (e.g. Padel and Das 2009: 267–92). In addition, despite the biggest transnational mining corporations being powerful enough to overrun weak states, international institutions and organizations heavily subsidize the industry. Funding flows from central international financing institutions like the World Bank especially for larger projects. Moreover, many of the costs of constructing essential infrastructure, such as big dams for electricity supply, or railways or deep-water ports necessary for transportation, are not necessarily financed by the industry, but at least partly by the local, probably already severely indebted governments (Padel and Das 2009: 455–95). Negotiations about the use of resources and land tend to take place between markedly unequal parties.

Despite the problems discussed above and growing awareness of the destructiveness of the continuous depletion and degradation of the land and natural resources, it seems as if there is nothing else to be expected as long as there are minerals to extract. For the time being, dominant economic agendas remain based on the necessity of economic growth, which historically has been intimately tied to increased mineral consumption (Theis and Tomkin 2012: 226). Thus nations as well as companies compete with each other for diminishing raw materials and energy resources (Harvey 2011). At the same time, governments also compete for foreign investment, which makes them prone to (or forced to), sell off natural resources at a cut-rate price. In this way, they allow polluting industries into their countries, and indeed subsidize such industries through conditional loans (Padel and Das 2009, 455–95).

Finland, Odisha and the Mining Industry – Parallels and Distinctions

As stated, in the case of Finland and Odisha my interest lies in the less often recognized similarities and convergences between the two locations, especially regarding resource conflicts and mineral extraction. For example, as Odisha is one of the world's leading producers of aluminium foil, many potatoes baked in their jackets in Finnish ovens are covered in foil that has travelled from India. In the mining industry there may also be direct business contacts. Finnish companies which provide mining technology, such as Metso, Outotec and Sandvik Mining and Construction, are global actors transacting business in India – although their websites do not indicate whether this includes Odisha. Other companies with Nordic ownership, such as Larsen and Toubro and Norsk Hydro have been active in Odisha. Larsen and Toubro, started by two Danish businessmen in Goa in 1938, and now headquartered in Mumbai, is a construction, engineering and arms company that also produces mining equipment. At present, while active also in many other states of India, the company has an office in Rourkela, Odisha's major steel industry town, and is involved in Bauxite-Alumina plans in Kashipur in southwest Odisha (see Padel and Das 2009: 220).

The Norwegian company, Norsk Hydro, owned the Utkal Alumina International as a joint venture with the Indian companies Tata and Indal. The joint venture started in 1993 with the aim of extracting the bauxite of the Babla Mali Mountain in Odisha. The site is located in the midst of an Adivasi area and the locals strongly resisted the project at one stage, detaining three Norsk Hydro officials for a short time in November 1998. As the administration and police adhered strongly to the company agenda, the resistance was answered with severe police and *goonda* (hired gangster) intimidation, culminating on 16 December 2000 when the police fired indiscriminately without warning into a gathering of tribal protestors near Maikanch. This attack became known as the Maikanch Police Firing and in it three Adivasis were killed and 30 were seriously injured (e.g. Dash and Samal 2008: 642–3). This incident, together with earlier changes in Utkal ownership, and also the pressure of Norwegian human rights' campaigners, led to Norsk Hydro withdrawal from Utkal[12] (Padel and Das 2009: 111–19, 220). Civil society connections also exist between Odisha and Finland. In the Finnish Social Forum of 2013, for example, Mining-Induced Displacement was one of the panel topics; with invited Adivasi speakers from Odisha and from the equally mineral-rich neighbouring state, Chhattisgarh.[13]

While geological reasons dictate the sites of mining industry operation in the first place, every region in which mineral extraction takes place has its own specific histories, including how it, as well as different groups and individuals within it, have been positioned in relation to each other and to the state or equivalent. In other words, the resource extraction is enmeshed with different temporal and political contests (Nixon 2011: 11, 99). In Finland the mining activity is largely concentrated in the northern and eastern parts of the country; in Odisha it is undertaken in the state's western interior. Northern Finland (Finnish Lapland) was officially constructed when the eastern part of Swedish Lapland was annexed to Russia in 1809 (Moisio 2012: 13; Lähteenmäki 2005: 147). In terms of environmental history, Ilmo Massa, a pioneer of social scientific environmental research in Finland, divides the history of Northern Finland into four phases, the Sami people's Lapland, the backwoods settlers' Lapland (*korvenraivaajien Lappi*), the forest industry's Lapland, and the state's Lapland (1994: 142–263). The area was originally home to the Sami, whose most important livelihoods were fishing and hunting. Northern Finland was initially only loosely tied to the state that claimed it. Gradually, the Sami and their livelihoods were disturbed by settlements spreading from the south. The settlers, while relying on animal husbandry and farming, also adopted Sami livelihoods, so reducing the Sami share of fish and game and forcing them into reindeer herding (155, 161–81).

12 Padel and Das (2009: 124) also state that in India, 'Norsk's insistence on human rights had been "frustrating for the Indal"' [the company with a controlling stake in Utkal after several ownership changes after Tata had left the consortium in the late 1990s] 'and the administration, which were not used to taking these considerations seriously, and considered them as a sign of "weakness"'.

13 They were invited to Finland to talk about the situation from their own perspective by the Finnish NGO Emmaus Aurinkotehdas.

Effectively, northern Finland was integrated with the rest of the country only after the Second World War (Moisio 2012: 14). Even then, the region was largely conceived as a resource pool of timber and hydropower for the rest of the nation. According to Massa (1994: 261–6), Finnish Lapland was clearly a locale of ecological colonialism, which became welfare state colonialism by the 1970s, when state subsidies to local municipalities 'nationalized' Lapland. Massa comments that this nationalizing or welfare state colonialism took place during the 1970s and 1980s via various forms of economic incentives, such as subsidies for agriculture and forestry, and other forms of state sponsorship channelled to the region. While these brought a greater level of social security, as well as employment opportunities in the public sector, especially infrastructure development also improved access to the natural resources of the region. Later on, the downsizing of the welfare state, as well as the increasing mechanization and structural changes in the forestry sector have hit Lapland particularly hard (262–3).

Subsequently, the role ascribed to northern Finland has often been that of an exoticized northern place with high unemployment and, proportionally, limited opportunities, diminishing population (approximately 180,000 inhabitants of a total Finish population of 5.4 million in an area roughly one third of Finland). Accordingly, in spite of the acknowledged opportunities in tourism, the region was in late 1990s and early 2000s often labelled a burden for the national economy (Moisio 2012: 277). At the same time, many welfare services have been reduced to bare minimum especially outside the main population centers of Northern Finland. According to Moisio (2012: 191–5, 226–31, 277–9) this signals a move toward metropolitan centric development.

In India, since British sovereignty over the commons and the forests, practically all those relying on the land for their way of life, including hunter-gatherers, peasants, artisans and nomads, have suffered great distress because of resource depletion. In modernizing India, the increasing number of people and their growing needs for living room, industry and transport has led to further materials usurpation to the benefit of the state and the commercial-industrial sector of the country. There is a scramble for remaining resources, which then has either caused or intensified inter-communal and caste conflicts, when communities that earlier had functioning relations with each other now struggle against each other (Gadgil and Guha 1992: 213–15). Particularly for people 'at the receiving end of ecological degradation' the essence of the history of development in independent India has been a process of resource capture by the resource omnivores at the expense of the ecosystem people (Guha and Martinez-Alier 1997: 12). To a great extent, people who are driven out or who are too impoverished to survive elsewhere now flock to cities (Gadgil and Guha 1992: 215).

In Odisha, the mining boom has significantly accelerated Odisha's growth rate and total income, but this has been growth that has circumvented the poorest. A high incidence of poverty remains particularly among the groups that were destitute and vulnerable to start with (e.g. Panda 2008: 12–15). In addition, mining has brought numerous adverse effects, such as air and soil pollution, contamination and evaporation of water bodies, loss of lands and livelihoods, and deterioration of community structures. As noted, these effects are substantial for the Adivasi peoples of the state, as many Adivasi communities reside at the very mountains where the mineral resources are located (e.g. Guha 2007: 707–9). At any rate, Padel and Das view the official version of the state's modern history 'focusing on various monuments of modernity' as biased because it omits '... the realities on the ground, such as displacements, cultural genocides in the making, and the interconnectedness of many calamities from terrible floods to communal violence' (2008: 581). There is an increased polarization within the society between those who believe in or promote industrial development models, and those who resist them (Padel and Das, 2008: 589).

In Odisha, polarization fuels violence. In addition to the above-mentioned Maikanch Firing in 2000, the conflict between reclaiming and exploiting the mineral resources and utilizing other resources from the same soil has led to gross human rights violations and violent deaths. For example, in Kalinganagar in January 2006 the local police opened fire against a group of tribal people protesting against the Tata steel plant construction on their lands, killing 12 (Padel and Das 2009: 405–8). Yet, in the political rhetoric of the state, and its instruments, the police and security forces, those resisting their own displacement and impoverishment are increasingly, and interchangeably, labelled Maoists or Naxalites.

The term Naxalism refers to a Maoist insurgency movement, which originated from a 1967 land dispute case in the state of West Bengal (North of Odisha), but which now consists of a number of left-wing insurgent groups waging an armed guerrilla struggle against the Indian state to which the state has responded with violence. On one hand, the Naxalites claim to be supported by the rural poor and the Adivasis, whose freedom to choose sides or benefit from the situation can easily be questioned. On the other hand, politically 'Naxalism' and' Maoism' are much abused names used 'to brand anyone crying for social and economic justice and justify using repressive measures against him' (Singh 2006: ix–xiv). Ramachandra Guha (2013) argues that Odisha, 'a State once completely free of Naxalites' has seen them acquiring considerable influence only because of 'lack of efforts by the State to make the Adivasis stakeholders in mining projects' and 'the complete mismanagement of democracy and governance in tribal areas' (Guha 2013; see also Roy 2013).

In Finland, similar violence is unheard of. However, instances of displacement are not; environmental refugees have been produced in the name of development. As Aikio states (2012: 165), the construction of the reservoirs of Porttipahta and Lokka in the 1960s and 1970s as part of hydropower development in northern Finland drowned half a dozen Sami villages, destroying the natural economy of these communities. The hydropower company, Kemijokiyhtiö, utilized unethical means to speed up land acquisition including providing free alcohol to buy consent, corrupting regional police, and accessing local bank records to use knowledge about individual debt (Aikio 2012: 164). In the end, the reservoirs' construction displaced 650 people, damaging cultural and language networks irreparably.

The displaced were herded into Vuotso village, as if onto a reservation area, a move followed by several suicides (Aikio 2012: 165). Aikio labels the process as a cultural genocide that destroyed the social and cultural organization of the Sami reindeer herding system based on communal use of land; a loss that the Finnish state has neither recognized nor compensated (166–7) (see also Massa 1994: 238–46).

Downstream from the project, a number of people who lived off the River Kemi were also impoverished, with men being particularly affected. As a result of the changing environment and unable to continue fishing and other river-related men's activities, at least a generation of men lost their sense of purpose, many of them turning to alcohol.[14] The 1949 damming of the river virtually emptied the river of fish (see Massa 1994: 241). Kananen reports his personal experience of displacement in a place that has been blocked and left with constant pollution and altered environment due to the proximity of the Talvivaara Mine (2012: 89–97). While seen from the perspective of the company as an unfortunate individual case, the enormous size of new and planned mines suggests that the history of mining-induced displacement is far from fully written in Finland. While on a different scale than in Odisha, local resistance to mining also exists in Finland, where there is an active environmental movement, distrustful of the state (Moisio 2012: 314) and the companies involved.

In both Finland and Odisha, the mining booms have been established in the context of neoliberal states, both states having adopted neoliberal politics from the early 1990s. In Finland, the major goal of the boom has been to increase Finland's viability as a competitor in the international marketplace. At the same time, within the country, the neoliberal ideology and the kind of competition it entails has in respect of welfare service provision been largely constricted by a competitiveness that operates to disadvantage those who dwell outside urban centres. In similar fashion, the political discourse around 2010 has often presented globalization as ever increasing competition between states. Finland's future is cast as either successful or as suffering a gradual deterioration of its earlier status as European periphery. In this paradigm, competition is constructed as self-evident and non-political (Moisio 2012: 167, 204–6). At the same time, Finnish social policy has remained committed to a productivist model of welfare, in which economic growth and consumption are seen as crucial to the national economy, whereas issues of ecological sustainability and the connections between poverty, inequality and environmental destruction receive little attention (Helne, Hirvilammi and Laatu 2012: 44–50).

In Odisha, the leading political idea seems to be that industrialization, primarily geared towards harnessing the vast natural resources of the state, is necessary to

14 While research on the issue is still lacking, the experience has been dealt with in fiction and in theatre. A widely popular play, recognized for its capacity to capture and perform the local people's views, has been *Mustan Joen Syke* (*The Beat of the Black River*, my translation) by Olli Tiuraniemi and Sami Parkkinen (2007).

eradicate the poverty, to open up employment opportunities and to enhance the state's revenue (Dash and Samal 2008: 627). While there are many fine words acknowledging the region's biodiversity and recommending inclusive growth, a nationally powerful and oft-expressed view is that people attached to the land belong to the past and should not hinder India's development. One example of this attitude is the cover story (Kumar and Bhuchar 2012: 19–22) in *India Today*, 15 October 2012, 'Green Terror' which accuses the Minister of Environment and Forests, Jayanti Natarajan as well as her predecessor, Jairam Ramesh, of obstructing India's development through their ministerial portfolio.

As the above examples from Finland and Odisha attest, when balanced against the desire for investments, economic growth, and development in the name of the common good, vulnerable communities can be adversely harmed by investment in mining and the products of mining. Simply depriving them of the natural environment they depend on destroys the lifestyles of the inhabitants of mining areas. When environmental policy privileges the short-term interest of those who benefit from resource-mining policies at the expense of longer-term sustainability and the interests and dignity of the people suffering from the imposed changes, the underpricing of environmental resources and their value for local communities constitutes a structural problem (Samal 2007: 23).

Conclusions

As Viken and Nyseth (2009) argue, places provide not only material, but also discursive contexts. When places are produced and performed, their construction involves materialities, politics and imaginations, as well as geometries of power (Bærenholdt and Granås 2008; Eriksson 2010). Rather than making direct comparisons between the situation in Finland and Odisha, the idea behind my writing has been that these two locations offer two localized perspectives into mineral extraction in areas constructed as peripheral. In the case of the Finnish and Odishan mining regions, their constructed peripherality also include derogatory elements in the sense that they have for long been considered as marginal, left behind places, reproducing the idea that periphery has less value than centre (Brennan 2006: 101). Yet, as I argue throughout the chapter, the question about the use of natural resources, including minerals, and managing the subsequent environmental and social problems is a global one, and closely connected to issues of underdevelopment, inequalities within and between countries, social justice and human rights (e.g. Piguet, Pécoud and de Guchteneire 2011: 25).

Mining is an issue that divides opinion on moral, economical and philosophical grounds. Opinion depends on how individuals situate themselves in relation to the benefits and losses associated with the industry. The industry in Finland and Odisha has clearly positive and negative consequences. In northern Finland, mining has already increased employment opportunities, brought in investments, as well as raised the population of towns like Sodankylä. The estimation is that the present mining boom may significantly improve the economic status of the region as long as it lasts, presumably for the next 20–30 years. For these reasons, the local inhabitants in northern Finland are happier about the mining industry than those who come to the region for recreation (DILACOMI 2013). As such, this is no surprise, as in northern Finland, as in other peripheral places at the rim of northern Europe (Nyseth and Viken 2009: 222), the overarching aim has for long been job creation, and the main concern how to sustain or indeed create industry.

Conversely, mining is expected to have negative consequences for other significant industries in northern Finland, such as; tourism, fishing and reindeer herding, in addition to which present claims for mines also threaten several nature conservation areas. In Odisha, mining has enhanced the state revenue and has thus contributed to the building of highly needed basic infrastructure as well as financing welfare programmes in the state. At the same time, the effects of mining are catastrophic. Mining erodes natural resources and pollutes the environment, offering limited scope for employment (the number of people employed in the industry has decreased from the early 2000s). Therefore, any jobs created would need to be measured against the loss of livelihoods caused through the large-scale displacement of poor, particularly tribal, people from their native lands (Dash and Samal 2008; Padel and Das 2009). In Finland and Odisha alike, one of the lessons learned is that the costs of the industry for local people and the natural environment are rarely taken into account in cost benefit calculations. If they had been, the conclusion would be that most minerals are underpriced (Padel and Das 2009).

The above review of the mining boom in Finland and Odisha supports the idea that the age of colonialism and industrialism is not over. Similarly to Karl Benediktsson's analysis (2009: 16) of aluminium smelter towns in Iceland, in a time of an alleged 'second modernity', in these regions 'the solutions seem to have more in common with the "first"'. In the case of Odisha, and to some extent Finland (e.g. Talvivaara), present-day practices of mineral extraction also highlight rent-seeking behaviour typical of capitalism, that is, the drive to maximize the chasm between the market value of the resource and the cost of its extraction (Nixon 2011: 41, 71). In fact, as Brennan (2006: 117) indicates, for companies the present nation-state system, in all its variety, functions 'as a political smorgasbord of locally varied legal options: in one place offshore accounting, in another, relaxed environmental laws, in a third decent transit infrastructure'. The whole system is based on the existence of 'zones of invisibility', that is, a willingness not to see or not to care about problematic chains of exploitation behind the production of commodity products (Brennan 2006: 117). However, particularly third-world peripheries are often 'wielded as an image of the fearful potential' dystopian future also for the affluent, unless they play their cards wisely (Brennan 2006: 101).

Finally, my review on mining industry also supports the notion that instead of focusing merely on 'classic colonialism' it is also important to look at processes that create contemporary structural inequalities within states (e.g. Eriksson 2010: 1). For example, in situations of conflict over the use of natural resources, even well-meaning mediating governmental programmes may contain colonial-like disciplinary modes of domination in their attempts to educate the desires of local people and configure their relations with each other, as well as with land, wealth, resources, and means of subsistence. It is not uncommon that political questions of land, resources, jobs and wages are rendered nonpolitical by rephrasing them as seemingly technical issues (Cameron 2012). Moreover, 'where corruption, hierarchy and exclusion are the norm', the situation is ever more problematic. In the case of Odisha, the view of Padel and Das is that 'mining companies, and banks investing in them, are poised to become the effective owners of some of Odisha's best-forested mountains and their minerals, with a view to rapid extraction' (2009: 457).

Overall, there is a clear need for postcolonial, environmentally conscious research and, as Brennan (2006: 106) demonstrates, the development of an (updated) postcolonial theory on contemporary world economy, actual relations of production, and changing forms of imperialism is vital. The experiential impacts of extractive businesses at the beginning of the chain, are made invisible. Mining materializes as smells, sounds and dust, some of them toxic. It disfigures landscapes indelibly and denies access to the inhabitants of a mined area to all that was familiar or sacred. At the same time, as Pietarinen writes, many living in the over-consuming end of the economic chain would actually like not to live and consume as they do. Yet, still doing so is grounded deeply in the present immensely strong conditioning to see the world as something that can be consumed and sacrificed (Pietarinen 2012: 8–9).

Works Cited

Acharya, Pritish (2008) *National Movement and Politics in Orissa 1920–29*. New Delhi: Sage.

Aikio, Pekka (2012) 'Tekojärvet hukuttivat ja tuhosivat ...', in Kati Pietarinen (ed.), *Sijoiltaan menneet. Kulutuksen häätämä elämä.* Helsinki: Siemenpuu-säätiö, 161–7.

Bærenholdt, Jørgen Ole and Brynhild Granas (eds) (2008) *Mobility and Place. Enacting Northern European Peripheries*. Aldershot: Ashgate.

Benediktsson, Karl (2009) 'The Industrial Imperative and Second(hand) Modernity', in Nyseth, Torill and Arvid Viken (eds) *Place Reinvention: Northern Pespectives.* Farnham: Ashgate, 15–31.

Brennan, Timothy (2006) 'The Economic Image-Function of the Periphery', in Loomba, Ania, Suvir Kaul, Matti Bunzl, Antoinette Burton and Jed Esty (eds), *Postcolonialism and Beyond.* Delhi: Permanent Black, 101–22.

Cameron, Emilie S. (2012) 'Securing Indigenous Politics: A Critique of the Vulnerability and Adaptation Approach to the Human Dimensions of Climate Change in the Canadian Arctic' in *Global Environmental Change* 22, 103–14.

Connell, Raewyn (2007) *Southern Theory*. Cambridge: Polity.

Daniele, Vittorio (2011) 'Natural Resources and the "Quality" of Economic Development', in *Journal of Development Studies* 47 (4), 545–73.

Das, P. (2001) 'Undermining Welfare'. *The Hindu* (Online Edition) Sunday, 7 January 2001, opinion section, viewed 30 July 2013, http://hindu.com/2001/01/07/stories/05071344.htm.

Dash, L.N. (2007) 'Economics of Mining in Orissa' in *Orissa Review*. November, 69–76.

Dash, K. and K.C. Samal (2008) 'New Mega Projects in Orissa: Protests by Potential Displaced Persons', in *Social Change* 38 (4), 627–44.

DILACOMI (2013) *Avoin tutkimus lisää kaivosten hyväksyttävyyttä paikallisyhteisöissä*, a notice by the DILACOMI – Mines, land use, and local communities – research project, viewed 18 September 2013, http://www.ulapland.fi/loader.aspx?id=3272d390-31f0-4180-9abf-700654291438.

Dominelli, Lena (2012) Green Social Work, From Environmental Crises to Environmental Justice. Cambridge: Polity Press.

Eriksson, Madeleine (2010) *(Re)producing a Periphery. Popular Representations of the Swedish North*. Umeå: Department of Social and Economic Geography, Umeå University.

Europa (2009) *Summaries of EU Legislation* http://europa.eu/legislation_summaries/justice_freedom_security/free_movement_of_persons_asylum_immigration/l33020_en.htm, retrieved 11.7.2013.

Gadgil, Madhav and Ramachandra Guha (1992 [2013]) *This Fissured Land: An Ecological History of India*. New Delhi: Oxford India Perennials.

— and — (1995) *Ecology and Equity: The Use and Abuse of Nature in Contemporary India*. London: Routledge.

Gibson, Katherine (2011) 'Foreword', in Lahiri-Dutt, Kuntala (ed.) *Gendering the Field: Towards Sustainable Livelihoods for Mining Communities*. Canberra: ANU E Press, ix–xi.

Government of Odisha, Department of Steel and Mines (2014) *Resource Statistics/Mineral Production/Production of Pres/Minerals in the State During Last 15 Years (1994–95 to 2008–9)*, viewed 25 January 2014, http://orissaminerals.gov.in/website/MineralProduction.aspx?GL=resstat&PL=1.

Guha, Ramachandra (2007) *India After Gandhi: The History of the World's Largest Democracy*. London: Macmillan (Picador India imprint).

Guha, Ramachandra (2013) 'The Continuing Tragedy of the Adivasis', *The Hindu*, 28 May, (Opinion), viewed 28 May, 2013, www.thehindu.com/opinion/lead/the-contining-tragedy-of-the-adivasis/article4756954.ece.

Haapala, Pertti (2009) 'Modernization of Finland 1800–2000', in Perkiö, Mikko (ed.) *Perspectives to Global Social Development*. Tampere: Tampere UP, 48–66.

Hall, C. Michael (2007) 'North-South Perspectives on Tourism, Regional Development and Peripheral Areas', in Muller, Dieter K. and Bruno Jansson (eds), *Tourism in Peripheries. Perspectives from the Far North and South*. Wallingford: Cabi 19–38.

Harris, G (2013) 'Children Toil in India's Mines, Despite Legal Ban', *The New York Times*, 25 February 2013, viewed 23 January 2014, http://www.nytimes.com/2013/02/26/world/asia/in-india-missing-school-to-work-in-the-mine.

Harvey, David (2011) *The Enigma of Capital and the Crises of Capitalism*. London: Profile Books.

Helne, Tuula, Tuuli Hirvilammi and Markku Laatu (2012) *Sosiaalipolitiikka rajallisella maapallolla*. Helsinki: Kelan tutkimusosasto.

Hentilä, Seppo (1999) 'Independence between East and West. How Did Finland Survive as a Democracy?' in Lehtonen, Tuomas M.S. (ed.), *Europe's Northern Frontier, Perspectives on Finland's Western Identity*. Jyväskylä: PS-Kustannus, Jyväskylä, 86–116 trans. by Philip Landon.

Human Rights Watch (2012) *Out of Control. Mining, Regulatory Failure, and Human Rights in India*, Human Rights Watch June, http://www.hrw.org/sites/default/files/reports/india0612ForUpload_0.pdf.

ILO (2013) 'Indigenous and Tribal Peoples' viewed 6 December 2013, viewed 6 December 2013, http://www.ilo.org/indigenous/lang--en/index.html.

Kalia, Ravi (1994) *Bhubaneswar: From a Temple Town to a Capital City*. Delhi: Oxford UP.

Kananen, Ari (2012) 'Talvivaaran takana', in Pietarinen, Kati (ed.), *Sijoiltaan menneet. Kulutuksen häätämä elämä*. Helsinki: Siemenpuu-säätiö, 87–97.

Kanungo, Trilochan (2004) 'Agony of Orissa' in Panda, Rabindra Kumar (ed.), *Reviving Orissa Economy. Opportunities and Areas of Action*. New Delhi: A.P.H. Publishing, 99–115.

Keeling A. (2012) 'How long is forever?' Blog posted at *Abandoned Mines in Northern Canada* 1 March, viewed 18 May 2012, http://www.abandonedminesnc.com/.

Kumar, D. and P. Bhuchar (2012) 'Green Terror' in *India Today*, 15 October, 19–22.

Kuokkanen, Rauna (2007) 'Saamelaiset ja kolonialismin vaikutukset nykypäivänä', in Kuortti Joel, Mikko Lehtonen and Olli Löytty (eds), *Kolonialismin jäljet, keskustat, periferiat ja Suomi*. Tampere: Vastapaino.

Lahiri-Dutt, Kuntala (2006) *Gendered Livelihoods in Small Mines and Quarries in India: Living on the Edge*, Working Paper, Rajiv Gandhi Institute for Contemporary Studies, New Delhi and Australia South Asia Research Centre, Canberra, July 2006, viewed 23 January 2014, http://crawford.edu.au/rmap/pdf/-docs/smalscalemining.pdf.

— (ed.) (2011) *Gendering the Field: Towards Sustainable Livelihoods for Mining Communities*. Canberra: ANU E Press.

Lähteenmäki, Maria (2005) 'Suomen Lapin synnystä alueiden Lappiin', *Terra* 117 (3), 147–58.

Laita, Samuli (2013) Talvivaaran kipisakka-allas vuotaa jälleen. *Helsinging Sanomat*, Kotimaa 8.4.3013, viewed 25 January 2014, http://www.hs.fi/kotimaa/Talvivaaran+kipisakka-allas+vuotaa+jalleen/a1365384661260.

Lehtonen, Veli-Pekka (2002) *The Sámi People: Traditions in Transition*. Aanaar-Inari: Kustannus-Puntsi.

Löytty, Olli (2006) *Ambomaamme, Suomalaisen kirjallisuuden me ja muut*. Tampere: Vastapaino.

Majumder, Kunal (2010) 'Half-life of the Coal Child'. *Tehelka Magazine*, 7, (26) 3 July 2010, viewed 23 January 2014, http://archive.tehelka.com/story_main45asp?filename=Ne030710coalchild.asp.

Massa, Ilmo (1994) Pohjoinen luonnonvalloitus: Suunnistus ympäristöhistoriaan Lapissa ja Suomessa. Helsinki: Gaudeamus.

Mathur, Hari Mohan (2008) 'A New Deal for Displaced People: Orissa's Involuntary Resettlement Policy', in *Social Change* 38 (4), 553–75.

Moisio, Sami (2012) *Valtio, alue, politiikka: Suomen tilasuhteisen sääntely toisesta maailmansodasta nykypäivään*. Tampere: Vastapaino.

Nixon, Rob (2011) *Slow Violence and the Environmentalism of the Poor*. Cambridge: Harvard University Press.

Nyseth, Torill (2009) 'Place Reinvention at the Northern Rim', in Nyseth, Torill and Arvid Viken (eds), *Place Reinvention: Northern Perspectives*. London: Ashgate, 1–14.

Padel, Felix and Samarendra Das (2008) 'Orissa's highland clearances: The reality gap between R and R', in *Social Change* 38 (4), 576–608.

— and — (2009) *Out of This Earth, East India Adivasis and the Aluminium Cartel*. Hyderabad: Orient Black Swan.

Panda, M. (2008) *Economic Development in Orissa: Growth without Inclusion*. Mumbai: Indira Gandhi Institute of Development Research (IGIDR), viewed 16 November 2009, www.igidr.ac.in/pdf/publication/WP-2008-025.pdf.

Pandey, Balaji (2008) 'The Kalinganagar Tragedy: Development Goal or Development Malaise', in *Social Change* 38 (4), 609–26.

Pasanen, Jarna and Marko Ulvila (2009) *Sustainable Futures. Replacing Growth Imperative and Hierarchies with Sustainable Ways*. Helsinki: Ministry for Foreign Affairs of Finland, http://www.sustainablefutures.fi.

Pietarinen, Kati (2012) 'Aluksi: Sijoiltaan menneet', in Pietarinen, Kati (ed.), *Sijoiltaan menneet. Kulutuksen häätämä elämä*. Helsinki: Siemenpuu-säätiö, 7–11.

Piguet, Étienne, Antoine Pécoud and Paul de Guchteneire (2011) 'Introduction: Migration and Climate Change', in Piguet, Étienne, Antoine Pécoud and Paul de Guchteneire (eds) *Migration and Climate Change*. UNESCO and Cambridge University Press, 1–33.

Pöyry (2011) *Kaivostoiminnan edellytysten kehittäminen*. Pöyry C.M. Oy.

Ranta-Tyrkkö, Satu (2010) *At the Intersection of Theatre and Social Work in Orissa, India: Natya Chetana and its Theatre*. Tampere: Tampere University Press.

Ranta-Tyrkkö, Satu (2011) 'High Time for Postcolonial Analysis in Social Work', in *Nordic Social Work Research* 1 (1), 25–41.

Roy, Arundhati (2013) *Broken Republic*. New Delhi: Penguin.

Samal, Kishor C. (2007) *Poverty, Social Capital and Natural Resource Management*. Jaipur: Rawat Publications.

Singh, Prakash (2006) *The Naxalite Movement in India*. New Delhi: Rupa.

Talvivaara Mining Company Plc (2014) Stock Exchange Release 17 January 2014, viewed 25 January 2014, http://hugin.info/136227/R/1755457/592729.pdf.

Theis, Tom and Jonathan Tomkin (eds) (2012) *Sustainability: A Comprehensive Foundation*. Houston: Connexions, viewed 15 April 2013, http://cnx.org/content/col11325/1.40/.

THL (2012) Talvivaaran kaivoksen ympäristö- ja vesitalousluvan lupamääräysten tarkistaminen sekä uraanin talteenottolaitoksen ympäristölupa ja toiminnan aloittaminen muutoksenhausta huolimatta, Sotkamo, Kajaani. Lausunto 14.12.2012. Viewed 25 January 2014, http://www.thl.fi/thl-client/pdfs/bbee98bc-3a29-41d1-bbfd-c8409c686862.

Tukes (2012) *Kullanhuuhdonta, malminetsintä ja kaivokset*, viewed 14 September 2013, http://www.tukes.fi/Tiedostot/kaivokset/tilastot/VUORI2012.pdf.

UNRIC (2013) 'The Sami of Northern Europe: One People, Four Countries' viewed 14 September 2013, http://www.unric.org/en/indigenous-people/27307-the-sami-of-northern-europe--one-people-four-countries.

Uusisuo, Maija (2012) 'The Mining Industry Report', A Presentation at Suomen Kaivosyrittäjien http://www.kideve.fi/luentomateriaalit-6-76-kaivosseminaari-2012-luostoKaivosseminaari 6.–7.6.2012, Luosto, viewed 18 September 2013.

Vuorela, Ulla (2009) 'Colonial Complicity: The "Postcolonial" in a Nordic Context', in Keskinen, Suvi, Salla Tuori, Sari Irni and Diana Mulinari (eds), *Complying with Colonialism, Gender, Race and Ethnicity in the Nordic Region*. London: Ashgate, 19–33.

Chapter 7

Saving Guatemala's 'Mayan Forest': The Environmental Crisis and Contested Development

Margit Ystanes

Like the disturbing pictures of polar bears clinging to melting icebergs, the destruction of tropical forests provides us with a powerful imagery of the unfolding environmental crisis; the earth's very lungs are being destroyed at a staggering pace. Yet, this depiction of ecological destruction is not neutral. As Nancy Leys Stepan points out in her work *Picturing Tropical Nature,*

> … all representations and pictures of the world, even the most technical and scientific ones, are partial and selective. We see the world by means of and through such representations and system of communication, which allow us to make sense of landscapes and objects (2001: 15).

The fierce debate about the scientific basis for climate change in contemporary *Western* societies emphasizes the difficulty in establishing an overarching Western conception of the crisis. I nevertheless use this term to refer to ideas about nature conservation that have gained political dominance in Euro-America, and have been exported globally through various conservation and development efforts. While ideas about nature conservation have complex historical trajectories (see e.g. Slater 1996; Tsing 2005), their current form incorporates the notion that nature conservation can be achieved without compromising economic growth. A case in point is Norway, where intensified consumption made possible by oil-driven economic growth coexists with the cultivation of a self-image as global promoters of nature conservation.

The prevalence of the notion that environmentalism and economic growth can be reconciled does not mean that all conservation efforts involve ambitions of profitmaking. As this chapter will show, however, such aspirations may combine with widespread ideas about tropical forests and human difference to complicate critical assessment and make conservation projects more easily understandable and marketable to a global audience. In the following, I explore the struggle over different narratives for legitimizing development and conservation interventions in the tropical forest of Petén, Guatemala. The existing conservation model in this area includes the granting of forest concessions to local communities. Such concessions represent modest economic gains through the sale of forest produce; yet are favoured by most concession holders as it provides them with ownership of their own development process. Notwithstanding, the current conservation regime is challenged by a proposal to combine forest preservation with highly profitable 'archaeo-tourism'.

These two conservation strategies value profit-making differently, and contrast in their degree of articulation with what Candace Slater (1996) has called 'Edenic narratives' about tropical forests. She argues that contemporary 'Western' conceptions of such places are profoundly influenced by our ideas about the Amazon – which are underpinned by the biblical story of the Garden of Eden. There are two main strands of Edenic narrative. The first establishes an initial state of harmony and perfection and eventual loss. The second centres more closely on a sense of bereavement and nostalgia for paradisiacal origins. In either case, there is a need for human labour to regain mastery over nature to re-establish a harmonious state. Humans' role in these stories is paradoxical; they are at once integral parts of the natural world they seek to dominate, and simultaneously alien to the rest of nature, which appears to turn against them in the garden. This paradox is reflected in the interchangeable representations of tropical forests as vulnerable places of immense beauty, and veritable 'jungle hells' marked by disorientation, wild beasts, decay and illness. Slater argues that the ambiguous function of humans in these conceptions is played out in powerful ways in Western societies; our representations of tropical forests tend to obscure the people and places they actually contain, yet they also invite us to dominate and protect these fragile zones (Slater 1996: 114–16).

For example, indigenous inhabitants are often seen as embodiments of the forest and discussed in similar ways as endangered species (Slater 1996: 114, 118–21). Non-indigenous forest dwellers, by the same token, are commonly considered destructive intruders, while more influential outsiders to these forest zones, whether local or international, can more easily establish themselves as potential rescuers. In many ways, this tropical imagery of environmental destruction evokes the racism of the colonial past. Whether cast as 'ecologically friendly noble savages' (Kalland 2003) or destructive elements (Ystanes 2011), locals tend to be represented as impoverished and without opportunities – to be assisted, spoken for and sometimes even removed. The prevalence of this imagery is problematic as it builds on out-dated ideas about indigenous people as pure, authentic communities living in harmony with nature, and ties in with stigmatizing notions of poverty. The agency of forest dwellers is disregarded, as is the actual variation in their life situations; for instance, some consider themselves to suffer from material want and lack of opportunities, while others reject such characterizations. Consequently, Edenic imagery of tropical forests contributes to making the lives of forest peoples less legible to 'Western' publics. And ironically, the assumption that local people need assistance in establishing sustainable livelihoods has paved the way for a number of destructive, yet profitable, activities in such areas by strategic reference to nature conservation and/or development (Slater 1996; see also Sawyer 2003).

These issues are relevant also in the Nordic context. Here, involvement in efforts to reduce poverty, conflict, racism and environmental destruction has become part of national identities (Loftsdóttir and Jensen 2012a, see also Hübinette, Chapter 4, this volume). In Norway, transfers towards the preservation of tropical forests, so-called 'rain forest millions'[1] have become a highly publicized part of the country's development aid.[2] However, Norway's involvement in addressing the climate crisis is far from unequivocal. While the state hands out 'rain forest millions' the partly state-owned Statoil extracts oil from the controversial tar sands in Alberta, Canada, and the daily *Dagens Næringsliv* claims that 'Rainforest billions open oil doors' (Nerdal 2010). Hence, the existence of 'rain forest millions' testify perhaps more than anything to the power of tropical forest preservation as symbolic of 'doing something' about the crisis.

It is problematic that so many of the representations underpinning tropical forest preservation efforts obscure power relations and pave the way for neo-colonial interventions. Reflection upon such matters is perhaps particularly important in the Nordic countries, as the complicity and involvement in colonialism – as well as the discursive residue of such endeavours – have largely gone unrecognized here (Loftsdóttir and Jensen 2012b; Keskinen et al. 2009; Gullestad 2004; Gullestad 2005). It may be symptomatic that Norway's generous gifts of 'rain forest millions' are subject to such strict control mechanisms that intended recipients have complained they are virtually impossible to release – the money is held in a World Bank account until results are documented (see e.g. Bakken 2011).

Forest Preservation in Petén, Guatemala

In Petén, Guatemala illegal logging, oil extraction agriculture, ranching, poaching, looting of archaeological treasures and *narcoganadería* (cattle ranching as a façade for drug trafficking) threaten the existence of the remaining forest, its wildlife and the Mayan ruins it contains. Petén is considered a frontier zone marked by the presence of drug traffickers, *invasores* ('invaders'; people who settle illegally the protected areas), and others who operate outside the law, while the state is largely absent (Hurtado Paz y Paz 2007). Most of Petén's forest communities are inhabited by *Ladinos* who have migrated to this area throughout the last century. While Ladinos are people of mixed origin, who tend to emphasize their European ancestry and downplay their indigenous heritage, they are often associated with 'national culture'. They have also traditionally oppressed the indigenous Mayan population and been excluded from the Euro-Guatemalan elite (see e.g. Hale 2006; Nelson 1999; Smith 1990).

---

1 Regnskogmillioner.

2 Despite Norway's long-term development involvement in Guatemala (see e.g. Norad 2011), 'rain forest millions' have not been made available to any of the actors involved in the case explored here.

Between 1994 and 2002, forest concessions were granted to a number of local communities in order to increase state control, engage forest dwellers in protecting their areas, halt the influx of new migrants, and provide economic opportunities through sustainable extraction activities. Although the implementation of this policy has not been smooth, and long-term outcomes remain to be seen, it has so far yielded promising results.[3] Nevertheless, a proposal to establish tourism in the ancient Mayan city of El Mirador, which is still mostly hidden beneath the forest, has called the concession model into question. This idea is promoted by the US archaeologist heading the excavations in El Mirador, Dr Richard Hansen, and a consortium of Guatemalan and international businesses and foundations.[4] The proposal to establish tourism there is controversial; both because it means bringing significant numbers of people into a protected forest area and because it has involved continuous campaigning to overturn the concession legislation. Even the name of the project, Mirador Basin, is controversial; it mirrors an attempt to establish a new protected area entitled 'Mirador Basin' (*Cuenca Mirador*, in Spanish), where tourism and research would be the only legal activities. According to environmental organizations working in Petén, this area is not a recognized geographical or political demarcated zone. Many therefore consider the use of 'Mirador Basin' to be a deliberate attempt to undermine the concession model. Hence, concession communities have opposed this proposal. Nevertheless, the promoters of tourism have rather successfully created political space and legitimacy for their idea by claiming it will save Petén's remaining forest and archaeological treasures and at the same time, create economic growth for local communities.

In the following discussion I will show how Edenic narratives are used to make these claims by obscuring the perspectives and contributions of local communities. The analysis I present in this chapter is based on 11 months of ethnographic fieldwork in 2007 and 2008. Although my initial aim was to gain equal insight into the perspective of all sectors, this proved difficult. Most of my time was spent with

3 See, for example, Cronkleton et al. (2008), Hay-Edie and Halverson (2006), Hurtado Paz y Paz (2007), Stoian and Rodas (2006), Taylor (2009), Taylor and Cheng (2009), Taylor et al. (2008).

4 The excavations are headed by Dr Richard Hansen, affiliate professor at Idaho State University and president and founder of FARES (Foundation for Anthropological and Environmental Studies). Among the most prominent contributors to the Mirador Basin Project were, at the time of fieldwork, the California based Global Heritage Fund (not to be confused with the UNESCO World Heritage Centre) and PACUNAM (Fundación Patrimonio Cultural y Natural Maya – Foundation for Cultural and Natural Mayan Patrimony). The latter is a consortium of elite-owned Guatemalan and multinational businesses, including Cementos Progreso, Walmart México and Centroamérica, Cervecería Centroamericana, Banco Industrial, Citi, Disagro, Cofiño Stahl, Samsung, Fundación Pantaleon, Blue Oil, Pica, Ingenio Madre Tierra and Claro (Jaramillo and Guerra 2008a; Jaramillo and Guerra 2008b; Jaramillo and Guerra 2008c; PACUNAM 2010). At the time of writing, however, PACUNAM's support for the Mirador Basin Project appears more uncertain (see Escalón 2012).

representatives of the concession communities, some civil society representatives and meetings involving all 'stakeholders'. Gaining access to state bodies and the promoters of tourism proved more complicated; partly because a considerable number of them were located in Guatemala City or abroad. In general, it is difficult for researchers to gain access to the Guatemalan elite.[5]

Representations of the Mirador Basin Project have been consulted in interviews with the above mentioned Dr Hansen in various international news media,[6] their project website (miradorbasin.com) and that of a significant and active donor, Global Heritage Fund (globalheritagefund.org). Such representations illustrate how the tourism project is promoted to an international public, and helps contextualize the Mirador case. Local concession-holding communities also receive funding from abroad;[7] this case therefore reaches well beyond the scope of ethnographic fieldwork in Petén. The promotion of the tourism project internationally is a crucial part of the context – and one that speaks about the kinds of tropical deforestation narratives that easily gain ground with a Western audience.

Conceptualizing the Unthinkable

In teasing out the less legible aspects of forest conservation in Petén, I take inspiration from Michel-Rolph Trouillot's (1995) work on the Haitian Revolution against the French colonial power (1791–1804). Drawing on Pierre Bourdieu's definition of the unthinkable: 'that for which one has no adequate instruments to conceptualize', Trouillot argues that for Europeans at the time, such occurrences were unthinkable (1995: 82). The justification for colonial slavery rested upon the idea that Africans were not fully human, and therefore did not desire freedom in the same way as 'white' men. Therefore, as news of the rebellion reached France and the rest of Europe, it was impossible for people to form the idea that African slaves were staging an organized revolution. The events of the revolution were often considered too unlikely to be true, or were thought of as isolated and exceptional cases. Very few were willing to consider the possibility that the rebellion was an outcome of a natural desire for freedom in the enslaved

---

5 Although see Casaús Arzú (2007) and Schirmer (1998).

6 The Mirador Basin Project has been featured in a *National Geographic* documentary, The Dawn of the Maya (2004), as well as in several well-known publications such as *The New York Times* (Schmidt 2010), *The Wall Street Journal* (Davis 2005), *The Smithsonian Magazine* (Brown 2011), *The Guardian* (Syz 2006) and *The Los Angeles Times* (Brazil 2007).

7 The founding and running of ACOFOP, the local communities' umbrella organization, has been financially supported by Ford Foundation, Interchurch Organization for Development Cooperation (ICCO) of Holland, Deutcher Entwicklungsdienst (German Development Service, DED), Helvetas – The Swiss Association for International Cooperation and Cristina Romero Initiative (CIR).

(Trouillot 1995: 92). Although these events took place over 200 years ago, there are continuities between the way Europeans received the news of the French revolution, and the way contemporary forest peoples are portrayed in Euro-American media communication (see e.g. Slater 1996; Sawyer 2003). The most significant continuity for the case explored here is the way international media outlets present locals as unfit to take on Petén's deforestation problems.

Thus, I will argue that for many *Westerners* as well as global elites, the role Petén's concession holders have taken on in addressing the deforestation crisis is unthinkable – i.e., impossible to conceptualize. The existing conservation model falls into this blind zone because it explicitly upsets local and global hierarchies of power, wealth and 'race'. However, precisely such contestation of the *status quo* is a prerequisite for successful development projects (see e.g. Willson 2010). It is therefore problematic, as the Mirador case illustrates, that challenging the *status quo* may make a project 'unthinkable', even to a well-meaning global public eager to address the environmental crisis.

This case does not only involve 'Western' interventionists, however, as some of the wealthiest and most powerful people in Guatemala have, at least at the time of my fieldwork in 2007/2008, supported the Mirador Basin Project (see footnote 4). Guatemala's complicated entanglement between notions of 'race', ethnicity and socio-economic status therefore also comes into play. Here, as in many other contexts, it is common among the elites and middle class to think of poverty as an outcome of personal failure, deviance, laziness, promiscuity and irresponsibility. This is a conception of poverty with long roots; it has been used to legitimize colonial and social engineering projects around the world and continues to hold ideological relevance (Brown 2010; Broch-Due 1995; Milton 2007; Casaús Arzú 2007; Castellanos Cambranes 1985; Haney 2000; O'Connor 2002). Within Guatemala, it is mainly the indigenous Mayan population who has been labelled in this way, however as the biological racism of the past is increasingly rejected, many now consider the most important hierarchical distinction to be rich and poor, not Mayans and ladinos (see also Hale 2006). Many ladinos are stigmatized because of material hardship and darker skin tones, while others are more socially and economically mobile, aided by greater access to monetary means, education or 'whiteness'. The boundary between Mayans and ladinos is somewhat unstable, but remains relevant; poverty rates are still significantly higher among the indigenous population (INE 2002) and social segregation along ethnic lines persists. This contradictory state of affairs is not entirely new, or limited to Guatemala, but builds on a degree of flexibility that has been an aspect of Latin-American 'racial' hierarchies since colonial times (see e.g. Lokken 2001; Martinez-Alier 1989; Twinam 1999).

Consequently, the ladino concession holders whose situation is explored in this chapter is complex; they are not the indigenous 'quintessential other', however, their marginalized social and economic circumstances mean that they are not too distant from it. In global discourses about tropical forest preservation, they are not exotified as indigenous people living in harmony with nature, but are instead cast as destructive elements. Furthermore, their situation exemplifies that although 'participation' is a buzzword in contemporary development efforts, the legacy of local and global hierarchies established during the colonial era often works to limit the roles of intended beneficiaries (see also Green 2003; Willson 2010).

Crisis as Context

The deforestation crisis in Guatemala is unfolding against a background of multifaceted, chronic crisis; it is a 'crisis embedded in crisis' (Nordstrom cited in Vigh 2008: 13). Indeed, the sense of crisis has not yielded in Guatemala, although the 1996 Peace Accords formally ended three decades of internal conflict between the government and the guerrillas of the Guatemalan National Revolutionary Unity (URNG). The country still experiences serious problems related to the workings of democracy, poverty, inequality and hunger, environmental destruction and the proliferation of new forms of violence – many of them related to organized crime (see e.g. Thomas et al. 2011). Consequently, a full implementation of the peace accords has not been possible, and the increase in violent crime has led to higher murder rates in recent years than during the internal conflict (Norad 2011: 38).

In such contexts, crisis is more meaningfully understood as a 'condition of instability' (Vigh 2008: 10), than a rupture or turning point. These circumstances are characterized by somatic, social or existential incoherence, yet do not necessarily lead to passivity. Rather, they frame the possibilities for acting (Vigh 2008: 9–11). Thus, as this volume's introduction clarifies, a state of crisis does not only bring about destruction, but also the potential for new ways of acting upon the world. There is a tendency for the opportunities this represents to be gathered at the hands of global elites (Klein 2007), yet, a crisis can also bring opportunities for marginalized people to improve their situation (see for example, Jensen, Chapter 8, this volume). In Petén, the concession system, which was initiated by the Guatemalan state as a response to the deforestation crisis, presents marginalized forest dwellers with opportunities for economic and social improvement; it provides employment, promotes the sharing of knowledge and enhances social cohesion through joint projects and the inclusion of women as cooperative members. It is also a source of pride and identity for those who embrace the role of 'forest guardians'. In contrast, the deforestation crisis also presents more lucrative opportunities for those who have the resources to invest in upscale tourism infrastructure. The possibility of the latter not only threatens the concession system from without – as it would involve overturning existing legislation – but also from within. A few inhabitants of concession villages have placed their hopes in the more profitable prospect of tourism, and reject the moderate gains conceivable through forest management. The struggle over the opportunities presented by Petén's deforestation crisis is therefore at the centre of the case explored here – and indeed, constitutes a crisis in its own right.

Saving La Selva Maya

The forest of El Petén is often informally referred to as *La Selva Maya* (the Mayan Jungle), evoking the ancient Mayans who used to inhabit the area and the archaeological remains of their settlements. One ancient city, Tikal, has been excavated and reconstructed for decades, and was declared a UNESCO World Heritage Site in 1979. Since then, it has been turned into the most profitable tourist attraction in Guatemala – bringing in approximately 200 million US dollars a year. Many hope that El Mirador can create comparable revenue.

While still only partially excavated, it is already clear that El Mirador contains architectural achievements that are at least as impressive as those of Tikal. The most spectacular example is perhaps *La Danta* (the Tapir), considered one of the world's largest pyramids. Other factors further enhance El Mirador's mystery and allure. It is believed to have been both the earliest and largest of the Mayan city-states; archaeological findings indicate that people settled here as early as the Middle Preclassical period (1000–350 BC), and that at its height, El Mirador had between 100,000 and 200,000 inhabitants. For reasons not yet fully established, the Mayan cities went into decline and were eventually abandoned around 700–800 AD (Global Heritage Fund 2009; Mirador Basin Project 2010; Bremer and Murray 2009). The contemporary fascination with this history has been fuelled by Mel Gibson's 2006 film *Apocalypto*[8] and the alleged Mayan prophecy that the world (as we know it) would end in December 2012. Many have been drawn to the scene, hoping to be part of the developments in tourism this interest may generate.

As outlined above, Petén's forest, its wildlife and the Mayan ruins have long been under threat. One of the efforts intended to address this situation, was the establishment of the Mayan Biosphere Reserve in 1990,[9] and the subsequent granting of concessions to forest communities. The biosphere model involves three levels of protection: core zones, multiple-use zones and buffer zones. In buffer zones, the protection regime is relatively liberal, and several agricultural practices are permitted. In multiple-use zones, concessions can be awarded. Concession holders may engage in sustainable extraction of forest resources in exchange for control and vigilance of their area, and the process is monitored by the National Council for Protected Areas of Guatemala (CONAP).[10] Marriage to a concession holder is the only legal way for newcomers to settle in these communities, and the land here is publicly owned; it cannot be legally bought or sold. Core zones are national parks, where research and low-impact tourism are the only legal activities.

---

8 Dr Richard Hansen, the archaeologist leading the Mirador excavation project, was a technical advisor for Mel Gibson during the production of *Apocalypto*. Furthermore, Mel Gibson has served on the board of Hansen's Foundation for Anthropological Research and Environmental Studies (Archaeological Institute of America 2007).

9 See Perera (1993: 217–68) for some of the complications involved in this undertaking.

10 Consejo Nacional de Áreas Protegidas de Guatemala.

El Mirador is located in the Mirador-Río Azul National Park, and concession areas do not stretch into this part of the forest.

Deforestation has slowed in concession areas, while it has continued exponentially in other parts of the reserve. In addition, concession communities have also achieved some degree of economic development through the sale of forest produce (see e.g. Cronkleton et al. 2008: 10). Representatives of CONAP, as well as representatives of local environmental organizations, agree with this assessment. In conversations and interviews, they often pointed out that: 'the concession model is not perfect, but it is the best we have come up with so far'. Notwithstanding this evaluation, the Mirador Basin Project and their supporters argue that tourism is better suited to halt deforestation and create economic growth than the current conservation regime (GHF Public Relations 2008). The current conservation model constitutes an obstacle for this vision as it gives concession holders exclusive access to the areas they control. It also limits the possibilities for establishing hotels, restaurants and other forms of tourism-related infrastructure. Although the rhetoric used to promote tourism does not focus on these points, concession holders understand them to be the reason why their activities have been consistently attacked as unsustainable.

The idea of overturning the existing conservation regime was first introduced in 2002, in a proposal put forward by the Mirador Basin Project and their donors. The story circulating in Petén is that President Alfonso Portillo (2000–2004)[11] was flown to the excavation site by helicopter, and was impressed by what he saw. So much so, that upon his return to the capital city he promptly issued a presidential decree (*Acuerdo Gobernativo 129-2002*) overturning the existing legislation in favour of the tourism proposal. Concession communities feared for their livelihoods, and with the help of their umbrella organization ACOFOP (the Association of Forest Communities of Petén)[12] they challenged the validity of the decree. A long, conflict-ridden and difficult process followed. The Constitutional Court rejected the decree as unconstitutional in 2004, and it was finally revoked by President Oscar Berger in 2005.

A roundtable discussion forum called *La Mesa Multisectorial* was established at the end of 2006, assisted by a seed grant from the Wildlife Conservation Society (Wildlife Conservation Society 2009). WCS also formed the secretariat of the forum together with the local environmental NGO *Asociación Balam*. The purpose of *La Mesa*, as participants called it, was to turn the conflict into collaboration. Thus, represented in La Mesa were the archaeological project and

11 Since leaving office in 2004, Portillo has been on the run from and later standing trial for embezzlement charges in Guatemala. He was absolved of these charges in 2010, but the prosecution have announced their intention to appeal the verdict. Since he was acquitted, however, Portillo has been imprisoned in an US military base, waiting to stand trial in the US where he is accused of money laundering (CNN México 2011b; CNN México 2011a).

12 Asociación de Comunidades Forestales de Petén.

their donors (including members of some of Guatemala's most elite families as well as foreigners), various civil society organizations, the presidency, state bodies on cultural and natural heritage, protected areas, tourism and the environment, in addition to concession holding forest communities. The forum was to meet once a month for discussion and decision-making by consensus, and in theory, all participants had an equal say in the settling of any point. In practice, however, the representatives of different sectors had unequal access to contacts and networks within and outside the forum, their experience with political work varied, as did the degree to which they were comfortable voicing their opinions in this forum. Because of this, the cooperation was marked by suspicion between the different groups and difficulty in overcoming hierarchical boundaries.

Meetings were held more or less according to plan during my fieldwork in 2007 and 2008,[13] but decision-making was complicated as there was little trust between the participants. When I first met Javier, a representative of the Carmelita concession community,[14] he summed up the situation in the following way: 'People here are perpetually deceived' (*Aquí la gente vive engañada*). By this he did not only refer to the present situation, but also to a host of other 'developers' – international NGOs as well as Guatemalan government representatives – who had at some point or other came to his community and made promises, but had not delivered them. His hopes for a favourable outcome of the Mirador process were low.

A point of contention was that the ideas presented in the Presidential Decree of 2002 had yet to be abandoned by the Mirador Basin Project and their supporters who argued that logging, the most important economic activity undertaken in the concession system, cannot be sustainable, and so must be abandoned altogether in the zone they have termed the 'Mirador Basin'. The proposed Mirador Basin is considerably larger than today's Mirador-Río Azul National Park, and would absorb large parts of the concession areas. As stressed in this chapter's introduction, the very use of the name 'Mirador Basin' is considered a deliberate attempt to undermine the concession model, and according to an NGO representative I interviewed, carries a loud and clear message in favour of overturning the existing legislation.

---

13 I have not been able to follow the developments of La Mesa since 2008, yet ACOFOP's recent social media activity indicates that the forum may still be in function. As it is unclear how or if La Mesa operates at the time or writing, however, I use the past tense here to emphasize that the description refers to the fieldwork period.

14 Carmelita is one of the communities most affected by and involved in the Mirador process – they stood to lose as much as 60 per cent of their concession area according to the Presidential Decree of 2002.

Edenic Narratives and the Obscuring of Forest People

The position of concession holders as lower-class forest labourers, most of them ladinos, marginalizes them socially and politically. The ways concession holders make a living in Petén's tropical forests also clash with Western, Edenic narratives about such places. As one civil society representative emphasized in a meeting with concession holders in Carmelita; 'we all know that the idea of a harmonious relationship between humans and nature is *una paja* (bullshit)'. Carmelita was originally established about a century ago by *chicleros*; extractors of the *chicozapote* tree resin, which was traditionally used to produce chewing gum, or *chicle*, in Spanish. Local nature conceptions have thus developed along with *la chiclería* and other extractive activities, and their interaction with the natural surroundings is not imbued with spiritual meaning as it is for Mayan peasants (see e.g. Green 1999), or notions about transforming the landscape according to their vision. Whereas they enjoy being in the forest and take great pride in their ability to survive in it, the concession holders' approach is ultimately more practical – the forest must be sustained because it constitutes their livelihood.

By comparison, Richard Hansen, the archaeologist leading the Mirador excavations, relates a fascinating theory – that the historical collapse of Mayan lowland city states was caused by deforestation (see e.g. Davis 2005; Syz 2006). His descriptions of the forest's history follow the Edenic structure of a state of initial harmony followed by loss and the need for human labour to restore the original paradisiacal state (Slater 1996). Hansen explains how the original forests of Petén were destroyed by the ancient Mayans mainly due to 'a speedily growing population and an excessive, competitive opulence between rival cities' (Syz 2006). How the forest later regenerated as these cities were abandoned, is not elaborated upon, the point being, the forest is once again threatened by its inhabitants. According to Hansen there is an urgent need for the international community to intervene and halt the concession activities:

> If the Mirador Basin doesn't get Unesco heritage protection and logging is allowed to continue, the forest will disappear in front of our eyes and the precious ruins within it will be destroyed. (Syz 2006)

According to *The Guardian* reporter Francesca Syz quoted above, the film *Apocalypto* (2006) also intends to convey this message. The director Mel Gibson's friendship with Hansen and his involvement in the Mirador Basin Project are cited in support of this reading of the film. Syz interprets *Apocalypto* in light of its opening quote; 'A great civilisation is not conquered from without until it destroys itself from within.' She concludes that

> [The film] attempts to draw parallels between the collapse of the ancient Mayan world with the chaos of the present day – to warn the world of impending

> ecological and moral disaster while entertaining us with violent, high-octane action. (Syz 2006)

Apocalypto has been interpreted as racist by scholars of the ancient Mayans, contemporary Mayan activists, as well as Guatemalan officials (see e.g. *The Guardian* 2007; Arden 2006). Traci Arden, for example, argues that the arrival of Christian missionaries at the film's conclusion carries a 'blatantly colonial message that the Maya needed saving because they were rotten at the core' (2006). She further notes that the success of Jared Diamond's best-selling book *Collapse* made it 'fashionable to use the so-called Maya collapse as a metaphor for Western society's environmental and political excesses' (2006). While Arden dismisses the usefulness of this metaphor, the public communication supporting the Mirador Basin Project illustrates how seamlessly it can change from messages about 'Western' urban opulence to labelling impoverished forest dwellers in the Global South destructive – and simultaneously promote continued 'Western' consumption through tourism. The racism of this metaphor thus reinforces the potential for neo-colonial intervention already embedded in Edenic narratives.

In other public statements by spokespeople for the Mirador Basin Project, the concession holders are consistently vilified and presented as people without hope of any dignified future in the absence of outside intervention. For example, Global Heritage Fund, a California-based foundation contributing considerable resources to the Mirador Basin Project, claimed in a 2008 press release that the primary economic activities of local populations were looting, poaching, trafficking and logging. To repair this situation, they stated, 'we are working to enable local communities to be the stewards for Mirador's long-term protection'. The press release also declares that 'Two of the most important prerequisites for successful long-term protection are community *involvement* and private-sector *leadership*' (GHF Public Relations 2008, emphasis added). Finally, in a 2010 interview Hansen emphasized that 'receiving the benefits of tourism' would be key to ensuring the inhabitants of local communities are 'involved and interested in the conservation of these resources that generate their well-being' (*Revista de la Red de Expertos Iberoamericanos en Turismo* 2010).[15]

In these statements, multiple contradictory ideas meet. On the one hand, we find the Edenic notion of humans as alien to nature – the forest dwellers are portrayed as naturally destructive. They are also presented as economically and morally impoverished criminals, in need of outside assistance. On the other hand, however, these claims are based on the idea that locals have the capacity to be masters over nature, once this potential has been released by submission to private sector leadership and the economic benefits of tourism. Thus, we find here the contradictory ideas about the role of humans in Edenic narratives, together

15 Original in Spanish: ... para que las comunidades próximas reciban el beneficio del turismo ... y que en consecuencia se vean involucrados e interesados en conservar esos recursos que les generan bienestar.

with the discursive residue of 'racializing' colonial hierarchies, the stigma of poverty, and the popular contemporary hope that environmental destruction can be counteracted by consumption, thus not compromising economic growth nor undermining private sector interests. This entanglement licences the thought that 'Westerners' can consume their way out of the environmental crisis, while simultaneously critiquing the efforts of economically marginalized people in the Global South to create development for themselves (see also Ranta-Tyrkkö, Chapter 6, this volume).

However, it remains unstated that through the concession system, these communities are already stewards of Petén's forest and the archaeological treasures it contains. They are also both involved and interested in their own development process, which hinges on the sustainable management of the forest. By not ceding this stewardship any recognition in their public statements, those speaking for the Mirador Basin Project appear to understand the potential contributions of forest dwellers as limited to a role of 'client' or 'beneficiary' of outside aid.

Contested Development

The Guatemalan elites have traditionally not taken much interest in improving the life conditions of the impoverished majority, but have instead exploited them as cheap labour (see e.g. Casaús Arzú 2007; Castellanos Cambranes 1985). Further, the stigma and racist exclusion associated with poverty continue to reproduce social barriers between the economically marginal and the wealthy. Thus, it is difficult for concession holders to trust that they will genuinely be included as equal partners in the tourism project. They find it worrying that the promoters of tourism favour a conservation model that renders their skills irrelevant, and imagine that their intended role is that of unskilled, minimum wage service workers. The lack of clarity as to how profits will be distributed reinforces such concerns. As a result, the whole process is permeated by ambiguities and mutual mistrust. A few months after La Mesa had been founded, one of the facilitators told me they expected to spend the first year establishing trust between the participants, before any decisions could be made. During this year, however, people from all sectors complained that an absence of trust made it impossible to drive the process forward; '*el proceso no anda*' ('the process goes nowhere'), they would say.

From my initial encounter with representatives of concession-holding communities and their umbrella organization ACOFOP, they made it clear that their overall perspective on the Mirador process was one of conflict. At first, a couple of people tried to place me in the role of someone who could 'represent their view', yet most of them quickly embraced my intention to try to understand the perspectives of everyone involved. They considered their disadvantage to be so excruciatingly obvious that any neutral outside observer would recognize it. This disadvantage was understood as exclusion from powerful networks and insufficient knowledge on a few crucial subjects; tourism, public relations and political work in a middle-class and elite context.

For example, the staff of ACOFOP considered it their greatest weakness in this regard that they do not know anything about tourism. Their main assignment was to assist the community organizations in forestry related production processes. Therefore, an external consultant was asked to carry out an analysis of the concession areas, and concluded that several of the villages had great potential for developing eco-tourism projects. 'The problem now is that we have this document [the report], but we have no idea how to approach it, we don't even know what a tourism product might be', one of them explained. ACOFOP staff therefore aspired to have someone help them formulate a good proposal for a tourism project – one that would actually benefit the concession holders. They also struggled to make their version of events available to a wider audience; unlike the archaeological project and their donors, they did not have easy access to local and international news media, a command of the English language, an impressive amount of economic and public relations resources or the support of some of the most powerful people in Guatemala.

ACOFOP staff emphasized that the political activism they had engaged in because of the Mirador process had in many ways strengthened their organization and enhanced their profile. Nevertheless, the experience of disadvantage was frequently emphasized. It constituted one of the most prominent and stable aspects of the Mirador process throughout the fieldwork, even though at times it was relieved by moments of optimism in which concession holders or ACOFOP staff declared that they were more inclined to view tourism as an opportunity than as a threat. However, the threat-or-opportunity discussions continued throughout my fieldwork. Although their participation in La Mesa gave them '*voz y voto*' (voice and vote), this was not sufficient to remove the experience of living in a perpetual state of deception. Because of this, the idea that it would perhaps be better to withdraw from La Mesa altogether, as their participation might be used to legitimate unfavourable decisions, regularly surfaced.[16]

At the end of 2010, the perception of this process as an on-going crisis deepened (*Comunicación y Relaciones Públicas ACOFOP* 2010). The trigger was the presentation of two legislation initiatives to Congress by Manuel Baldizón, a member of parliament representing Petén. One of these initiatives intended to establish a new protected area in the so-called 'Mirador Basin'. The other one aimed to prepare for the investment in large tourism enterprises through tax exemption. In September 2012, the online newspaper *Plaza Pública* published a critical article about the Mirador process (Escalón 2012). It argued that these legislation initiatives replicate point by point the Presidential Decree of 2002. If they are passed by Congress, the concession contracts will be cancelled, the Mayan Biosphere Reserve reconfigured, and a new protected area named

16 Unfortunately, it has not been possible to establish how this experience of disadvantage has developed since the end of fieldwork in 2008.

'the Mirador Basin' established. Ironically, this will constitute a downscaling of protection in the areas immediately surrounding El Mirador, as the existing protection regime hinders the construction of hotel infrastructure or new routes of access. The Guatemalan Institute for Anthropology and History, IDAEH,[17] which is responsible for managing the country's cultural heritage (and represented in La Mesa), therefore argues that it is absurd to present this legislation initiative as a conservation law, when in reality it promotes tourism in the area.

Conclusion

This case illustrates that the discourse of environmental crisis is a malleable tool that can be used for various purposes. In the *Plaza Pública* article, environmental researchers working in Petén accuse the leader of the archaeological project of consistently exaggerating the problems of deforestation in the areas surrounding El Mirador in order to promote tourism. The ease with which the Edenic narratives and the Maya collapse metaphor gains ground with the international public, demands attention. It still appears 'unthinkable' to many 'Westerners' that tropical forest dwellers may have the capacity to address environmental crises unfolding in in their surroundings. Rather, they are often portrayed as impoverished in numerous ways; in opportunities, voice, capacity and agency, to mention a few. The local view, however, is different; every single person I asked, both in Petén and Guatemala City, explained that the concession model was something intrinsic to Guatemala. Concession holders frequently expressed pride in their role as protectors of Petén's forests and developers of their own communities. Some rejected altogether the idea that they were poor or needy. During my fieldwork, ACFOP received delegations from other Latin American countries who had come to learn from them, and bodies of considerable authority have extended formal recognition of their work. This includes the United Nations Development Programme (UNDP), the US Agency for International Development (USAID), the Guatemalan Government, the Rainforest Alliance and National Geographic (ACOFOP 2010). Despite this acknowledgement, however, the concession holders contesting the Mirador Basin Project have found that their work consists of complicated political manoeuvring on various levels within Guatemala, as well as public relations work directed towards an international public. Their international recognition does not speak quite as loudly as the media stories of impending collapse and high-profit solutions.

This case illustrates the struggle over the opportunities that such a state of 'crisis embedded in crisis' (Nordstrom cited in Vigh 2008: 13) represents. The concession model explicitly upsets local and global hierarchies, thus challenging the entitlement of foreigners and Euro-Guatemalan elites to promote their interests unhindered in this region. It is perhaps because of this that the concession holders'

17 Instituto de Antropología e História de Guatemala.

perspectives are so readily overlooked in international media representations; critical questions about the environmental benefits of tourism-based conservation, or about whether a 'Western' project's presentation of itself as benevolent can be taken at face value, are few and far between.

In the Nordic countries, such ideas about 'Western' benevolence may be based on the blindness that dominates the understanding of Nordic involvement in colonial endeavours and the residue of such activities in the use of language and imagery (Loftsdóttir and Jensen 2012b, see also Hübinette, Chapter 4, this volume; Keskinen et al. 2009; Gullestad 2004; Gullestad 2005). Thus, while critical researchers have long argued that Norway's involvement in development aid and peace negotiations is primarily motivated by the advancement of national interests, this type of intervention has overwhelmingly been understood as altruistically motivated by the Norwegian public (Waage 2008; Tvedt 1995). It appears that development aid is firmly encompassed by what Jill M. Loga has called 'the goodness discourse', characterized by an invitation to 'care' and to display goodness by 'acting' (2003: 65–7). However, the goodness discourse also provides the speaker with the power to define the problem and characterize other speakers. It is not easy to argue against someone claiming to do good, without being cast as uninterested in goodness. In addition, not all attempts at doing good produce favourable outcomes. The authority to define what is good, or how to solve a crisis comes with considerable responsibility. Norwegian politicians' recent claims that 'realism' rather than pure altruism should form the basis for development aid (see e.g. Støre 2011) and the accentuation of 'results' rather than intentions in their rainforest policy, may represent opportunities for critical discussion of this difficulty. However, as the Mirador case illustrates, the goodness discourse sits well with contemporary concerns about economic growth, environmental destruction and human difference, thus producing powerful messages about the need to intervene in ways that those at the receiving end may not necessarily find beneficial. Indeed, such interventions may be experienced as a crisis in its own right by intended recipients. Those aiming to alleviate crises, as they unfold in distant locations, would therefore be wise to look for the blind zones, be open to unthinkable solutions, and to scrutinize dominant narratives critically.

Works Cited

ACOFOP (2010) 'Reconocimientos'. Available at: http://www.acofop.org/reconocimientos.html.

Archaeological Institute of America (2007) 'Conversations: Mel Gibson's Maya'. *Archaeology* 60 (1).

Arden, Traci (2006) 'Is "Apocalypto" Pornography?', *Archaeology*, 5 December. Available at: http://archive.archaeology.org/online/reviews/apocalypto.html.

Bakken, Laila Ø. (2011) 'Regnskogmillioner står ubrukt', NRK. Available at: http://www.nrk.no/nyheter/verden/1.7572017.

Brazil, Ben (2007) 'Atop the World of the Maya'. *Los Angeles Times*. Available at: http://articles.latimes.com/2007/jan/07/travel/tr-mirador7.

Bremer, Catherine and Kieran Murray (2009) 'Guatemalan Mayan City El Mirador May Have Ended in Pyramid Battle'. *Maya and Aztec. Ancient Mesoamerican Civilizations*. Available at: http://www.maya-aztec.com/2010/06/22/guatemala-mayan-city-el-mirador-may-have-ended-in-pyramid-battle/.

Broch-Due, Vigdis (1995) *Poverty Paradoxes: The Economy of Engendered Needs*. Occasional Papers, The Nordic Africa Insitute Uppsala: Nordiska Afrikainstiuttet.

Brown, Chip (2011) 'El Mirador, the Lost City of the Maya'. *Smithsonian Magazine*. Available at: http://www.smithsonianmag.com/history-archaeology/El-Mirador-the-Lost-City-of-the-Maya.html – ixzz1LE6T1LZf.

Brown, Marvin (2010) 'Free enterprise and the economics of slavery'. *Real-world Economics Review* 52, 28–39.

Casaús Arzú, M.E. (2007) *Guatemala: Linaje y Racismo*. Ciudad de Guatemala: F. and G. Editores.

Castellanos Cambranes, J. (1985) *Cafe y Campesinos. Los orígenes de la economía de plantación moderna en Guatemala, 1853–1897*. Guatemala: Editorial Universitaria. Universidad de San Carlos.

CNN México (2011a) 'Alfonso Portillo, el Primer Expresidente de Guatemala Juzgado en EU'. Available at: http://mexico.cnn.com/mundo/2011/11/17/alfonso-portillo-el-primer-expresidente-de-guatemala-juzgado-en-eu.

— (2011b) 'La Justicia de Guatemala Absuelve al Expresidente Alfonso Portillo'. Available at: http://mexico.cnn.com/mundo/2011/05/10/la-justicia-de-guatemala-absuelve-al-ex-presidente-alfonso-portillo.

Comunicación y Relaciones Publicas ACOFOP (2010) 'Proyecto Cuenca Mirador..¿Beneficio para las Concesiones Comunitarias?'. Available at: https://www.facebook.com/notes/asoc-de-comunidades-forestales-de-peten/proyecto-cuenca-miradorbeneficio-para-las-concesiones-comunitarias/136459049738707.

Cronkleton, Peter, Peter Leigh Taylor, Deborah Barry, Samantha Stone-Jovicich and Marianne Schmink (2008) *Environmental Governance and the Emergence of Forest-Based Social Movements*. CIFOR Occasional Paper No. 49. Bogor, Indonesia: Centre for International Forestry Research.

Davis, Bob (2005) 'In Guatemala, A Battle Over Logs And a Lost Kingdom'. *The Wall Street Journal*. Available at: http://www.miradorbasin.com/resources/misc/printmedia.php.

Escalón, Sebastián (2012) 'El Mirador: El Incierto Futuro de unas Ruinas'. *Plaza Pública*. Available at: http://www.plazapublica.com.gt/content/el-mirador-el-incierto-futuro-de-unas-ruinas.

GHF Public Relations (2008) 'Global Heritage Fund Announces Continued Sponsorship From Leading Private Companies For The Preservation Of The Cultural and Natural Heritage Of Mirador Basin'. Available at: http://globalheritagefund.org/in_the_news/press_releases/ghf_announces_continued_sponsorship_of_mirador_basin.

Global Heritage Fund (2009) 'Mirador, Guatemala. Cradle of Mayan Civilization'. Available at: http://globalheritagefund.org/what_we_do/overview/current_projects/mirador_guatemala.

Green, Linda (1999) *Fear as a Way of Life*. New York: Columbia University Press.

Green, Maia (2003) 'Globalizing Development in Tanzania. Policy Franchising through Participatory Project Management'. *Critique of Anthropology* 23 (2), 123–43.

Gullestad, Marianne (2004) 'Blind Slaves of our Prejudices: Debating "Culture" and "Race" in Norway'. *Ethnos* 69 (2), 177–203.

— (2005) 'Normalising Racial Boundaries: the Norwegian Dispute about the Term Neger', *Social Anthropology* 13 (1), 27–46.

Hale, Charles R. (2006) *Más Que un Indio (More Than an Indian). Racial Ambivalence and Neoliberal Multiculturalism in Guatemala*. School of American Research Resident Scholar Book Santa Fe, New Mexico: School of American Research Press.

Haney, Lynne (2000) 'Global Discourses of Need: Mythologizing and Pathologizing Welfare in Hungary', in Burawoy, Michael, Joseph A. Blum, Sheba George, Millie Thayer, Zsuzsa Gille, Teresa Gowan, Lynne Haney, Maren Klawiter, Steve H. Lopez and Sean Riain (eds) *Global Ethnography: Forces, Connections, and Imaginations in a Postmodern World*. Berkeley, Los Angeles and London: University of California Press, 48–73.

Hay-Edie, Terence and Halverson, Elspeth (2006) *Acciones Comunitarias para la Conservación de la Biodiversidad. Creación de Vínculos entre la Conservación del a Biodiversidad y el Desarrollo de Mejores Medios de Sustento*. New York: Grupo de Ambiente y Energía del PNUD.

Hurtado Paz y Paz, Margarita (2007) *Sólo para medio vivir. La importancia actual de las actividades extractivas de recursos forestales no maderables en los hogares de Carmelita y Uaxactún*, Petén. Guatemala: FLACSO Guatemala/Editorial de Ciencias Sociales.

INE (2002) *Características de la Población y de los Locales de Habitación Censados*. Instituto Nacional de Estadística, República de Guatemala. Censos Nacionales XI de Población y VI de Habitación.

Jaramillo, V. and Guerra, H. (2008a) 'Descubridor de Tesoros'. *Estrategia & Negocios* 106, October, 48.

— and — (2008b) 'Por Una Nueva Visión', *Estrategia & Negocios* 106, October, 40–46.

— and — (2008c) 'Rescatando el Patrimonio Maya', *Estrategia & Negocios*, 106, October, 34–9.

Kalland, Arne (2003) 'Anthropology and the Concept "Sustainability": Some Reflections', in Roepstorff, Andreas, Nils Bubandt and Kalevi Kull (eds) *Imagining Nature: Practices of Cosmology and Identity*. Aarhus: Aarhus University Press, 161–77.

Keskinen, Suvi, Diana Mulinari, Sari Irni and Salla Tuori (eds) (2009) *Complying with Colonialism: Gender, Race and Ethnicity in the Nordic Region*. Farnham and Burlington: Ashgate.

Klein, Naomi (2007) *The Shock Doctrine: the Rise of Disaster capitalism*. London and New York: Penguin.

Loftsdóttir, Kristín and Lars Jensen (2012a) 'Introduction: Nordic Exceptionalism and the Nordic "Others"', in Loftsdóttir, Kristín and Lars Jensen (eds) *Whiteness and Postcolonialism in the Nordic Region: Exceptionalism, Migrant Others and National Identities*. Farnham and Burlington: Ashgate, 1–11.

— and — (2012b) *Whiteness and Postcolonialism in the Nordic Region: Exceptionalism, Mirgrant Others and National Identities*. Farnham: Ashgate.

Loga, Jill Merethe (2003) 'Godhetsdiskursen', in Berge, Kjell Lars, Siri Meyer and Tom Are Trippestad (eds) *Maktens Tekster*. Oslo: Gyldendal Akademisk, 62–81.

Lokken, Paul (2001) 'Marriage as Slave Emancipation in Seventeenth-Century Rural Guatemala', *The Americas* 58 (2), 175–200.

Martinez-Alier, Verena (1989) *Marriage, Class and Colour in Nineteenth-Century Cuba. A Study of Racial Attitudes and Sexual Values in a Slave Society*. Ann Arbor: The University of Michigan Press.

Milton, Cynthia E. (2007) *The Many Meanings of Poverty. Colonialism, Social Compacts, and Assistance in Eighteenth-Century Ecuador*. Stanford: Stanford Universty Press.

Mirador Basin Project (2010) 'The Mirador Basin Project'. Available at: http://www.miradorbasin.com/about.php.

Nelson, Diane M. (1999) *A Finger in the Wound. Body Politics in Quincentennial Guatemala*. Berkeley, Los Angeles: University of California Press.

Nerdal, Roar (2010) 'Regnskog-milliarder åpner oljedører'. *Dagens Næringsliv*. Available at: http://www.dn.no/energi/article1975276.ece.

Norad (2011) *Norads Resultatrapport del 1: Bistand og Konflikt*. Oslo: Norad.

O'Connor, Alice (2002) *Poverty Knowledge: Social Science, Social Polity, and the Poor in Twentieth-Century U.S. History*. Princeton: Princeton University Press.

PACUNAM (2010) '¿Quiénes Somos?'. Fundación Patrimonio Cultural y Natural Maya. Available at: http://www.pacunam.org/index/quienes_somos.

Perera, Victor (1993) *Unfinished Conquest. The Guatemalan Tragedy*. Berkeley, Los Angeles: University of California Press.

Revista de la Red de Expertos Iberoamericanos en Turismo (2010) 'Entrevista. Dr. Richard Hansen. Especialista en la Cultura Maya Temprana, Director del Proyecto de Investigación Científica Cuenca El Mirador, ubicado en El Petén, Guatemala, Centroamérica', 5–9. Available at: http://globalheritagefund.org/in_the_news/mirador/interview_with_dr_richard_hansen.

Sawyer, Suzana (2003) 'Subterranean Techniques. Corporate Environmentalism, Oil Operations, and Social Injustice in the Ecuadorian Rain Forest', in Slater, Candace (ed.) *In Search of the Rain Forest*. Durham and London: Duke University Press, 69–100.

Schirmer, Jennifer (1998) *The Guatemalan Military Project: A Violence Called Democracy*. Philadelphia: University of Pennsylvania Press.

Schmidt, Blake (2010) 'Ranchers and Drug Barons Threaten Rain Forest'. *New York Times*. Available at: http://www.nytimes.com/2010/07/18/world/americas/18guatemala.html?_r=2&th&emc=th.

Slater, Candace (1996) 'Amazonia as Edenic Narrative', in Cronon, William (ed.) *Uncommon Ground. Rethinking the Human Place in Nature*. New York: W.W. Norton & Company, 114–31.

Smith, Carol A. (1990) 'Origins of the National Question in Guatemala: A Hypothesis', in Smith, Carol A. (ed.) *Guatemalan Indians and the State: 1540–1988*. Austin: University of Texas, 72–95.

Stepan, Nancy Leys (2001) *Picturing Tropical Nature*. London: Reaktion Books.

Stoian, Dietmar and Aldo Rodas (2006) 'Community Forest Enterprise in Guatemala: A Case Study of Cooperativa Carmelita R.L.'. *CATIE-CeCoEco*, 1–21. Available at: http://orton.catie.ac.cr/repdoc/A2439i/A2439i.pdf.

Støre, Jonas Gahr (2011) 'Godhet og Realisme', Dagbladet. Available at: http://www.regjeringen.no/nb/dep/ud/aktuelt/taler_artikler/jgs_taler_artikler/2011/godhet_realisme.html?id=642441.

Syz, Francesca (2006) 'The Mystery of Maya's Jungle Heart' *The Guardian*, 31 December. Available at: http://www.guardian.co.uk/travel/2006/dec/31/guatemala.honduras.culturaltrips.

Taylor, Peter Leigh (2009) 'Conservation, Community, and Culture? New Organizational Challenges of Community Forest Concessions in the Maya Biosphere Reserve of Guatemala'. *Journal of Rural Studies*, doi:10.1016/j.jrurstud.2009.09.006.

— and Antony Cheng (2009) 'Reflexive Resource Governance as Embedded Process: A Comparison of Two North American and Central American Community-Based Forestry Organizations'. Conference on the Human Dimensions of Global Environmental Change, Amsterdam.

—, Peter Cronkleton, Deborah Barry, Samantha Stone-Jovicich and Marianne Schmink (2008) *'If You Saw it With My Eyes': Collaborative Research and Assistance with Central American Forest Steward Communities*. Bogor, Indonesia: Center for International Forestry Research.

The Guardian (2007) '"Racist" Apocalypto Accused of Denigrating Mayan Culture', 10 January. Available at: http://www.theguardian.com/film/2007/jan/10/news.melgibson.

Thomas, Kedron, Kevin Lewis O'Neill and Thomas Offit (2011) 'An Introduction', in Thomas, Kedron and Kevin Lewis O'Neill (eds) *Securing the City: Neoliberalism, Space and Insecurity in Postwar Guatemala*. Durham and London: Duke University Press, 1–21.

Trouillot, Michel-Rolph (1995) *Silencing the Past. Power and the Production of History*. Boston: Beacon Press.

Tsing, Anna L. (2005) *Friction. An Ethnography of Global Connection*. Princeton and Oxford: Princeton University Press.

Tvedt, Terje (1995) *Den Norske Samaritan: Ritualer, Selvbilder og Utviklingshjelp.* Oslo: Gyldendal Norsk Forlag.

Twinam, Ann (1999) *Public Lives, Private Secrets. Gender, Honor, Sexuality, and Illegitimacy in Colonial Spanish America.* Stanford: Stanford University Press.

Vigh, Henrik (2008) 'Crisis and Chronicity: Anthropological Perspectives on Continuous Conflict and Decline'. *Ethnos* 73 (1), 5–24.

Wildlife Conservation Society (2009) *The Global Conservation Program. Achievements and Lessons Learned from 10 Years of Support for Threats-based Conservation at a Landscape and Seascape Scale. Maya Biosphere Reserve Living Landscape (Guatemala).* Flores, Guatemala: Wildlife Conservation Society.

Willson, Margaret (2010) *Dance Lest We All Fall Down. Breaking Cycles of Poverty in Brazil and Beyond.* Seattle and London: University of Washington Press.

Waage, Hilde Henriksen (2008) 'Postscript to Oslo: the Mystery of Norway's Missing Files', *Journal of Palestine Studies* 38 (1), 54–65.

Ystanes, Margit (2011) *Precarious Trust. Problems of Managing Self and Sociality in Guatemala.* Dissertation submitted for the degree of philosophiae doctor (PhD) at the University of Bergen.

Websites

miradorbasin.com – Website of the Mirador Basin Project
globalheritagefund.org – Website of the Global Heritage Fund

Chapter 8
Crisis as Opportunity – Opportunity as Crisis: Greenlandic Independence and Sustainability

Lars Jensen

Sovereignty is an interesting term. It means different things to different people, and to different countries. ... Inuit have their own definition of sovereignty. ... We have a history that spans thousands of years across the Arctic that others now claim. This question is an old one for Inuit. While we are uncomfortable with the word 'own', I say it is all Inuit who 'own' much of the Arctic, if I must use a non-Inuit word.

Aqqaluk Lynge, former President of the ICC (Inuit Circumpolar Council), Address to the Ministerial Summit of Arctic Oceans, Agenda Item: issues relating to the local inhabitants and indigenous communities, Illulissat, Greenland, 2008. (Powell 2010: 76)

The gateway through which we must pass is now wide open.

Kuupik Kleist, Greenlandic Premier, 21 June 2009, the day Greenland achieved self-government. (Emmerson 2010: 289)

Introduction

Societal crisis is customarily discussed in terms of society's existing order coming under strain. This is particularly true of the three overlapping crises (economy, multiculturalism and environment) discussed in this book. Crisis can in a similar but more abstract vein be read as a permanent condition of modernity (see Tikka and Sumiala, Chapter 1). Permanence, however, is not the same as statis, but reflects that crisis in modernity is a symptom of an unsustainable order, and that this order is incapable of transcending itself. In other words, while crisis signals the possibility of change, it cannot necessarily occur within modernity in its hegemonic form. Within Marxist thought, however, crisis is more than a signal of a challenged order. Here crisis is the sign of the impending inevitable death of an unjust order that paves the way for a new and better balanced one (Bauman 2011). In the case of the three crises listed above it is hard to see that there is much to bemoan in the passing of the order they refer to. If the crisis of multiculturalism refers to an inadequately developed aspiration towards a genuinely inclusive society then why complain about multiculturalism's demise, when it has failed both as an idea and in terms of delivering inclusion as a political reality? If the attempts at responding to what Gilroy (Gilroy 2011) has labelled a planetary environmental crisis caused by the exhaustion of resources and the damage caused by their extraction are at best random, then why complain about the collapse of the neoliberal regime that orchestrates them? Why regret the disappearance of an order that merely allows patchy responses to a full-scale assault on the environment? If the economic crisis is the inevitable result of capitalism's self-destructive drive, then why complain about the demise of an unjust economic order, built on the back of historical and contemporary physical and economic slavery, colonialism and general exploitation?

The provocative observations above are based on the assumption that crisis as an overlapping phenomenon between three central driving mechanisms of late modernity (labour mobility, exploitation of nature and neoliberalism) is the symptom of an impending collapse of an overall order rather than its unfortunate by-product. To label the observations as provocative hinges on their being in radical opposition to prevailing ways of addressing the crises. But what drives predominant ways of responding to the crises? In western societies, or the global north, suggestions to how the crisis – or each of the crises – can be solved, rest solidly on Liberal notions about what drives society, nationally, regionally and globally, which means the responses to the crises are systemic rather than outside. And through the west's historical and contemporary dominance western Liberalism has become global. This means that if, as I claim, Liberalism is part of the problem rather than the solution, the various Liberal-derived responses are not only inadequate, but will in effect prolong and deepen the crisis. My argument is not that Liberalism can come up with only one uniform response to the crisis, rather the problem is that even when Liberalism suggests radical responses to the crises, it puts its faith in the best future society, both in terms of multiculturalism, economy and the environment, in the individual as that has been conceptualized in western epistemological thought since the Enlightenment. The rebuilding of the economic system after each crisis continues on the same premises as those put forward by Adam Smith in *The Wealth of Nations* (1776), which remains the economic Bible of Liberalism. Smith's ideology governs economic thought from financial institutions to the vast majority of professors of economy. The choice is limited to one between Keynes and Friedman, or as Walden Bello (2013) argues in relation to the post-2008 financial collapse, between Keynesianisms and a resurrected extreme right advocating against public spending. Seen through the prism of economic crisis multiculturalism in crisis is the result internally in western societies of the failure of the trickling-down-effect, so central to Liberalism's ethos. Externally, the flows of migrants and refugees from the lesser affluent parts of the world are dramatically stopped at the borders of self-proclaimed Liberal societies brandishing human rights, and human equality. The divisions between the global north and south over environmental concerns have become ritualized in the COP-meetings which have increasingly emerged as futile exercises, even the rhetoric is flagging. In all three crises it is precisely the economic rationalism of Liberalism, coupled with the Enlightenment thought paradigm and its accompanying idea of western supremacy that has produced the three crises in the first place. It is the desire to look for a response to these profound ruptures in global relations outside the confines of Liberalism that motivates my analysis here. The chapter seeks to develop an integral perspective on the three crises, even as it places most emphasis on the crisis of the environment and economy, as a way of looking beyond the individual crisis regime. It focuses on Greenland,[1] which represents an interesting geopolitical border case in the global north, also with respect to the crises.

Greenland is a postcolonial nation still partially ruled from Denmark. Denmark retains control in the areas of defence and foreign policy. Even if it is stipulated that Denmark is required to liaise with Greenland in matters deemed of importance to Greenland, it remains a Danish prerogative to decide when this is the case, since Denmark has sovereignty. Greenland is marginal to the global north, in so far as it still harbours many colonial traits in its administrative system originally installed by Denmark. Hence it can be seen as a piece of global south, incidentally placed in the extreme north. One way to begin to define its position on the margins of the north is to think in terms of degrees of agency. Agency in its most powerful articulation suggests that crisis represents an opportunity for change and in its most circumscribed form points to the dilemma that speaking of the order as hegemonic against which the pressure for change is directed, threatens to make pointless resistance. My purpose is to discuss contemporary Greenland as inhabiting a space between these polarized positions. On the one hand I wish to challenge the idea that Greenland's role can be reduced to one of passive recipient of economic opportunity and environmental disaster. On the other hand, I wish to keep in view the globalizing order and the enormous pressures it brings to bear upon any society including Greenland whose resources for countering these pressures are clearly limited.

Greenland as a semi-autonomous agent navigating in the choppy waters of neoliberal capitalism is like any country capable of opposition, consent and reinterpretation. Even if it also has a volatile economy, dependent on subsidies from Denmark, which uses the subsidies to keep Greenland under Danish sovereignty. The opening of the Arctic sea lanes and the potential of a resource boom can potentially deliver sovereignty to Greenland, but may replace the dependence on Denmark with a new dependence on transnational companies with far bigger resources than Greenland. How can Greenlandic responses to this

1 It is not that multicultural society is non-existing in Greenland, or an uninteresting analytical object. Greenland is split in a number of ways; between urban centres and small settlements, linguistically between speakers of different variations of Greenlandic, and between Greenlandic and Danish. Historically, inter-marriage between Danes, Norwegians, Germans (connected to Danish administrators from present-day northern Germany) and Greenlanders produced a typical colonial form of multiculturalism. Today there are around 6,000 Danes (or 10 per cent of the local population) living in Greenland, while people born outside of Greenland and Denmark number around 650 (http://www.groenlandskehus.dk/media/4134/Det%20gr%C3%B8nlandske%20arbejdsmarked%202011.pdf.).

unfolding scenario of opportunities and threats be understood? In the wide gap between readings suggesting that what is happening in Greenland is potentially disastrous and others focusing on it mainly as economic opportunity, one risks forgetting that it can be both. To read the resource boom in the Arctic solely in terms of a neoliberal onslaught on indigenous communities, fails to consider the point that Arctic peoples, such as Greenlanders, also engage with the world outside the Arctic. Because the outside world has arrived in the Arctic, and continues to arrive, in many different forms; from tourism, over transnational companies to anthropocentric climate change and pollution. Agency is a constructive way of approaching the issue of Greenland's role in the global order, but limited due to agency's conceptual roots in sociological, philosophical and anthropological literature. When speaking of agency in relation to political systems, or the international political order, sovereignty is the key to deliver internationally recognized agency. Yet, sovereignty in its conventional definition in political science and international relations literature and discourse is too narrow for my purposes here, because, as I will discuss later, it is a product of Liberal political philosophy and therefore again framed in a Eurocentric discourse. What is required instead is sovereignty understood far more broadly as a way of conceptualizing the relationship between in this case indigenous peoples and the land, not in the received political philosophical understanding as the relationship between state and territory. It is this necessary rewriting of sovereignty Lynge voices in the opening quotation of the chapter, where he displaces the normativized relationship between ownership and territoriality. Deceptively simple by drawing attention to the foreignness of this concept to an Inuit epistemology, while insisting on the right to reclaim geographical spaces that European colonialism through sovereignty had laid claim to against the interests of Inuit. In Lynge's problematization of the concept it is easy to identify how received understandings of sovereignty are a direct consequence of a colonialism that is not finished at the moment in which Greenland is no longer named or defined within political science discourse as a colony, but has become, for want of better words, a postcolony (Mbembe 2001). Lynge's reading raises a number of related epistemological issues; a) sovereignty is still in the hands of Denmark, even if Greenland is no longer a colony; b) the international political system invented in Europe and exported to the world through colonialism continues to favour the old imperial powers (in this case, Denmark); c) a transition of sovereignty from Denmark to Greenland will only solve the problem of agency in a limited way confined by the international political system – and its accompanying broader system of capitalism. It will not dissolve the relationship between state and territory or dismantle the capitalist system, which continues to produce the relationship between humans and nature in ways that are alien to indigenous peoples and seen as environmentally destructive.

Environment can be seen as a sub-division of sovereignty in so far as sovereignty is a way of governing relations with nature. Environment in crisis in a Greenlandic context initially signals natural disasters as the result of global developments over which Greenland has little control. Some of the more highly profiled elements include melting glaciers and ice cap, pollution from the run-off from large-scale mining, the disappearance of traditional food sources, the accumulated toxins in the food chain as a result of industrial waste flowing with ocean currents and the potential disasters from oil-drilling at sea and the transport of goods through Arctic waterways. Yet, global warming will locally also produce beneficial side effects in Greenland. Rising temperatures may lead to conditions similar to those which enabled agricultural Viking settlements during the warm period 1,000 years ago. Greenland can within limits adjust itself to the effects of climate change locally. What is often missed in debates on climate change is that even if glaciers are melting in Greenland, the potentially disastrous consequences are global rather than local – or rather localized far from the geographical origin of the specific form of climate change. In our reading of climate change and, more broadly, environmental destruction we remain local in our interpretations of its consequences. This attitude is exacerbated by the circulation of climate change 'footage'. When international top politicians visit the Sermeq Kujalleq/Jakobshavn Glacier to watch the breaking off of vast chunks of ice, they are watching a *naturally occurring* phenomenon whose *accelerated speed* is evidence of global warming in action. There is a long way from this Arctic spectacular to the combination of elevated sea levels, flooding, and increasing extremes of the monsoonal season that create havoc in places like Bangladesh and which are linked to the melting Greenlandic ice.

Setting the Stage of Greenlandic Sovereignty in Relation to Denmark

In the summer of 2012, the Danish broadsheet newspaper, *Politiken*, carried a series of interviews with the political leaders of *Rigsfællesskabet*.[2][3] *Rigsfællesskabet* is the official name for the association of Denmark and two of its former colonies/dependencies, Greenland and the Faroe Islands, under Danish sovereignty. Three aspects about the interviews immediately stood out. First, Bo Lidegaard, the chief editor of Denmark's leading national newspaper, *Politiken*, conducted the interviews, which added a touch of journalistic statesmanship to the interviews. Secondly, the interviews, even as they explored possible future directions of

---

2 The interviews were brought under the headlines, 'If I was Danish Prime Minister, I would do my utmost to keep the Faroe Islands and Greenland within the Danish realm' (Bo Lidegaard interview with Greenlandic Premier, *Kuupik Kleist*, 19 August 2012), 'I see three independent countries (Bo Lidegaard Interview with Kaj Leo Johannesen, 12 August 2012), and *Rigsfællesskabet* makes us all a little greater and stronger in the world' (Bo Lidegaard interview with Danish PM Helle Thorning-Schmidt, 26 August 2012).

3 *Rigsfællesskabet* [Literally 'The Society of the Realm'] has been translated in various ways into English. However, it is a unique construction, where the three members participate in upholding sovereignty over the shared realm. I have therefore kept the original Danish name.

Rigsfællesskabet, worked from the clear premise that all three nations needed to give their consent to any future framework for collaboration. Thirdly, the continuation of *Rigsfællesskabet* represented only one possible future scenario. Independence for the Faroe Islands and Greenland was another, while a looser umbrella organization for the three countries represented a third. Hence, in the context of the interviews the Danish majority society, historically the unilateral decision maker, had been reduced to one of three *Rigsfællesskab* partners, dependent on the acceptance of its two 'junior' partners for the conditions underpinning future collaboration. The alternative would be to face up to their unilaterally declared independence. While the possibility of the non-future of *Rigsfællesskabet* is a scenario which would pose demonstrable challenges for the future navigation of an independent Greenland and Faroe Islands, it also holds an emancipatory potential, which is more than mere identity politics. For Denmark, however, the prospect of independence for its North Atlantic dependencies cannot meaningfully be seen as anything but a major blow to its international status. Without the North Atlantic partners and particularly the gateway to the Arctic provided by Danish sovereignty over Greenland, Denmark is just another small European state. If *Rigsfællesskabet* faces a new crisis, it is very much a Danish crisis about how to redefine its role as the Faroe Islands and Greenland insist on a new relationship based on mutual recognition as equal partners.

The interviews focused on speculations regarding the future, and they harboured no illusions that independence was around the corner or an emerging scenario whose details were ready to be discussed. But they also demonstrated that the stumbling block of the Danish constitution, put in place by the Danish government through the constitutional reform of 1953, which annexed Greenland and the Faroe Islands to the Danish realm, no longer works as an automatic doorstopper to either partners' future aspirations for independence.

This is a radical change since Danish politicians historically have routinely referred to the Danish constitution as the sole arbiter of sovereignty. This position has been bolstered by official Danish publications relating to *Rigsfællesskabet* which routinely open by establishing the amount of funds transferred annually to the associate members in the North Atlantic.[4] It is difficult not to see this as an attempt to sustain the implicit Danish claim that the rule over the North Atlantic is an altruistic enterprise, rather than a colonial, or neo-colonial form of dominance ensuring Danish interests in the North Atlantic and Arctic. At the same time it works as a reminder for the junior partners that they are dependent on Denmark. The pervasiveness of the image of benevolent Denmark in Denmark is not limited to official discourse. It is also a popular sentiment among Danes, just as the Danish media traditionally does little to question the assumptions underlying this assertion (Togeby 2002: 139; Bryld 1998; Graugaard 2009: 40–44). Now two

4 See for example *Focus*, March 2012, 41. *Focus* is a magazine published by the Danish Foreign Ministry, which is supposedly both the Foreign Ministry of Denmark and *Rigsfællesskabet*.

far more self-assured North Atlantic members of *Rigsfællesskabet* articulate their position within *Rigsfællesskabet* as one defined by their own choice, not by what is considered historically settled or desirable by the Danish majority partner. Hence they reject the Danish claim that the constitution is the document that unilaterally defines the terms of the partnership. This shift in attitude has been brought on by a number of factors. In Greenland it is the two interlinked factors of resource boom/emerging economic opportunity and climate change which stand out. These two factors have together helped place the Arctic, and hence Greenland, solidly at the centre of the world's attention. Both of them are the result of crisis. The hunt for non-renewable resources is caused by the exhaustion of more easily available resources closer to the power centres. To extract them in the Arctic can potentially do immense damage to the environment (Nowlan 2001: 1). The existing record of mining companies' environmental credentials have been under attack for many years, even in less fragile areas of the world (Evans et al. 2002; see also Ranta-Tyrkkö and Ystanes' chapters). Global warming, of course, constitutes its own environmental predicament. The perceived relocation of Greenland from a remote and forbidding north to the centre of international attention elevates the discussion from the framework of *Rigsfællesskabet* to the question of international sovereignty.

Sovereignty on Thin Ice

Existing political science and international relations literature dealing with sovereignty is limited by its automatic reference to 'statehood' as understood in a conventional Westphalian, and hence geographically and historically specific European context. To deal with sovereignty outside Europe raises a range of issues, which collectively amount to an epistemological crisis. Places with very different – often colonial – histories cannot be addressed as postcolonial 'misfits', but are evidence of the need for a wider political theoretical debate on the inadequacies of the Westphalian-derived concept of sovereignty which the international system continues to be based on.

Some of this work has been done, although certainly not at the centre of political science/international relations discourse. The more critical approach to instrumentalized sovereignty reduced to singular statehood can be divided into two groups. Those that seek to accommodate challenges to what is simultaneously a politically received and conceptual model of sovereignty (i.e. the tenets of the territorial integrity and supremacy of the (nation) state) through a broader or less confined definition of sovereignty. And those that think the model of sovereignty defined as stemming from the Westphalian Peace (1648) has either been made redundant, is based on falsehood or is simply inadequate to such an extent that its basic assumptions have to be altered if it is to be useful beyond the purely instrumental with all that this entails in terms of the reproduction of power relations.

Jessica Shadian's work belongs to the former camp, and is relevant, because she works on sovereignty in relation to the Arctic, not least in her article, 'From State to Polities: Reconceptualizing Sovereignty through Inuit Governance' (2010). Although critical of mainstream international relations literature's tendency to reproduce the discourse of Westphalian discourse her critique is not premised on the dismantling of the Westphalian system. Rather, her argument about a 'post-Westphalian reality' rests solidly on the continued recognition of indivisible state sovereignty. She points out that 'sovereignty as a concept … does not diminish nor does the state disappear' (Shadian 2010: 502). She finds it more productive to think of ways to link sovereignty to a more inclusive form of governance:

> Through the incorporation of new non-state political entities, the traditional political architecture upon which international politics has played out is being remade. Within this structure the boundaries determining who governs and how governance proceeds is in a process of redefinition in which non-state political myths are creatively attaining new ways to attain institutional sovereignty. (Shadian 2010: 502)

In Shadian's analysis the state is not the oppressor but the arbiter that is capable of reformulating its attitude to its execution of sovereignty when it comes under pressure from disenfranchised groups. It would appear out of an interest to accommodate for example indigenous groups, although one could wonder why such an interest has not manifested itself earlier given the calls for self-determination are as old as colonialism itself. Correspondingly, she identifies strategies in indigenous movements not seeking sovereignty (for example statehood) that meet their desires for increased influence on their own situation. Even if statehood is clearly not an option in all cases, the question how the state rules over indigenous communities, and particularly the history of state oppression of indigenous communities which can be identified throughout the Arctic, ought to be a crucial concern. Yet her analysis is silent regarding the question of colonial oppression which in all parts of the Arctic paved the way for an outside dominating influence. Nor is this merely a historical omission since the same states continue to exercise their power, for example, when it comes to control over resource extraction, or territorial surveillance. Here, the state's own interests clearly outrank those of local indigenous communities and this raises quite fundamental questions about the premise of her argument concerning political agency.

In the fundamentally sceptical camp regarding the productiveness of engaging with the existing way of defining sovereignty, we find an article by Andreas Osiander (2010), who dismisses the repeated claim that sovereignty can be dated back to the Westphalian peace of 1648 where national governments (including the Danish and the Swedish) supposedly stood up against the Holy Roman Empire. He concludes that the idea of the sovereign territorial integral state rising against the empire is a reconstruction of nineteenth- and twentieth-century nationalistic historiography, which takes its departure in an emphasis on the territorial integrity of the (nation) state as the explanatory framework (Osiander 2010: 252). This reconstructed model becomes then a manifestation of what Benedict Anderson (1991) would render as the expression of the idealization of the imagined community as a progressive, secular, modern national society pitted against the historically redundant idea of a more pan-European identity. Anderson, like Osiander, stresses this imagined community is a construction. For the model to work, as Anderson also points out, members of the nation must subscribe to it. However, the construction of the imagined community also in the sovereignty literature serves as a way of legitimizing the conceptualization of a political community as a territorial political entity. The nation provides the cultural identitarian justification for the state, which in turn emerges as the only way of organizing a society that will be internationally recognized. Political theory and political reality through this is conflated into one and the same. Consequently, theorizing sovereignty within the established discourse of political science and international relations is unable to accommodate forms of sovereignty beyond the confines of the (nation) state. This conceptual trap is undoubtedly related to anxieties that if we were to abandon the currently accepted international model of sovereignty recognition anarchy would follow. While this may be a legitimate concern, this implicit understanding raises at least two quite fundamental questions, which are particularly pertinent to indigenous communities. First, why should indigenes (but also other groups), who have no historical relationship with the construction of Westphalian sovereignty, let alone a say, be subjected to it or subscribe to its conventions? In particular since sovereignty, as colonialism has demonstrated again and again, in this form has been used in active service of their repression? Secondly, and this is more of an epistemological objection, why can there be only one system of recognizing sovereignty, when clearly that definition is deeply flawed, because it depends on the instrumental approach that bears out the international system of mutually recognized states at the cost of other ways of understanding sovereignty, which are clearly more fair to specific communities? The state's exercise of sovereignty can in no way be said to have been a guarantor of fundamental societal issues such as environmental, economic or societal sustainability, not at 'home' nor in its administration of 'remote' indigenous areas. State bureaucracy works against dealing with interconnected and overlapping crises, because it is geared towards working for specific solutions to specific delimitated problems. Sovereignty can be read as an extension of a bureaucratic state order, and as the combined order of states based on mutual recognition. Here, Greenland's position can either be seen as one that fails to meet the criteria required for sovereignty, or, as a nation that has not yet emerged as a state. It is these conditions underpinning this emergence made possible by climate change and the scramble for the Arctic that I now turn to explore.

Greenlandic Futures

Climate change and the global, neoliberal driven search for ever more remote resources have conjointly brought Greenland global attention on an unprecedented scale. Greenland's emergent hub status on the climate change scene and resource front was captured by a world map which adorned the Danish-Greenlandic pavilion for the 2012 Venice Biennale, *Possible Greenland.* The map shows Greenland at the centre of the world and all the continents sprawling along a single axis away from an Arctic middle.[5] In this cartographic representation all continents are orientated towards the Arctic. The imagined naval highway was also a theme captured in Greenlandic Professor of Geology and curator of the Danish-Greenlandic Pavilion, Minik Rosing's opening speech, in which he stated 'The Arctic Ocean will become the new Mediterranean Sea, when the Northwest Passage is opened up. Greenland will be in the middle of the world.'[6] Rosing probably had not thought that his depiction echoed age-old European imperial desires, not least those of the British Empire. It devoted enormous resources to the search for the Northwest Passage, based on the conviction that beyond the ice barrier blocking the ships' passage lay a Mediterranean Sea (see Berton 1988, and Williams 2003). The search for the Northwest Passage marked the first time the Arctic occupied centre stage in a globalizing economy. Later, during the cold war, Greenland's position at the front line first as a launching pad for bomber planes and later on missiles became the latest manifestation of imperial ambitions in the Arctic. With the opening of the Arctic to resource exploration, military and global economic ambitions will intensify Greenland's significance. Read in this vein it is easy to detect in the renewed focus on the Arctic – and Greenland – yet another scramble and yet another colonialism in the making. The theme of the hunt for resources as an age-old preoccupation of the global economy is outlined in the introduction to Richard Sale and Eugene Potapov (2010), *The Scramble for the Arctic.* More concretely, in Greenland the scramble includes Cairn Energy's oil drilling off the Greenlandic coast in volatile Arctic sea conditions, Greenland Minerals and Energy's proposed extraction of rare earths and uranium and London Mining Greenland's proposed iron ore mine. The scramble, however, takes place against a backdrop of a growing degree of local Arctic political autonomy, not least in Greenland. It is the Greenlandic government which negotiates with the mining companies, since Greenland took over the natural resource administration from Denmark in 2009. The Greenlanders have an opportunity of directly influencing the debate on climate change, the process of securitizing navigation through the Arctic waters and as well regulating the scramble for resource extraction in contrast to earlier when their priorities could be outright ignored. This is an important qualification to keep in mind, even if few Greenlanders harbour any illusions regarding their ability to call the scramble for the Arctic off with reference to the fragile environment for example.

The complexities in responding to the international opportunities and concerns brought on by the resource scramble are not the only challenges faced by Greenland.

---

5 The map decorating the Danish pavilion can be seen here: http://miedinesen.dk/storage/media/portfolio7/img_6772.jpg.

6 Minik Rosing quoted in Andersen (2012) (my translation).

The country seeks to strike a balance between, on the one hand, the need for domestic development to generate jobs and build an independent economy, and, on the other hand, the insistence on identifying itself as an indigenously rooted culture, where development hinges on traditional and sustainable practices. Development within the existing global order is required if Greenland is to generate its own prosperity and remove itself from the long shadow cast by Danish rule and interests. A political agenda supported by Greenland's major political parties. But development in its existing form has already deeply compromised a Greenlandic way of life built on the art of long-term survival in an extremely tough environment. Even if this problem is not of Greenland's own making since it derives generally from Danish colonial rule since the mid-nineteenth century, and more specifically from the large-scale Danish modernization programme initiated in the 1950s. The modernization programme was launched in a speech by the Danish Prime Minister in 1948 during his visit to Greenland, meant to show the world the Danish determination to remain in Greenland.[7] The modernization programme initially gained support from parts of the Greenlandic population, who saw the programme as a way to achieve recognition by the Danes as 'modern' citizens in their own country, and as such the long held desire to become equal partners. Relations soured when the Greenlanders experienced what they saw as largely a continuation of the old Danish colonial thought paradigm, where Danes provided unilateral solutions. This brought protest and the formation of modern political parties in Greenland was a direct result of this discontent. The political organization of Greenlanders eventually brought pressure to bear on the Danish government, which resulted in Home Rule in 1979, and 30 years later, self-government. However, despite the power over Greenland's 'modernisation' gradually passing from Denmark to Greenland, the problems embedded in the established practice coupled with a continued dependence on Danish expertise have continued to haunt Greenlandic governments.

The Greenlandic dilemma between development and sustainability has as mentioned above, had both domestic and international repercussions, and they tend to overlap. One example of the debate between development and sustainability concerns is the angry exchange between the then Greenlandic Premier, Kuupik Kleist, and Greenpeace over its campaign to block oil drilling in the Arctic (Carrell 2010). Others include warnings against opening an aluminium smelting plant (Nuttal 2008), and all types of major development projects in Greenland, with reference to its pristine environment. Greenland has had a difficult relationship with international environmental organizations, not least Greenpeace. This may initially appear odd to outsiders given the linked interests between indigenous and environmentalist activism directed against transnational companies over environmental concerns. However, one needs only to revisit the argument between Greenland and Greenpeace over the latter's campaign in the 1970s

7 The modernization programme is discussed in Lars Jensen (2012), *Danmark: Rigsfællesskab, tropekolonier og den postkoloniale arv*. Copenhagen: Reitzel, chapter 3.

and 1980s to ban the import of sealskins, which hit the Greenlandic economy hard, to understand how deeply divided their interests have been historically (Lynge 1992). This campaign still brings up bitter Greenlandic responses today whenever new Greenpeace campaigns take place. Whaling is another bone of contention. Seen from Greenpeace these issues are examples of a highly effective form of campaigning, while to many Greenlanders they represent a form of environmentalist fundamentalism, which is completely ignorant or careless of the consequences for local livelihoods. To many Greenlanders Greenpeace represents yet another example of the West lording it over an indigenous population whose means of existence and cultural life it fails to understand. Greenpeace has apologized to the Greenlanders over a partially misguided anti-fur campaign, and have learnt to emphasize a distinction between indigenous, sustainable killings of seals and whales, and major whaling and seal furring nations. Japan, Norway and Canada's economies are clearly not dependent on this activity, whereas for indigenous economies these practices are both a traditional way of life and sustainable. Even so, a problem remains in specific environmental organizations' campaigns targeting specific animals or environments, both because they cannot guarantee that such campaigns do not spill over into a general campaign against for example all hunting practices related to specific animals, and because the campaigns are driven by wholesale protection of animals, rather than discussions about hunting rights.

Yet, if environmental organizations' focused campaign strategies reveal their limitations in terms of achieving a more sensitive approach to sustainability, Greenland has its own sustainability problems as can be quickly established in the current economic political climate. Greenland promotes its national identity, both in terms of domestic policy, but also in terms of its relationship to the world outside through an organically defined cultural identity, complete with its cultural baggage of traditionally living in harmony with nature in one of the world's most pristine environments. A highly profiled example of this is the Greenlandic Premier, Kupiik Kleist's speech on the day Greenland achieved self-government (June 21, 2009):

> We stand here today because we the Greenland people believe that all things are interconnected. We believe in the powers of the universe and that these are inseparable from the individual's soul. We believe in the power of nature and that we must live in harmony with nature. This belief is crucial to our way of life. (Kleist 2009)

Kleist's narrative grants Greenland a position as specifically well suited to make decisions concerning future directions in its Arctic environment with reference to its indigenous culture. Yet how does this sit with Greenland's simultaneous, proactive search for partners carrying out potentially extremely environmentally damaging large-scale resource extraction. Though large-scale mines are not operating yet, London Mining which has signed an agreement with the Greenlandic government (2013) has been criticized for its mining activities in Sierra Leone (see Franks and Erskine 2012; *Cocorioko* 2013). This critique is particularly disturbing since large-scale industry, or resource extraction, cannot be monitored by Greenland's small population with its limited resources, but would have to be left in the hands of outside experts, who do not possess this localized/indigenous knowledge. This simple fact raises a range of questions both on a political practice level and at a broader epistemological level. Local environmentalist groups in Greenland have protested against the government's development plans. The Inuit Circumpolar Conference protested against the licence given to Cairn Energy to drill for oil in Baffin Bay. Local environmental groups (Avataq, Nuuk Fjords Venner and Foreningen 16. August) have protested against the large-scale law and mining projects.

Placing Greenland in the Broader Picture

So, how can one begin to problematize the incompatibility between development and sustainability in Greenland. To begin to answer this complex question, we have to return to the theoretical level to see how scholars have sought to deal with this complexity, which obviously isn't unique to Greenland, but in relation to which Greenland occupies a unique position as I have sought to outline above. These theories occupy a space where the disciplines of anthropology, political science/ international relations, geography, international law and philosophy intersect. It is beyond the scope of this chapter to stage the process by which these disciplines come to intersect. But it is important to state that the search for productive engagements begins by looking for approaches that preoccupy themselves with debilitating disciplinary boundaries in order to question whether issues regarding the complexity of say place and space articulation of indigenous populations can actually be addressed adequately by any single discipline. My brief exploration of this question here is inspired by Noel Castree's work, and in particular his article 'Differential Geographies: place, indigenous rights and "local" resources' (2004), where he searches for the borders of the self-interrogatingly critical abilities of Geography. Castree defines a shift in critical Geography in the work of a group of scholars dedicated:

> to bring about a paradigmatic shift in human geographers' conception of place. This shift has seen the move away from what are variously described as Cartesian (Merrifield 1993), neo-Kantian (Harvey 1990) or Newtonian (Massey 1999a) conceptions of place towards relational ones. These relational conceptions are not all of a piece, of course … Nonetheless, at a more abstract level, relational imaginaries together contest a view of places as 'locations of distinct coherence' (Massey, 1999a 14). Instead, they depict places as 'nodes in relational settings' (Amin 2002: 391), as 'specific yet globalized sites' (Watts 1991: 10) and as 'articulated moments in networks' (Massey 1994: 5). (Castree 2004: 134)

Castree is sympathetic to this move, particularly because on the one hand they strive to emphasize 'locatedness', while steering clear of treacherous 'boundedness'. On the other hand they also remain acutely aware of the dangers of abstracting globalization from its very concrete contextualizations. However, in spite of his sympathy for their work, he moves on to question 'three ideas about place that seem to be axiomatic of their approach' (Castree 2004: 134).

The first is that attempts to put 'strong' boundaries around places – that is to enclose peoples, resources or knowledges within a 'local' domain – are invariably misguided because such boundary acts are always false attempts to shut-out (or at least ameliorate the impacts of) translocal ties that in part constitute those places. They are, in other words, a denial of a fundamental ontological fact of our time: namely, that the global is in the local. Secondly, such denial, it is further argued, typically engenders actions that are politically regressive.

> The third shibboleth I wish to question is almost the mirror opposite of the previous two. It is the idea that there is something morally 'progressive' about insisting that people on the ground work with, rather than disavow or deflect, the inter-place connections that irrevocably bind them to distant others. Put differently, it is the idea that a geographical politics that proactively weds agendas in one place to those in myriad others – what Katz (2001: 724) calls a 'rooted translocalism' – is to be preferred to one that is placebound. (Castree 2004: 135)

These observations call for a brief look at what repercussions Castree's three shibboleths might have for considering Greenland. The first suggests one has to be careful about automatically assuming Greenland's pro-development and indigenous focused identity discourses to be only about exclusivist nation-building. While it is a factor, it has also to be seen at least partially as a strategic manoeuvre against historical Danish domination. Additionally, it has to be seen in the context of environmental organizations whose work is premised on the defence of the environment against any potentially damaging consequences. Environmental organizations, whose work builds on a view of nature and humans as dichotomies, risk failing to consider that indigenous peoples' relationship with nature are differently configured and cannot be reduced to this dichotomy. Furthermore, as environmental organizations have risen in response to the destruction of nature caused by capitalism, their own response is necessarily entangled with the discourse of modernity. These observations could help explain why environmental organizations are often at loggerheads with indigenous organizations. Indigenous organizations work towards gaining control over their land and on their own terms against their 'guardian' states. In their view, international environmental organizations represent another Western modernity-driven land management system.

Castree's third shibboleth raises the issue who is the rightful representative of Greenland, the government with its indigenous identity/development platform or the Inuit Circumpolar Council (ICC), which claims a more pan-Arctic approach to defining 'Inuit' – including Greenlandic – interests. Here Greenland's different path from those of its Arctic neighbours in North America as a circumscribed polity within the space of *Rigsfællesskabet* becomes an interesting exercise in articulating increasing degrees of autonomy, that is, the right to define and decide over its resources, environment and knowledges. ICC with its focus on identifying a pan-Arctic polity is not necessarily directed against a Greenlandic government following its own nation-building trajectory. It may be more productive to see ICC as an organization that seeks to secure *all* Inuit/Arctic peoples the best means of representing themselves through the dissemination of successful strategic manoeuvres that have given particular polities in the Arctic greater degrees of autonomy. It is this space for acknowledging strategic manoeuvring that Castree argues for, when he warns against jumping to conclusions regarding indigenous groups' articulations of a position which may appear to be a form of ethno-nationalism. Part of Castree's warning is directed at those critical exponents of cosmopolitanism, who pay inadequate attention to the forms of historical oppression against which the articulations for self-determination are made. Furthermore, if the historical trajectory is insufficiently acknowledged it runs the risk of underestimating currently unfolding oppressions as the transformation of earlier strategies of domination. This assertion would appear to be borne out by practice. Where state control remains largely intact in the Arctic and elsewhere, there is little evidence that indigenous groups have any real influence over their own situation in relation to resource extraction. As Castree argues:

> Given the sometimes appalling histories [Indigenous peoples] have suffered at the hands of majoritarian populations, it is understandable (and pragmatically useful) that they might, in certain cases, wish to underpin claims to territory, artefacts and knowledges with plenary statements about 'their' identity and difference. Such statements can provide a platform for indigenes to interact with named 'outsiders' on their own terms. It is therefore interesting that Left-wing academics in geography and the social sciences have called into question traditional concepts of place, culture and identity at the very moment when marginal populations worldwide need them more than ever. As Coombe (1998: 93) notes, these concepts and the practices they license might 'be the last legitimate ground for political autonomy and self-determination' for indigenous peoples. (Castree 2004: 156)

To Castree, 'indigenism is both a reaction to and an embrace of translocal connectivity (or "globalization" as it is now commonly termed)'. It would seem that Castree's reading suggests a way of understanding the Greenlandic self-government's attempt to deal with the pressures of transnational companies and powerful states on the one hand while seeking to ensure a sustainable development, with a focus on environmental consequences on the other. As such it is not in opposition to the declarations and charter of the ICC, which also points to sovereignty and self-determination and cross-polar collaboration as the way forward. It is difficult to escape the conclusion that small populations scattered across the Arctic with no direct backing of a state with 'Arctic sovereignty' will be ill-equipped to face the onslaught on the Arctic, which seems to be on the brink of occurring. To ask the 'guardian' states to look after the interests of its 'remote' indigenous peoples fails to consider the historical record of those same states' imperial interventions in these areas. Self-determination ultimately has no attractive alternatives.

Works Cited

Andersen, Marianne Krogh (2012) 'Grønland – det nye Middelhav', in *Weekendavisen*. 31 August.

Anderson, Benedict (1991 [1983]) *Imagined Communities: Reflections on the Origin and Spread of Nationalism*. London: Verso.

Bauman, Zygmunt (2011) 'The Triple Challenge', in *Postcolonial Europe*, a special issue of *Moving Worlds* 11 (2), 7–11.

Bello, Walden (2013) *Capitalism's Last Stand? Deglobalization in the Age of Austerity*. London: Zed Books.

Berton, Pierre (1988) *The Arctic Grail. The Quest for the North West Passage and the North Pole, 1818–1909*. New York: Viking.

Bryld, Tine (1998) *I den bedste mening*. Nuuk: Atuakkiorfik.

Carrell, Severin (2010) 'Greenland's Prime Minister Lambasts Greenpeace for Raiding Arctic Oil Rig' *The Guardian*, August 31. http://www.theguardian.com/environment/2010/aug/31/greenland-greenpeace-arctic-oil-rig.

Castree, Noel (2004) 'Differential Geographies: place, indigenous rights and "local" resources', in *Political Geography* 23, 133–67.

Cocorioko newspaper (2013) 'Open Letter to London Mining – Sierra leone' *Cocorioko* newspaper, July 12. http://www.cocorioko.net/?p=49796).

Comaroff, Jean and John Comaroff (2011) *Theory from the South: Or, How Euro-America is Evolving Towards Africa*. Boulder: Paradigm Publishers.

Danish Foreign Ministry (2012) *Focus*, March.

Emmerson, Charles (2010) *The Future History of the Arctic*. London: The Bodley Head.

Evans, Geoff, James Goodman and Nina Lansbury (eds) (2002) *Moving Mountains: Communities Confront Mining & Globalisation*. London: Zed Books.

Franks, Daniel and Peter Erskine (2012) *Mine Site Rehabilitation in Sierra Leone – A Rapid Appraisal of Selected Sites*. International Mining for Development Centre (Australian Agency for International Development) and United Nations Development Programme. http://www.csrm.uq.edu.au/Portals/0/docs/mine-site-rehabilitation-sierra-leone.pdf.

Gilroy, Paul (2011) 'Shameful History: The Social Life of Races and the Postcolonial Archive', in *Postcolonial Europe*, a special issue of *Moving Worlds* 11 (2), 19–34.

Graugaard, Naja Dyrendom (2009) *National Identity in Greenland in the Age of Self-Government*. Working Paper CSGP 09/5. Peterborough, Ont.: Trent University.

Jensen, Lars (2012) *Danmark: Rigsfællesskab, tropekolonier og den postkoloniale arv*. Copenhagen: Reitzel.

Kleist, Kupiik (2009) 'Speech by Premier Kuupik Kleist on Inauguration of Greenland Self-Government 21st of June 2009 in the Morning' http://naalakkersuisut.gl/~/media/Nanoq/Files/Attached%20Files/Engelske-tekster/Kuupik%20Kleist%20tale.pdf.

Lidegaard, Bo (2012) 'Hvis jeg var dansk statsminister, ville jeg udfolde mit yderste for at beholde Færøerne og Grønland inden for det danske rige' [If I Was Danish PM, I Would Do My Utmost to Keep the Faroe Islands and Greenland within the Danish Realm], interview with Greenlandic Premier, Kuupik Kleist, *Politiken*, August 19 http://politiken.dk/politik/ECE1730971/hvis-jeg-var-dansk-statsminister-ville-jeg-udfolde-mit-yderste-for-at-beholde-faeroeerne-og-groenland-inden-for-det-danske-rige/.

— (2012) 'Jeg ser tre selvstændige lande' [I see three independent nations], interview with Kaj Leo Johannesen, *Politiken*, August 12 http://politiken.dk/politik/ECE1731165/jeg-ser-tre-selvstaendige-lande/.

— (2012), 'Rigsfællesskabet gør os alle sammen lidt større og stærkere i verden' [The Commonwealth Makes Us All a little Greater and Stronger in the World], interview with Danish Prime Minister, Helle Thorning-Schmidt, *Politiken*, 26 August, reprinted in *Sermitiaq* http://sermitsiaq.ag/node/135896.

Lynge, Finn (1992) *Arctic Wars: Animal Rights, Endangered Peoples*. Hanover: University of New England Press.

Mbembe, Achille (2001) *On the Postcolony*. Berkeley: University of California Press.

Nowlan, Linda (2001) *Arctic Legal Regime for Environmental Protection*. Gland, Switzerland: IUCN.

Nuttall, Mark (2008) 'Self-Rule in Greenland: Towards the World's First Independent Inuit State?', in *Indigenous Affairs* 3-4, 64–70.

Osiander, Andreas (2010) 'Sovereignty, International Relations and the Westphalian Myth', in *International Organization*, 55 (2), 251–87.

Powell, Richard (2010), 'Lines of possession? The anxious constitution of a polar politics', in *Political Geography*, 29 (2), 74–7.

Sale, Richard and Eugene Potapov (2010) *The Scramble for the Arctic: Ownership, Exploitation and Conflict in the Far North*. London: Frances Lincoln.

Shadian, Jessica (2010) 'From State to Polities: Reconceptualizing Sovereignty through Inuit Governance', in *European Journal of International Relations* 16 (3), 485–510.

Togeby, Lise (2002) *Grønlændere i Danmark: En overset minoritet.* Aarhus: Aarhus University Press.

Williams, Glyndwr (2003) *Voyages of Delusion. The Quest for the Northwest Passage.* New Haven: Yale University Press.

Chapter 9
'The Enemy Outside and Within': The Crisis and Imagining the Global in Iceland

Kristín Loftsdóttir

> I mean, I think, one did not realize how maggots had eaten it up from inside out. You know; the *interiors* were rotten. Al l... you know ... many of those I have talked to about this [...] ... I think people [in her bank] were not crying because of the money. Trusting someone; that was just gone. (Natalía, interview with author)

Introduction

Natalía worked in one of Iceland's major banks during Iceland's economic collapse in 2008 and had years of experience in the fast emerging financial sector. As her words vividly reflect, economic crises are endowed with meaning and identity, never being 'only' about the money or financial losses (Schwegler 2009). The Icelandic 'economic miracle' – as it was labelled at the time – was initiated in the mid 1990s with the Icelandic government emphasizing neoliberal policies, which involved the gradual liberalization of banks and capital flows leading to intensive global integration (Ólafsson 2008; Sigurjónsson and Mixa 2011). At the time, social discourses in Iceland strongly emphasized that 'now' Iceland had become an important player in world politics and popularized essentialized images of Icelandic entrepreneurs as endowed with special characteristics that defined them, along with the rest of the Icelandic population (Loftsdóttir 2012a: 606). The economic crash created a paradigm shift in these discourses.

The glorification of Iceland's global involvements and economic prosperity lost its authority almost overnight when Iceland's then Prime Minister, Geir Haarde, announced at the beginning of October, 2008 the enactment of emergency laws. His statement revealed that the Icelandic government needed to bail out Iceland's three major commercial banks; they had been privatized only a few years earlier.[1] The shift in discourse is vividly reflected in suggestions by some individuals a few months later that the Icelandic entrepreneurs – celebrated so shortly before – were guilty of treason (Jóhannesson 2009). These voices echoed

1 The public was offered a share in two of the banks in 1997 and 1998 with the remainder sold to controlling interests in 2002 and the sales were finalized in 2003. The third bank was a combination of investment vehicles the government privatized in 1998 and in 2000 merged with another bank the government had salvaged in 1990.

wider sentiments within Iceland that the collapse could be seen as an outcome of corruption in the interconnected financial and political sector (Ragnarsdóttir, Bernburg and Ólafsdóttir 2012: 3). The banks' largest shareholders were also their largest debtors; in addition, the banks had invested their funds in shares in themselves (Hreinsson, Gunnarsson and Benediktsdóttir 2010: 4). As argued in the report compiled by a commission appointed by the Icelandic government to investigate the cause of the collapse of the three banks in Iceland, the reason for their collapse was primarily due to their expansion and size, not as a result of the global economic crisis *per se* (Hreinsson, Gunnarsson and Benediktsdóttir 2010; Flannery 2009: 171).

My discussion focuses on how global involvements look different through the prism of 'crisis'; how the crisis consequently can bring a shift in how individuals imagine the 'global'. The 'global' has become a part of most people's imagined worlds – a realm that they engage with and act on (Moore 2004: 74), which means that ideas of globalization are embedded in questions of identity and selfhood, creating new imaginations of the past and present (Appadurai 1996: 5–7). Imagination itself, as anthropologist Arjun Appadurai (1996) states, constitutes an important social force in a globalized world that mobilizes people in diverse ways. Imagination creates material actions and conditions where names can be turned into things, as phrased by Eric Wolf (1984), which are mobilized and acted on with direct consequences on livelihoods and subjectivities. I regard these insights on imagination, in the current global landscape, as useful tools with which to consider 'crisis'. They point to the importance of crisis narratives in current identity formation, as well as allowing a sense of crisis involving a particular way of imagining and engaging with the future.

In Iceland, the concept *kreppa* – referring literally to a contraction of some kind – is used to refer to the current crisis. *Kreppa* is not conceptualized so much as an economic or a social change accumulating in crisis but as a 'state' of things, something that *happened*, involving a rupture between past and present. Events in the recent past are often spoken about in daily conversations as happening either before or after the crash. 'The crisis' has become a way in Iceland of defining an historical moment though, which all events are measured by. I have often found it difficult to explain to people in other countries the radical transformation that the *kreppa* initiated – i.e. to people in countries where the economic situation has changed more gradually. This indicates how even when speaking of global events – as the economic crisis, which Iceland is a part of – these events are also inherently local, taking on a particular local texture.

The notion of a 'crisis' constitutes a part of how people conceptualize the world and their own position within it, even though 'crisis' is embodied and experienced in various ways. I explore these issues through an analysis of the Icelandic economic crisis, where the neo-liberalization processes that had started in the mid-1990s had successfully shaped Icelandic desires within a global economy. Natalía's words, the epigraph to this chapter, vividly express how this particular kind of global engagement – facilitated by the neoliberal transformations that occurred during the years before it – suddenly appeared different following an economic crisis. I emphasize that Icelandic national identity is generated in a fluid and dynamic conversation within a historical global environment, as well as shaped by an intensified neoliberal emphasis, which has increasingly also shaped the global economy. As I stress here, the erosion of identity is confronted by different positions of power where some benefit while others lose; the crisis thus entangled with power on multiple levels.

Scholars have approached crisis as necessary for change in society, in addition to being important in reproducing existing social structures in hierarchies. Karl Marx saw crisis in the classic sense of evolutionism of his time and so defined it as a force moving societies from one stage of evolution to another. Others defined crisis as reproducing the social system and dominant power structures (Rappaport 1968), almost constituting a ritualistic cycle of reproduction of existing hierarchies and elites (Gluckman 1956). Max Gluckman's phrase 'rituals of rebellion' showed that rebellions do not necessarily draw attention to the oppressive structures of the system itself but only to particular distributions of power, thus allowing for renewal of the 'unity of the system' (1954: 3). Crisis can signal change, while also constituting a loop where existing power structures are reproduced and enforced. As Naomi Klein (2007) has shown in her writing, economic crisis creates opportunities for multinational corporations, companies and institutions to initiate radical changes benefitting their own interests. Thus crisis does not necessarily mean that the power structures are contested or that they themselves are in crisis. This draws attention to how power operates in this new global economy, as simultaneously characterized by new and older boundaries, and more intensive fluidity (Nymnjoh 2000: 4–5), raising the question, to what extent is the new global economy based upon old and/or new hierarchies?

This discussion is based on an analysis of diverse materials that relate to the economic boom years and crisis in Iceland[2] but the two examples are founded on a body of media data collected in relation to two events heavily reported on, and discussed in Icelandic society. One was an application in 2011 for Icelandic citizenship for 10 wealthy individuals and their children, and the other discussion in regard to the businessman Huang Nubo's attempts to buy land in the northern part of Iceland in 2011 and 2012.[3] The analysis is also informed by broader media data collected for the project as a whole, and from interviews. Media analysis includes an analysis of two Icelandic business journals (*Markaðurinn* and *Viðskiptablaðið*)

2 The material for this analysis was collected and analysed in relation to the research project Icelandic Identity in Crisis which was funded by Rannsóknarsjóður Háskóla Íslands and RANNÍS (Icelandic Centre for Research) (grant number 130426-051).

3 I want to thank Sigrún Valdsóttir and Þóra Lilja Sigurðardóttir for assistance with collecting this data. For the first case study 32 articles were collected from various Icelandic newspapers at the time of the application (collected in June and July 2011) in addition to paying attention to 17 blog discussions. For the later case 53 articles were collected from various Icelandic newspapers and 38 blog discussions collected.

during 2006 and 2007. Interviews were undertaken with 28 Icelandic individuals; 18 worked in the financial sector (most of them in good positions as investors or in middle management in banks) and ten in international development, which was expanding extensively during the same time. The majority of the interviews occurred during 2011 and 2012 but some in 2013. I start with outlining briefly how engagement with the global world was conceptualized prior to the economic crash in 2008, and then focus in more detail on 'crisis' in the context of Iceland.

Neoliberalism, Globalization and Identities

Analysing economies holistically as a part of society has a long tradition in anthropology (Schwegler 2009), with scholars emphasizing finance as embedded in a larger nexus of social relations and history (Peebles 2010), as well as disjunctions between models of finance and their actual affects (Ho 2009: 180). The idea of *neoliberalism* has for many been valuable in theorizing the recent restructuring of the global economy as a social and political project, in spite of major disagreements in closely defining the concept itself and its historical transformation (see for example, Jessop 2013). I use the concept *neoliberalism* as involving rationality of governmentality where market values are extended to involve all social action and diverse institutions (Schwegler 2008: 682), rather than narrowly referring to the liberal operation of markets. Thus, the logic of neoliberalization, as defined by Gledhill, can be seen as a 'transformation of life itself into a marketable commodity and the imperative for us all to market ourselves' (2000: 342). The emphasis on governmentality signals that we have to look beyond the state, at more diverse ways in which governance is executed (Ilcan and Phillips 2006: 61). As such the term refers to diverse forms of governing which are based on rationalized programmes, techniques and even vocabularies which aim to shape the behaviour of people in coherence to particular objectives (Ilcan and Phillips 2008: 714–15). As Tara A. Schwegler describes, economic discourse is regularly separated from the political context in which it takes place that 'enables economic expertise to conceal political struggles and produce a veneer of technical neutrality' (2008: 686). It is generally well established among scholars that the close interconnection of the world does not simply lead to increased homogeneity but global processes gain localized meanings in different ways (Appadurai 1996; Gupta and Ferguson 1997: 5), being domesticated, redeployed and resisted (Comaroff and Comaroff 2000: 305). Angelique Haugerud (2003: 65) stresses that the understanding of global processes requires a more nuanced sense of the 'local' and the 'global', which involves a particular reworking of the notion 'local' where the local should not be seen as a category different from the global. Instead local transformations should be acknowledged as integral parts of globalization where it is even not always possible to distinguish between global and local processes (also Tsing 2000: 352).

The process of neoliberalization involves various changes in labour disciplines such as niche marketing, auditing and quality control. These have been used to change people into 'flexible, agile, self-regulating workers' who presumably then assist their companies to adapt to shifting conditions within the global markets (Dunn 2004: 7). More 'flexibility', as Elizabeth Dunn (2004) points out, often means that workers are taught to accept job insecurity and risk (19) where the worker needs 'continuous learning' in an 'endless process of reskilling to meet changing production requirements' (20). Scholars have also emphasized that neoliberalism involves particular reified notions of culture, where the concept has become reconfigured within neoliberal ideology as a commodity in a global market place (Lavie and Swedenberg 1996: 6), symbolized in ideas such as 'nation branding' where the nation becomes a brand in a similar fashion to the way company trademarks operate. Globalization has thus simplified and 'packaged' cultural stereotypes within an orderly world of manageable cultural difference. This reification of difference became quite important in Iceland prior to the crash, as I discuss later, along with other characteristics of neoliberalism in Iceland.

This reification of culture can also be contextualized towards a particular imagining of the past. The simplification which is involved in the claim that *now* the world is globalized and that the previous period was more embedded in national concerns, creates 'the illusion that we are now living in a unique period involving "new" spatial categories', thus leaving the global relations of the past out of the picture (Philips and Ilcan 2003: 436).

The Economic Boom Period

Iceland joined the European Economic Area (EEA) in 1994 and became part of the Schengen area in 2001 in addition to liberalizing its capital flows. In 1997 the process of the privatization of Icelandic banks began, and in 2003 the three largest banks had been fully privatized. This liberalization of Iceland's economy meant momentary economic prosperity, with finance as the main source of revenue in the 2000s (Sigurjónsson and Mixa 2011). The term 'Manic Millennium Years', which has been applied to the period from the turn of the millennium until the crash (Mixa 2009), is a useful term with which to capture this atmosphere. It also gives a sense that the turn of the millennium would be significant for Iceland, and includes the notion of forecasting Iceland's role as a leading global financial centre (Loftsdóttir 2010a and 2010b). This perception was supported by an extensive rise in the Icelandic stock index that rose 56 per cent for 2003, 59 per cent for 2004 and 54 per cent for 2005,[4] meaning

4 G. Magnússon 2006, Rannsóknir á íslenskum hlutabréfamarkaði – Presentation for Landssamtök lífeyrissjóða, 28 November 2006. Accessed 20 February 2012 from http://www.ll.is/files/bbgehddaaf/Gylfi_Magnusson.pdf.

that someone who had invested US100 dollars in the stock market[5] had almost 400[6] dollars only three years later.

The economic success of Icelandic entrepreneurs and the Icelandic financial market was explained by politicians, leading business people and the general media as part of Icelanders' intrinsic characteristics, often referring to Iceland's 'Viking' or settlement heritage and the survival of the population in an inhospitable country (Loftsdóttir 2010b). The casual reference to Icelanders as 'Vikings', indirectly or directly in official reports by the Icelandic government (Sigfússon and Þorbersson 2005: 21 and 33), and in business newspapers such as *Markaðurinn* and *Viðsiptablaðið*, reflect the general acceptance of these terms within Icelandic society. The reification of Icelandic culture is in itself not a localized phenomenon, as earlier discussed in relation to neoliberalization, but very much in line with how culture has increasingly been commoditized within the processes of globalization. As Henrietta Moore stressed, this becomes the means 'through which diversification is replicated through globalized processes, experiences and interconnections' (2004: 78). When Iceland became part of the Schengen agreement, certain populations could enter the country quite easily while others were kept more securely out. Steve Garner has pointed out how the categories of mobility on which Schengen is based overlaps with distinctions of geography and class and can be seen as racialized in the sense of clearly distinguishing rights on the lines of predominantly European 'white' and third world 'non-white' factors (2007: 69). The largest groups of immigrants during the boom period were Polish, primarily drawn to the ample work opportunities, even though many settled with their families (see discussion in Skaptadóttir 2004). Men in particular worked in the booming building industry, which included building the aluminum smelter in the eastern part of Iceland and the construction of the large power plant at Kárahnjúkar (Skaptadóttir 2010: 38–9). The power plant caused a dramatic change in a unique area of Iceland's interior, situated within the mountains in Iceland's highlands, nearly 200 metres high, providing energy to the new aluminum smelter (Benediktsson 2009).

In the early 2000s, the super rich appeared somewhat suddenly in Iceland, usually associated with the new business and finance elite, with extensive consumption practices that were unknown in Iceland at that time (Oddsson 2010: 8). In 1997, some discussion had begun in relation to the growing difference in salaries in Iceland, reflected in that 82 per cent replied in an opinion poll that they agreed with the statement that there were two 'nations' (*þjóðir*) living in the country due to the difference in salaries (Capacent Gallup 1997). Scholars have, nevertheless, shown that Icelanders have strongly seen themselves as a classless society, which has been an important idea to the national consciousness in Iceland for a long time (Oddson 2010: 7). This sentiment was mobilized in relation to the

5 Here the assumption is that the investment was in line with the distribution of the stock market index distribution.

6 The exact number is 382.

economic boom period in the 2000s, positioning 'Icelanders' against the rest of the world, and the Danish in particular, while simultaneously desiring recognition of Iceland's important international status (Loftsdóttir 2012a and 2012b). The characteristics of Icelandic entrepreneurs were seen as reflecting on the Icelandic character as a whole, leading to a strong identification as a unified nation – in spite of significant growing economic and class differences.

The intensification of nationalistic rhetoric engaged, furthermore, with Iceland's past as a Danish dependency and with older anxieties to gain recognition from more powerful European nation states during Iceland's demands for independence from Denmark (Loftsdóttir 2012a). This desire for Iceland's international recognition can be viewed as one of the key components in understanding the extensive public support that the economic adventure had until the collapse. This success was also celebrated by international rating companies and leading economists within the neoclassical model including Arthur Laffer, a member of Ronald Reagan's Economic Policy Advisory Board, who assured the Icelandic business community and the government that Iceland's fast economic growth, in spite of a large trade deficit and foreign debt, was a sign of its success (Wade 2009: 6). Any criticism of the 'economic miracle' was also attacked by the Icelandic government, business people and media, such as when a Danish national bank, Danske Bank, voiced serious concerns in 2006 (concerns which were actually also raised by the IMF) though these drew much less attention. The Icelandic Foreign Minister at that time, Valgerður Sverrisdóttir, for example, responded to the concern voiced by the bank that the criticism was resulting from 'unnatural motives' which had to be sought within the 'Danes' themselves (*Sjálfsímynd Dana farin að rispast* 2006). The category 'immigrant' was absent in these discourses of economic prosperity (Loftsdóttir 2010b), even though the heightened global integration during the boom period had meant a growing number of immigrants with foreign nationals steadily rose from 1.8 per cent in 1996 to more than 8 per cent of the national population of Iceland in 2008 (Statistics Iceland 2009).[7]

The Economic Crash

The economic collapse in Iceland was unprecedented in history, multiplying the State's foreign debt, in addition to the enormous losses suffered by individual and foreign creditors (Sigurjónsson and Mixa 2011). The crisis started with three of the main banks in Iceland defaulting on their external obligations, and lead to the passing of emergency laws. These banks had been privatized and deregulated in the boom period, being originally sold to 'owners friendly to the ruling political parties' (Wade 2009: 15) who had no prior experience in banking (Sigurjónsson

7 In 1996, 95 per cent of people with Icelandic nationality had both parents of Icelandic origin (Statistics Iceland 2009: 5). In addition, most immigrants came from Denmark and the other Nordic countries prior to this time (Statistics Iceland 2009: 11).

and Mixa 2011). It has been estimated that between 33–60 per cent of non-financial firms, 'became technically bankrupt' (Daníelelson and Zoega 2009: 16).

The cuts in purchasing power were also dramatic with the Icelandic krona falling from about 90 euros at the beginning of 2008 to 190 euros in November the same year (Wade 2009: 12). One of the Icelandic bankers that I interviewed, Hjálmar, worked at one of the larger banks. When hearing about the setting of the emergency law and realizing the situation that Iceland was in, Hjálmar tells me that he sent a SMS to his friend stating that 'This is finished.' He laughs somewhat hollowly, explaining that he thought that 'everything' would be gone. Another banker from a different bank tells me that what sticks in his mind as somehow symbolic of the crash was when he stopped at the red light and saw the woman in the car next to him reading the newspaper. Or as he phrased it: 'And she was just reading the paper and somehow this was just the last straw … The feeling was like everything was gone.' He is unable to explain why the image of the woman reading a newspaper was so unsettling but attempts to articulate that this was somehow the final thing, even as it hinges on a trivial detail.

The Icelandic government frantically tried for the months to come to secure loans to save Iceland's economy, which was made even more problematic because of the government's emerging dispute with the British and Dutch governments in relation to the Internet bank, Icesave, that was attached to Landsbanki, one of the collapsed banks (Danielson and Zoega 2009: 16). As some interviewees within the financial sector commented, there was a real shortage of foreign currency within the main banks to buy basic necessities, creating a panic in the bank. As this quote from an interview with a woman working in a senior position in one of the main banks reflects, the sense of insecurity became intense in the weeks after the crash: 'There was probably a week when I looked at the bottom of, you know, the shame, and you know, I was worried that the social security funds would disappear and the state and, you know, just seeing at it go down the drain.'

In November 2008, Iceland received an approval for US$ 2.1 billion assistance from the IMF (International Monetary Fund 2008) that made the country the first 'developed' country to seek IMF relief since 1976. As Aðalsteinn, who worked in investment in another bank tells me, 'I don't think we had any options on this. We were a bankrupt nation.' The government resigned in January 2009 after mass protest and riots. Prior to the collapse such protests and riots were almost unknown in Iceland. The protests reflected the discontent of the general public; they identified corruption in the financial sector as the reason for the collapse and saw that this had been made possible by failure of the government to regulate that sector (Ragnarsdóttir, Bernburg and Ólafsdóttir 2012: 6).

In many European countries, economic crises have led to a growing hatred of immigrants but this does not seem to have taken place in Iceland, or at least not in substantial way. One of the effects of the economic crash in Iceland in 2008 was the dramatic drop in employment opportunities. The extensive rate of unemployment among immigrants can in some cases be explained by other factors than anti-immigrant sentiments. For example, the high unemployment rate among

Poles by Icelandic standards (Sigurðsson and Arnarson 2011) seems largely due to the high representation of Polish workers in the construction industry, an industry adversely affected by the economic collapse (Wojtyńska, Skaptadóttir and Ólafs 2011). Anti-foreigner or racist sentiments cannot, however, be excluded. In my interviews with people from different African countries and from Lithuania, many speak about the increased difficulties of obtaining work. While some mention increased hostility, others mention feeling more understanding and friendliness from Icelanders after the economic crash. Anna Wojtyńska and Małgorzata Zielińska (2010: 8) in a discussion of Polish immigrants in Iceland also suggest that the attitudes towards Polish people do not seem to have changed significantly.

Crisis and Power

As I mentioned in the introduction the crash caused a paradigm shift in conceptualizing Iceland – internally and externally. The crisis not only constituted an economic downturn, but a radical change in perspective and ideology (Jónsson 2009: 286). My focus is on how the crash signals a more diverse kind of engagement with Icelanders, both in the sense that the consequences of these global involvements are uncertain, as well as in the sense that the mobilization of people in Iceland was not as strong as it was in the period prior to the crash. The concept disjuncture, theorized by Arjun Appadurai (1996), is useful here as a means of discussing what the contemporary landscape in Iceland looks like, where there are overlapping but still floating pieces that do not seem to fit together in the same way as they did before, i.e. not creating an apparently coherent ideological landscape. These new pieces mobilize different identities and engage with transformed kinds of subjectivities to those possible before the economic crash.

Primarily, there is a different way in seeing Iceland in the context of globalization. It is not regarded as self evident any more that Iceland will automatically be a 'winner' in globalization; global involvement prior to the crash was conceptualized by Icelanders as the Icelanders going 'out' and engaging with the global world (as if it existed externally to Iceland) and then bringing the benefits of that engagement back to Iceland. Such conceptualization retains a fairly rigid distinction between 'local' Iceland and a 'global' world. Ironically, neoliberalism and global integration were at their height, transforming Iceland's engagement with the world by changing the Icelandic banking system from the inside out by altering regulations in coherence with international ones. Today, one can suggest that the 'global' is in Iceland conceptualized as unpredictable, meaning different kinds of engagements, some of which are beneficial to Iceland as a nation state and others which are not. This is clearly reflected in my interviews in how often the concept 'smallness' comes up when discussing Iceland, often as synonym for vulnerability.

During the economic boom, smallness was probably more invoked in the context of how 'far' Iceland had been able to go. The sense of vulnerability in my interviews after the crash was expressed in various contexts, such as in relation to Iceland's disputes with Britain and Holland about the responsibility for the Icesave accounts. One women who I interviewed and who had held a management position at the bank told me that when Iceland was desperately trying to get foreign currency, she had realized, 'That we are actually a small island north in nowhere and if the British and the Dutch want it like that then we can be fenced off.' Her use of the term 'fenced off' expresses the isolation that she fears the British and Dutch governments can inflict on Iceland, and also Iceland's powerlessness in the face of that. Even though this smallness was often mentioned in context of the Icesave disputes, some interviewees mentioned it in relation to increased immigration to the country and foreign nationals buying up Icelandic land. One of the interviewees stated in that context that she was afraid of global influences because, 'We are just so few. We are so small and vulnerable.' She pauses and adds, 'This is what makes you afraid.' The 'global' has become real, intensifying a sense of Iceland being a small place, and vulnerable as well. Others, however, express optimism and a sense of relief that the economic collapse took place, leading to a breakdown of consumerist values and materialistic outlooks.

To expand on these disjunctures in mobilization of different identities and their entanglement with fear and desire, I briefly take two examples of contemporary discussions. I see them as intersecting – even though in some sense constituting quite different discourses – to the issue of who benefits and loses out in the process of crisis and globalization. As such both discourses reflect a sense of vulnerability or precariousness within a global economy. The former example was not addressed in my interviews, but many of those interviewed discussed the latter.

Wanting to Become Icelandic

In March 2011, a group of Icelandic entrepreneurs (*athafnamenn*) as they called themselves, placed an application to the legal authorities (*Allsherjarnefnd Alþingis*) for Icelandic citizenship on the behalf of a group of ten foreigners and their children, who would, in return, invest heavily in Iceland. According to *Kastljós*, a local news programme, the application stressed that by facilitating this, the Icelandic entrepreneurs – all of whom had important positions in Iceland's economy prior to the crash – wanted to help Iceland recover, and prevent the emigration of highly skilled, intelligent people from the country. While the names of the applicants themselves were not made public, their Icelandic spokesperson, Sturla Sighvatsson, advocated their cause in the media as did their Canadian-based lawyer, David Lesperance. The group of ten originated, according to news reports, from Canada and the USA. They did not fulfil the requirements for citizenship nor had they lived in Iceland but were extremely wealthy individuals. As is clearly stated on Lesperance's homepage,[8] he specializes in passport portfolio (where

8 http://lesperanceassociates.com.

individuals gain multiple citizenships and residencies) for extremely wealthy people who want to escape heavy taxation or litigation.

While the spokesperson for the Icelandic entrepreneurs emphasized the interest of these wealthy individuals in investing in Iceland, they simultaneously stressed that these inviduals were not interested in Iceland's natural resources (Þorgeirsdóttir 2011). Lesperance, by contrast, played more on the nationalistic feeling of Icelanders. In a media interview in Iceland, he claimed that these individuals wanted to 'join team Iceland' due to Iceland's non-engagement in wars and not having nuclear power plants, furthermore, he emphasized that the group of ten had been influenced by the Icelandic government tourist campaign entitled, 'Inspired by Iceland.' The interviewer had a hard time believing that there were no economic motives as can be seen in the following transcript:

> I[nterviewer]: But surely these people must be looking at financial gain as well?
> D[avid]: Well, there are people who have [pause] some of them are interested in making more money but for the most part they are motivated, kind of beyond money.
> I: Well, you specialize in helping people to um, avoid what they [pause] by collecting citizenship. Are you telling me that this is not the case with these ten people?
> D: Well, this is a kind of common misunderstanding that ... that people have. People, my clients, would never think of not paying taxes for services they use. It is when their tax money, over and beyond whatever they use, is used for things such as wars, which they do not, are philosophically opposed to, and where they are [hesitates] where the governments are not using them efficiently, um, for social programs, to help people [...] (Þorgeirsdóttir 2011).

The application for citizenship received a significant attention in Iceland, and blog and media discussions reflect that many regarded it with suspicion. Lesperance's arguments, emphasizing nationalistic reasons for the application, as well as the role and motives of the Icelandic entrepreneurs intensified these suspicions. The argument that the Iceland tourist campaign had been instrumental in the decision to apply for Icelandic citizenship would possibly have sounded more reasonable prior to the crash, but in the post-crash environment it functioned detrimentally. The use of this argument indicates a conscious, calculated and cynical manipulation of public opinion. The media labelled this as a 'selling' of citizenship and some bloggers emphasized Iceland's vulnerable situation with comments such as that the situation was not so bad that Iceland had to prostitute itself (*verða vændisríki*) (Vilhjálmsson 2011), and evaluating the application as a sign of that 'when a country bleeds, the sharks arrive' (Jónsdóttir 2011). At the end of April it was announced that the appropriate authorities had rejected the proposal and that citizenship could not be granted on these grounds.

Buying Land in Iceland

Like the example of the group of ten, the businessman Huang Nubo and his attempts to purchase land in the northern part of Iceland in 2011 and 2012 caused extensive reaction and even more intensified debates within Iceland regarding his motives. In July 2010, Nubo was first introduced in Iceland through media reporting. Emphasis was placed of his being a 'Chinese businessman and poet' who had along with his company, Zhongkun Group, established a cultural fund of one million US dollars entitled, *China Iceland Cultural Fund* with which he would also support a festival of poetry in Iceland. The role of the fund was to enrich cultural connections between the Nordic countries and East Asia (*130 milljónir til að kynna íslensk ljóð í Kína* 2010). Then in April 2011, another news story appeared about Nubo's trip to the South Pole with three Icelanders, in which readers were reminded that Nubo initiated the Chinese-Icelandic poetry festival in Iceland (*Afreksmaður á ferð* 2010). The Icelandic newspaper, *Morgunblaðið* reported in August the same year that Nubo has been investigating investment opportunities in Iceland, which – the reporter stated – had been confirmed by Nubo's friend Hjörleifur Sveinbjörnsson (Sveinbjörnsson was mentioned in relation to Nubo's trip to the South Pole). Nubo was introduced by the journalist as a Chinese 'friend of Iceland',[9] who then elaborated on his training as a mountaineer and interest in poetry, and mentioned that he is, according to Forbes, numbered 161 of China's richest people (Björnsdóttir 2010). Later it became apparent that these investment opportunities primarily involved the buying of a piece of land amounting to 0.3 per cent of Iceland (30,639 hectares) located at Grímsstaðir á Fjöllum, which is a marginal highland in the northern part of the country, in order to build a luxury tourist centre with a golf resort and villas.[10] In August 2011, Nubo's company, the Beijing Zhongkun Investment group, signed a binding sales agreement with the owners of the land but needed to get exemption from the Icelandic government from laws that prohibit companies outside the European Economic Area investing in Icelandic real estate (Huijbens and Alessio 2013: 5). The population in the area in question had been declining, and Nubo's investment would have been extensive (Huijbens and Alessio 2013: 5). In an announcement from the Ministry for Foreign Affairs (reported in the media) about Nubo's interest in investing in the land, it was stated that Nubo was willing to renounce water rights (*Funduðu um fjárfestingar* 2011), which is reminiscent of Lesperance's insistence that his super-rich were not interested in Icelandic natural resources. The government was,

9 In the Icelandic media there is a tradition of bestowing celebrities with the epithet, *íslandsvinur* (a friend of Iceland) if they have visited Iceland a few times or have special interest in the nation.

10 It is interesting still, how little coherence there is over these plans if news stories from different media at different times are compared. In August 2011 in an interview with Morgunblaðið Nubo for example says that he is planning on building a five-star, 300-room hotel in the centre of Reykjavík ('Ætlar líka að byggja upp í Reykjavík' 2011).

however, reluctant to give the necessary permission, leading to extensive disputes between the Icelandic government and Nubo, the government proposing instead that Nubo's company would lease it. An application for lease was, however, also subsequently rejected and the reason given was 'insufficient information'.

This case is complex and raises a number of issues, which I will not analyse here in depth but rather briefly outline. In the blog discussions, there were accusations that the continuing speculations about his motives for buying the land and the refusal to sell to him were racist, and also reflected on his Chinese nationality. Nubo stated in a media interview that the reason behind the government ratification of his purchase or leasing the land was 'anti-China ideology and rising trade protectionism' (Yuanyuan 2012). While there certainly were a number of racist remarks made in the blog discussions, it is difficult to dismiss all concerns with the relationship between Nubo and the Chinese government as an outcome of anti-Chinese sentiment.

The discussion touched on all kind of concerns, and included comments directed at Nubo as a desirable type of foreigner, being an investor, in which he is contrasted with the foreigners living now in Iceland, who are located within the framework of the crisis of multiculturalism (Þorsteinsson 2011). In addition the blogs are suspicious of Nubo's relationship to an Icelandic political party, perhaps because his Icelandic friend, Sveinbjörnsson, is the husband of a former government Minister and former leader of Samfylking, the ruling party at the time of the crash. To make these connections even more complex, the then acting Minister of Internal Affairs was the brother-in-law of Nubo's friend. Criticisms were also directed at the general issue of foreigners buying land; in these Nubo is primarily labelled 'foreigner' or 'foreign business tycoon'. Some commentators saw Nubo's prospective purchase as positive in terms of gaining investment into the country, while others expressed concerns with the means of such investment. Most of the people I interviewed primarily emphasized Nubo's role as a foreign investor whose investments could be positive for the economy, even though they were troubled by that his interest rose after the Icelandic economic fall. One woman stated in an interview that for her the whole thing smelled like a 'gold-rush', referring primarily to the Icelanders who had seen it as in their interest to advocate the sale of the land to Nubo. There were also concerns over the possibility that Nubo was a frontman for Chinese military interests, who saw the venture as an opening up of the Arctic, and thus granting Iceland new significance within a changing geopolitical map.

In addition, it is interesting to note the relatively strong positive focus on Nubo as a person in the Icelandic media. In different interviews and news stories three things were emphasized. Firstly, that Nubo became engaged with Iceland because of an Icelandic wool sweater he received as a gift from his Icelandic roommate during his University years. Secondly, that he sees himself more as a 'poet rather than investor', and thirdly, he was born poor and become an orphan in his childhood (Ragnarsdóttir 2011a). These three aspects of Nubo's life can also be seen in non-Icelandic media about the attempted land purchase. *The Asia Times* reports on them in relation to Iceland by quoting Nubo's comments in *The Shenzhen Daily*, where he remarks that like any 'poet, I am imaginative and not very practical'. *The Asia Times* also quotes the vice president of Zhongkun Group, Xu Hong, questioning why some people were skeptical since Nubo was 'a poet and the offer is totally in character'. Hong elaborates by stating that the project had to be put in context with Nubo's other hobby, 'mountain climbing', the project in Iceland thus constructed as being aligned with Huang's explorer characteristics (Chung 2011). Some of the bloggers reacted to this uncritical emphasis of the Icelandic media about Nubo, seeing it as making the whole project more suspicious, as the following comments indicate. They concern one of the interviews taken by the newspaper *DV* with Nubo. One commentator remarks that he 'obviously thinks we Icelanders are simple minded fools' (Þorgeir 2011),[11] and another asks 'how much did *DV* [a local newspaper] get for printing this sentimental propaganda nonsense?' (Tinna 2011).[12]

As with the application of the ten super rich individuals, there were suspicions raised not only regarding Nubo's motives, but also of any Icelanders associated with the project and concerns that there were some other interests being served other than those openly claimed. This overlaps with suspicions in regard to what interest those Icelanders had that were associated with these business opportunities, and so to some extent indicates the erosion of the assumption that all Icelanders have the same interests, which had seemed self-evident prior to the crash. The discussion of these two cases also takes place against a background of accumulating scandals in Iceland, where it has been difficult to prosecute the Icelanders seen as primarily responsible for the crash, and where a number of them have even returned to the economic market. Two brothers, Ágúst and Lýdur Guðmundsson, the main owners of Bakkavor – a company that was responsible for pension funds losing approximately US$90 million due to bond defaults (the stock losses were also immense)[13] – have begun re-investing in Iceland and receiving a 20 per cent discount on the Icelandic currency (krona) while doing so (Viðskiptablaðið 2012).

Discussion and Final Points

After years of presumed economic prosperity, the Icelandic society was in 2008 in ruins with the enormous individual and institutional debt, massive ecological disruptions and privatization of many services. Instead of being a 'winner' in an international power play of globalization, Iceland's position seems more ambiguous. In understanding the pre-crash period in Iceland, Ulrich Beck's (1992: 21)

11 In Icelandic: 'heldur greynilega *(sic)* að islendingar seu bara einfaldir afglapar'.

12 In Icelandic: Hvað ætli DV hafi fengið fyrir að birta þetta – sentimental propaganda bull?

13 See evaluation of the Icelandic Pension funds: http://ll.is/files/00_2012_Uttektarskyrsla/Slides.pdf.

discussion of 'risk' society can be useful, especially his observation that even though risk and risk management has always existed, we are no longer speaking of personal risk but rather of global danger and self-destruction. Beck is primarily referring to the global consequences of environmental risks but his identification of risk as having roots in 'industrial overproduction' and ideas of modernization, bring to mind the importance of neoliberalism in inducing and nourishing these processes by transformation of everyday reality and environment into marketable valuables. The concept 'self-destruction' also seems suitable when discussing the Icelandic millennium years, where individuals were encouraged to spend as if there were no tomorrow. Financial booms also leave behind massive ecological destruction through large-scale modernization projects. This is sadly becoming evident in Iceland now with the slow dying of the lake Lagarfjót – an outcome of its proximity to the Kárahnjúka dam. The whole Icelandic population will eventually carry the consequences of a risk that a few individuals decided to take.

Social discussions in Iceland addressing the country's global involvement symbolize how people try to understand changing international global landscapes, engaging with questions regarding Iceland's circumstances within a larger world and its 'defining role in the global economy' (Titley 2000: 80). Such readings of the present global circumstances must stand in a dynamic relationship with a notion of the past, which as underlined by Andreas Huyssen's (2001) work, can provide an important resource in understanding complex global interrelations in the present. As I have claimed elsewhere, the strong mobilization of the economic boom period has to be contextualized as being to some extent influenced by Iceland's past anxieties and desires (Loftsdóttir 2010b, 2012b). Increased immigration to Iceland was a part of the global processes taking place in the economic boom years in Iceland – even though at the time it was not recognized as being important – but after the economic crash, immigrants have not been extensive targets of anger and frustration in regard to the fall, even though they are racialized and discriminated against in various contexts. No political party has, for example, so far flourished after the crash with an open anti-immigration agenda. The anger seems still primary to be directed at the Icelandic business tycoons that are viewed as responsible for the crash.

Social discourses about the motives of Nubo and his company, about the ten super rich individuals, and about the possible and hidden benefits to the Icelandic spokespersons and facilitators of these economic adventures reflect, however, the uneasiness of this global engagement – which to some extent intersects with older Icelandic ambivalence about foreigners (see Loftsdóttir 2012a; James Rice Chapter 3, this volume). In sum, this indicates a sense of vulnerability towards global elites that have been particularly successful in using processes of globalization to their own advantage – justifiably or not in these particular cases. This 'transnational capitalist elite', as observed by Jean and John Comaroff (2000: 303), has its interest in globalized forms of capital, 'loop[ing] into and out of national economies', seeking to 'minimize the effects of legal regulations, environmental constraints, taxation and labour demands'. As many, however, have pointed out in blog discussions, the reason for the fall was not the 'foreigners' but rather Icelandic entrepreneurs, who successfully become a part of this global elite. In the crisis, as these voices point out, we should thus be no less aware of the Icelandic 'vultures' looming – which see the crisis as a signal of even larger possibilities for profits. After the crash there were strong demands for a 'new' Iceland. It remains to be seen how much of this 'rebellion' turns out to be reproduction in Gluckman's (1954) sense, then reproduction of intensified neoliberalization with mostly the same actors and the same agenda.

Works Cited

'130 milljónir til að kynna íslensk ljóð í Kína' (2010) *Morgunblaðið*, 7 July, viewed 5 July 2012, http://www.mbl.is/frettir/innlent/2010/07/07/130_milljonir_til_ad_kynna_islensk_ljod_i_kina/.

'Ætlar líka að byggja upp í Reykjavík' (2011) *Morgunblaðið*, 26 August, viewed 26 August 2012, http://www.mbl.is/frettir/innlent/2011/08/26/byggir_einnig_upp_i_reykjavik/.

'Afreksmenn á ferð' (2011) *Morgunblaðið*, 20 April, viewed 5 July 2012, http://www.mbl.is/folk/frettir/2011/04/20/afreksmenn_a_ferd/.

Appadurai, Arjun (1996) *Modernity at Large: Cultural Dimensions of Globalization*. Minneapolis: University of Minnesota Press.

Beck, Ulrich (1992) *Risk Society: Towards a New Modernity*. Los Angeles: Sage Publications.

Benediktsson, Karl (2008) 'Moving places: Emotional Politics of Nature', in Bæhrenholdt, Jørgen Ole and Brynhild Granås (eds) *Mobility and Place: Enacting Northern European Peripheries*. Aldershot: Ashgate, 206–16.

Björnsdóttir, R. (2010) 'Vill byggja upp ferðaþjónustu'. *Morgunblaðið*, 20 August, viewed 9 April 2013, http://www.mbl.is/frettir/innlent/2011/08/20/vill_byggja_upp_ferdathjonustu/.

Comaroff, Jean and John Comaroff (2000) *Millennial Capitalism and the Culture of Neoliberalism*. Durham NC: Duke University Press.

Capacent Gallup (1997) *Búa tvær þjóðir í landinu?,* Capacent Gallup, viewed 8 April 2013, http://www.capacent.is/frettir-og-frodleikur/thjodarpulsinn/thjodarpulsinn/?NewsID=74bc68b1-5136-4e32-b0be-8df544c45207.

Chung, O. (2011) 'Poet Huang's Iceland Purchase Too Big for Locals to Handle', *Asian Times*, 13 September, viewed 9 April 2013, http://www.atimes.com/atimes/China_Business/MI13Cb02.html.

Danielsson, J. and G. Zoega (2009) 'The Collapse of a Country'. Reykjavik: Institute of Economic Studies Working Paper Series, Institute of Economic Studies of the University of Iceland, viewed 31 July 2013, http://hhi.hi.is/sites/hhi.hi.is/files/W-series/2009/WP0903.pdf.

Dunn, Elizabeth C. (2004) *Privatizing Poland: Baby Food, Big Business and the Remaking of Labor*. Ithaca: Cornell University Press.

Flannery, Mark J. (2009) *Iceland's Failed Banks: A Post-mortem*. Annex 3. Reykjavik: The Icelandic Special Investigation Commission, viewed 31 July 2013, http://www.rna.is/media/skjol/RNAvefVidauki3Enska.pdf.

'Funduðu um fjárfestingar' (2011) *Morgunblaðið*, 24 August, viewed 24 August 2011, http://www.mbl.is/frettir/innlent/2011/08/24/fundudu_um_fjarf estingar/.

Garner, Steve (2007) 'The European Union and the Racialization of Immigration 1985–2006'. *Race/Ethnicity: Multidisciplinary Global Contexts* 1 (1), 61–87.

Gledhill, John (2000) *Power and its Disguises: Anthropological Perspectives on Politics*. London: Pluto Press.

Gluckman, Max (1954) *Rituals of Rebellion*. Manchester: Manchester University Press.

— (1956) *Custom and Conflict in Africa*. New York: Barnes and Noble.

Gupta, Akhil and James Ferguson (1997) *Culture, Power, Place: Explorations in Critical Anthropology*. Durham NC: Duke University Press.

Haugerud, Angelique (2003) 'The Disappearing Local: Rethinking Global-local Connections, in Mirsepassi, Ali, Amrita Basu and Frederick S. Weaver (eds) *Localizing Knowledge in a Globalizing World: Recasting the Area Studies Debate*. New York: Syracuse University Press, 60–81.

Ho, K. (2009) 'Disciplining Investment Bankers, Disciplining the Economy: Wall Street's Institutional Culture of Crisis and the Downsizing of Corporate America', *American Anthropologist* 111 (2), 177–89.

Hreinsson, Páll, Tryggvi Gunnarsson and Sigrídur Benediktsdóttir (2010) *Report of the Special Investigation Commission*. Special Investigation Commission, Seltjarnarnes, viewed 8 April 2013, http://www.rna.is/eldri-nefndir/addragandi-og-orsakir-falls-islensku-bankanna-2008/skyrsla-nefndarinnar/english/.

Huijbens, Edward H. and Dominic Alessio (2013) 'Arctic "Concessions" and Icebreaker Diplomacy? Chinese Tourism Development in Iceland'. *Current Issues in Tourism*, DOI: 10.1080/13683500.2013.837867.

Huyssen, Andreas (2001) 'Present Pasts: Media, Politics, Amnesia', in Appadurai, Arjun (ed.) *Globalization*. Durham NC: Duke UP, 57–77.

Ilcan, Suzan and Lynne Phillips (2008)'Governing through Global Networks'. *Current Sociology* 56 (5), 711–34.

— and — (2006) 'Governing Peace: Global Rationalities of Security and UNESCO's Culture of Peace Campaign'. *Anthropologica* 48 (1), 59–71.

International Monetary Fund (2008) 'IMF executive board approves US$2.1 Billion Stand-by Arrangement for Iceland: Press Release No.08/296'. *International Monetary Fund – News*, 19 November, viewed 8 April 2013, http://www.imf.org/external/np/sec/pr/2008/pr08296.htm.

Jessop, Bob (2013) 'Putting Neoliberalism in its Time and Place: a Response to the Debate'. *Social Anthropology* 21 (1), 65–74.

Jóhannesson, Guðni T. (2009) 'Þeir fólar sem frelsi vort svíkja: lög, ásakanir og dómar um landráð á Íslandi'. *Saga* 47 (2), 55–88.

Jónsdóttir, Jóna Ingibjörg (2011) 'Við komum í friði'. *Eyjan*, 1 April, viewed 8 April 2013, http://blog.pressan.is/jonaingibjorg/2011/04/01/vid-komum-i-fridi/.

Jónsson, Ólafur Páll (2009) 'Lýðræði, réttlæti og haustið 2008'. *Skírnir* 183 (2), 281–307.

Þogeirsdóttir, Brynja (2011) 31 March, interview in Kastljós with David Lesperance by Brynja Þorgeirsdóttir.

Klein, Naomi (2007) *The Shock Doctrine: the Rise of Disaster Capitalism*. Toronto: Knopf.

Lavie, Smadar and Ted Swedenburg (1996) 'Introduction: Displacement, Diaspora and Geographies of Identity', in Lavie, Smadar and Ted Swedenburg (eds) *Displacement, Diaspora and Geographies of Identity*. Durham NC: Duke University Press, 1–25.

Loftsdóttir, Kristín (2010a) 'Ímynd, ímyndun og útrásin: vegvísir fyrir rannsóknir á kreppunni ["Image, Imagination and the Economic Expansion"]', in Gunnar Þ. Jóhannesson and Helga Björnsdóttir (eds) *Þjóðarspegillinn 2010*. Reykjavik: Félagsvísindastofnun Háskóla Íslands, 185–93, viewed 8 April 2013, http://skemman.is/en/stream/get/1946/6789/18458/3/185-193_KristinLoftsdottir_FELMAN.pdf.

— (2010b) 'The Loss of Innocence: Identity, Economic Crisis and Colonial Past'. *Anthropology Today* 26 (6), 9–13.

— (2012a) 'Colonialism at the Margins: Politics of Difference in Europe as Seen through Two Icelandic Crises'. *Identities: Global Studies in Culture and Power* 19 (5), 597–615.

— (2012b) 'Belonging and the Icelandic Others: Situating Icelandic identity in a postcolonial context', in Loftsdóttir, Kristín and Lars Jensen (eds), *Whiteness and Postcolonialism in the Nordic Countries*. Farnham: Ashgate, 57–71.

Mixa, Mar Wolfgang (2009) 'Once in Khaki Suits: Socioeconomic Features of the Icelandic Collapse', in Hannibalsson, Ingjaldur (ed.) *Rannsóknir í Félagsvísindum X*. Reykjavik: Félagsvísindastofnun Háskóla Íslands, 435–47.

Moore, Henrietta L. (2004) 'Global Anxieties: Concept-metaphors and Pre-theoretical Commitments in Anthropology'. *Anthropological Theory* 4 (1), 71–88.

Nyamnjoh, Francis B. (2000) 'For Many Are Called But Few Are Chosen: Globalization and Popular Disenchantment in Africa'. *African Sociological Review* 4 (2), 1–45.

Oddson, Guðmundur Ævar (2010) 'Stéttarvitund Íslendinga í kjölfar efnahagshruns'. *Íslenska þjóðfélagið* 1 (1), 5–26.

Ólafsson, Stefán (2008) 'Íslenska efnahagsundrið: Frá hagsæld til frjálshyggju til fjármálahruns'. *Stjórnmál og stjórnsýsla* 4 (2), 233–56.

Peebles, Gustav (2010) 'The Anthropology of Credit and Debt'. *Annual Review of Anthropology* 39, 225–40.

Phillips, Lynne and Suzan Ilcan (2003) 'A World Free from Hunger: Global Imagination and Governance in the Age of Scientific Management'. *Sociologia Ruralis* 43 (4), 434–53.

Ragnarsdóttir, Sólrún Lilja (2011a) 'Dularfulli Kínverjinn sem kaupir Ísland'. *DV*, 2–4 September, 24–6.

— (2011b) 'Huang Nubo: sársaukafullt að rifja upp barnæskuna', DV, 7 September, viewed 9 July 2012, http://www.dv.is/frettir/2011/9/7/huang-nubo-sarsaukafullt-ad-rifja-upp-barnaeskuna/.

Ragnarsdóttir, Berglind Hólm, Jón Gunnar Bernburg and Sigrún Ólafsdóttir (2012), 'The Global Financial Crisis and Individual Distress: the Role of Subjective Comparisons after the collapse of the Icelandic Economy'. *Sociology* 46, 1–21.

Rappaport, Roy (1968) *Pigs for Ancestors: Ritual in the Ecology of a New Guinea People*. New Haven: Yale University Press.

Schwegler, Tara A. (2008) 'Take it from the Top (Down)? Rethinking Neoliberalism and Political Hierarchy in Mexico'. *American Ethnologist* 35 (4), 682–700.

— (2009) 'The Global Crisis of Economic Meaning'. *Anthropology News* 50 (7), 9–12.

Sigfússon, Þór and Halldór Benjamin Þorgeirsson (2005) *Útrás íslenskra fyrirtækja til Lundúna*, Ritröð Viðskiptaráðs Íslands um íslenskt viðskiptaumhverfi [Series by the Iceland Chamber of Commerce regarding Icelandic business environment]. Reykjavik: British-Icelandic Chamber of Commerce.

Sigurðsson, Karl and Valur Arnarson (2011) 'Erlendir ríkisborgarar á íslenskum vinnumarkaði árin 2010. Veitt atvinnuleyfi, áætlað vinnuafl og atvinnuleysi'. Vinnumálastofnun Íslands, Reykjavík, viewed 1 August 2013, http://www.vinnumalastofnun.is/files/Erlendir%20r%C3%ADkisborgarar%20á%20%C3%ADslenskum%20vinnumarkaði%202010_1178828625.pdf.

Sigurjónsson, Throstur Olaf and Mixa, Mar Wolfgang (2011) 'Learning from the Worst Behaved. Iceland's Financial Crisis and Nordic Comparison'. *Thunderbird International Business Review*, 53 (2) 209–24.

'Sjálfsímynd Dana farin að rispast' (2006) *Viðskiptablaðið*, 24 March, 12–13.

Skaptadóttir, Unnur Dís (2004) 'Mobilities and Cultural Difference: Immigrants' Experiences in Iceland', in Ingimundarson, Valur, Kristín Loftsdóttir and Irma Erlingsdóttir (eds) *Topographies of Globalization: Politics, Culture, Language*. Reykjavík: University of Iceland, 133–48.

— (2010) 'Integration and Transnational Practices of Filipinos in Iceland. Migrations dans la pays Nordiques', in Odden, Gunhild (ed.) *E-migrinter* 5, 36–45.

Statistic Iceland (2009) *Innflytjendur og einstaklingar með erlendan bakgrunn 1996–2008* ['Immigrants and Persons of Foreign Background 1996–2008']. Statistical Series, Reykjavík: Statistic Iceland.

Tinna comment to Ragnarsdóttir, Sólrún Lilja (2011b) 'Huang Nubo: sársaukafullt að rifja upp barnæskuna'. *DV*, 7 September, viewed 9 July 2012, http://www.dv.is/frettir/2011/9/7/huang-nubo-sarsaukafullt-ad-rifja-upp-barnaeskuna/.

Titley, Gavan (2000) 'Global Theory and Tourist Encounters'. *Irish Communications Review* 8, 79–87.

Tsing, Anna (2000) 'The Global Situation'. *Cultural Anthropology* 15 (3), 327–60.

Viðskiptablaðið (2012) 'Bakkavararbræður fara fjárfestingarleið Seðlabankans', *Viðskiptablaðið*, September 27, viewed June 13, 2013, http://www.vb.is/frettir/76602/.

Vilhjálmsson, Ingi Freyr (2001) 'Ísland þarf ekki að vera vændisríki'. *DV*, 4 May, viewed 8 April 2013, http://www.dv.is/blogg/ingi-freyr-vilhjalmsson/2011/4/5/island-tharf-ekki-ad-verda-vaendisriki/.

Wade, Robert (2009) 'Iceland as Icarus'. *Challenge* 52 (3), 5–33.

Wolf, Eric (1984) *Europe and the People Without History*. Berkeley: University of California Press.

Wojtyńska, Anna, Unnur Dís Skaptadóttir and Helga Ólafs (2011) *Report from the Research Project: The Participation of Immigrants in Civil Society and Labour Market in the Economic Recession*. Faculty of Social and Human Sciences, Reykjavík, viewed 1 August 2013, http://mark.hi.is/sites/mark.hi.is/files/filepicker/17/wojtynska_skaptadottir_olafs_participation_of_immigrants.pdf.

— and Małgorzata Zielińska (2010) 'Polish Migrants in Iceland Facing the Financial Crisis', in GÞ Jóhannesson and H. Björnsdóttir (eds), *Þjóðarspegillinn 2010*, Félagsvísindastofnun Háskóla Íslands, Reykjavík, 1–11, viewed 8 April 2013, http://skemman.is/en/stream/get/1946/6771/18418/3/1-11_Anna_Wojtynska.pdf.

Yuanyuan, Wang (2012) 'China Exclusive: Prejudice Dents Enterprises' Overseas Expansion', *Xinhuanet News*, 4 December, viewed 31 July 2013, http://news.xinhuanet.com/english/china/2012-12/04/c_132019238.htm.

Þorgeir comment to the article Ragnarsdóttir, Sólrún Lilja (2011b) 'Huang Nubo: sársaukafullt að rifja upp barnæskuna', *DV*, 7 September, viewed 9 July 2012, http://www.dv.is/frettir/2011/9/7/huang-nubo-sarsaukafullt-ad-rifja-upp-barnaeskuna/.

Þorsteinsson, Sigurður (2011) Fjölþjóðamenning á Íslandi, *Sigurður Þorsteinsson blog*, 26 August, viewed 5 December 2013, http://ziggi.blog.is/blog/ziggi/entry/1186906/.

Index